MUSICAL IDENTITIES

MUSICAL IDENTITIES

Edited by

RAYMOND A.R. MACDONALD

Glasgow Caledonian University

DAVID J. HARGREAVES

University of Surrey Roehampton

DOROTHY MIELL

Open University

OXFORD
UNIVERSITY PRESS

OXFORD

UNIVERSITY PRESS

Great Clarendon Street, Oxford OX2 6DP

Oxford University Press is a department of the University of Oxford.
It furthers the University's objective of excellence in research, scholarship,
and education by publishing worldwide in

Oxford New York

Auckland Cape Town Dar es Salaam Hong Kong Karachi
Kuala Lumpur Madrid Melbourne Mexico City Nairobi
New Delhi Shanghai Taipei Toronto

With offices in

Argentina Austria Brazil Chile Czech Republic France Greece
Guatemala Hungary Italy Japan South Korea Poland Portugal
Singapore Switzerland Thailand Turkey Ukraine Vietnam

Oxford is a registered trade mark of Oxford University Press
in the UK and in certain other countries

Published in the United States
by Oxford University Press Inc., New York

A catalogue record for this title is available from the British Library

Library of Congress Cataloging in Publication Data
(Data available)

ISBN 0 19 850932 4 (Pbk)

10 9 8 7 6 5 4

Printed in Great Britain
on acid-free paper by Biddles Ltd., King's Lynn, Norfolk

PREFACE

This book appears at a time when there is unprecedented interest in musical behaviour. Music is not only a pleasurable art form, but also plays an increasingly influential role in many aspects of daily life. This is partly because recent technological advances mean that music is more pervasive than at any other time in history. Indeed, recognition of its ubiquitous presence has been one of the factors motivating a growing body of research on the effects of music listening and participation on a range of psychological and physiological variables.

The origins of this book were in 1998, when we made a successful application to The British Psychological Society to host a series of research seminars entitled *Psychology of Music: Theoretical Advances and Practical Applications*. These seminars brought together many established and new researchers with a number of musicians, teachers and music therapists to present and discuss current issues in music psychology, particularly around the topic of musical communication and its link with developing identities. It quickly became clear that the research and ideas being discussed needed to be brought together in a book which explore the issues more widely than was possible at the seminars.

The question of what might constitute musical identity is followed up in some depth in our introductory chapter. Presentations by eminent music therapists Tony Wigram and Leslie Bunt at one of the seminars raised many topical issues regarding the relationship between therapy and identity. For example, the role that music therapy may have in developing communication skills, and the status of research within the music therapy profession were discussed in some detail. These and other issues are taken up in the final two chapters of the book. A number of key educational issues were also discussed at the seminars, and several chapters in this book have direct relevance to the way in which children are taught music. These and many other important topics were discussed at our seminars, and we developed the range of issues under consideration by inviting not only several of the presenters, but also other researchers with interests and expertise in this area, to contribute to the present volume. Our aim has been to produce a text which grapples with a set of key issues around the idea of musical identities rather than simply a collection of papers presented at seminars.

We were keen that the contributors to this book would in some way continue the dialogue and debates begun at the seminars and enhance the connections between the arguments they were each putting forward in their chapters. To achieve this, we held a further meeting at which the authors offered their thoughts on the first drafts of each of the chapters, and exchanged ideas about potential links and developing arguments across their different theoretical traditions or topic areas. We would like to thank all of our contributors for the time and effort they put into helping to make this process a very productive one. Martin Baum, our commissioning editor at Oxford University Press, has been encouraging, friendly and consistently accommodating throughout the whole process of completing this book: his input and support have been vital, and are greatly appreciated. Several others have also been very helpful in discussing ideas with us, and we would like to thank Gordon Dougall, Paul Flowers, Göran Folkestad, Linda, Jon and Tom Hargreaves, Tracy Ibbotson, David Miell, Patrick O'Donnell, Victoria O'Donnell, Ann Phoenix, Mark Tarrant, Stig-Magnus Thorsén, Margaret Wetherell and Graeme Wilson for their valuable contributions.

Those readers with a broad interest in psychological identities will be aware of the explosion of interest that has occurred in this topic over the past few years, and this is accompanied by a stimulating diversity of theoretical and methodological approaches to the topic. The book reflects this diversity and, whilst our approach is by no means exhaustive, we nevertheless feel that the wide range of theoretical perspectives and different research methods represented here will provide several points of departure for those interested in a deeper understanding of musical identities. We hope you enjoy reading the book as much as we enjoyed producing it.

R.A.R. MacDonald
D.J. Hargreaves
D.E. Miell
October 2001

CONTENTS

LIST OF CONTRIBUTORS

THE EDITORS

Raymond MacDonald Department of Psychology, Glasgow Caledonian University, Cowcaddens Road, Glasgow G4 0BA, UK. Lecturer in Psychology at Glasgow Caledonian University, and has been lecturing and researching in the psychology of music for a number of years. He has also been Artistic Director for a music production company, Sounds of Progress, working with individuals who have special needs, and is an experienced jazz saxophonist.

David Hargreaves Centre for International Research in Music Education, Faculty of Education, University of Surrey Roehampton, Southlands College, Roehampton Lane, London SW15 5SL, UK. Professor of Child Development at the University of Surrey Roehampton and Visiting Professor of Research in Music Education at the University of Gothenburg, Sweden. His publications, which have been translated into 13 languages, include *Musical Development and Learning: The International Perspective* (with Adrian North, Continuum, 2001).

Dorothy Miell Department of Psychology, The Open University, Walton Hall, Milton Keynes MK6 7AA, UK. Senior Lecturer in Psychology in the Social Sciences Faculty at The Open University. Her research interests lie in the study of close personal relationships, with the focus on two areas—accounts of identity development through relationships, and the effects of relationship level and communication patterns on the nature of children's and young people's collaborative working, especially in creative tasks such as music making.

CONTRIBUTORS

Sophia Borthwick Department of Music, The University of Sheffield, Sheffield S10 2TN, UK. Began her career in music as a viola player. She recently completed her PhD exploring children's musical development and is now working in the field of clinical psychology.

Jane Davidson Department of Music, The University of Sheffield, Sheffield S10 2TN, UK. Senior Lecturer in Music at the University of Sheffield. She researches and teaches in areas allied to musical performance and development. As a practitioner, she has performed in and directed music theatre works throughout Europe and South East Asia.

Nicola Dibben Department of Music, The University of Sheffield, Sheffield S10 2TN, UK. Lecturer in Music at the University of Sheffield, where she specializes in music psychology and popular music. Her research on the perception of music, and on representations of gender in popular music, has been published in a number of books and journals.

Göran Folkestad School of Music, Göteborg University, Box 210, S-405 30, Göteborg, Sweden. Professor of Research in Music Education at Göteborg University and Lund University, Sweden. His research interests are within the area of musical composition and Information and Communication Technology, in both formal and informal contexts. These interests include the study of young people's creative music making by means of computers.

Alexandra Lamont Department of Psychology, Keele University, Keele, Staffordshire ST5 5BG, UK. Lecturer in Psychology of Music at Keele University. She comes from a multidisciplinary background, and has carried out a broad range of research with infants, children and adults from perceptual, cognitive, social and educational perspectives in relation to music and musical understanding.

Wendy Magee Music Therapy Department, Royal Hospital for Neuro-disability, West Hill, London SW15 3SW, UK. Music therapy clinician, researcher and clinical supervisor working with adults with complex disabilities stemming from acquired brain damage and neurological illness. She holds a Visiting Lectureship at Goldsmiths College, University of London, and lectures on music therapy in the UK and abroad.

Adrian North School of Psychology, University of Leicester, University Road, Leicester LE1 7RH, UK. Lecturer in Psychology at the University of Leicester, and Director of the Music Psychology Research Group in the School of Psychology. His research investigates various aspects of the social psychology of music, including the effects of music on consumer behaviour.

Susan O'Neill Department of Psychology, Keele University, Keele, Staffordshire ST5 5BG, UK. Senior Lecturer in Psychology at Keele University, where she is Associate Director of the Unit for the Study of Musical Skill and Development and Director of the MSc in Music Psychology. She has been awarded a Visiting Research Fellowship at the University of Michigan from 2001 to 2003 to work with members of the Gender and Achievement Research Program. Her research interests include motivation, identity and gender issues associated with young people's engagement in music.

Mark Tarrant Department of Psychology, Keele University, Keele, Staffordshire ST5 5BG, UK. Lecturer in Psychology at Keele University, and has published studies of adolescents' motivations for listening to music, and the role of music in self-concept development. Current research interests include the relationship between social identity and group musical performance, and the role of music in the formation of national identities.

Colwyn Trevarthen Department of Psychology, The University of Edinburgh, 7 George Square Edinburgh EH8 9JZ, UK. Professor (Emeritus) of Child Psychology and Psychobiology and Honorary Research Fellow in the Department of Psychology at the University of Edinburgh, and has published widely on neuropsychology, brain development and communication in infancy. He is interested in how the rhythms and emotions of children's play and imagination, including musical games and songs, support cultural learning in pre-school years, and in the interpersonal foundations of language and meaning.

CHAPTER 1

WHAT ARE MUSICAL IDENTITIES, AND WHY ARE THEY IMPORTANT?

DAVID J. HARGREAVES, DOROTHY MIELL AND
RAYMOND A.R. MACDONALD

Music is a fundamental channel of communication: it provides a means by which people can share emotions, intentions and meanings even though their spoken languages may be mutually incomprehensible. It can also provide a vital lifeline to human interaction for those whose special needs make other means of communication difficult. Music can exert powerful physical effects, can produce deep and profound emotions within us, and can be used to generate infinitely subtle variations of expressiveness by skilled composers and performers.

At the same time, music plays a greater part in the everyday lives of more people than at any time in the past. This is partly the result of the extremely rapid technological developments that have occurred in the last two decades or so, allied to the increasing commercialization and economic power of the music industry. In the developed countries of the world at least, the widespread availability and relative inexpensiveness of the Walkman, the Internet, the MIDI interface, the video recorder and more means that a vast diversity of musical styles and genres is available to us as listeners. The ways in which people experience music—as 'consumers', fans, listeners, composers, arrangers, performers or critics—are far more diverse than at any time in the past, as are the range of contexts in which this takes place.

One result is that music can be used increasingly as a means by which we formulate and express our individual identities. We use it not only to regulate our own everyday moods and behaviours, but also to present ourselves to others in the way we prefer. Our musical tastes and preferences can form an important statement of our values and attitudes, and composers and performers use their music to express their own distinctive views of the world. Nicholas Cook (1998) puts this succinctly: 'In today's world, deciding what music to listen to is a significant part of deciding and announcing to people not just who you "want to be" ... but who you *are*. "Music" is a very small word to encompass something that takes as many forms as there are cultural or sub-cultural identities' (p. 5).

This concept of *identity* enables us to look at the widespread and varied interactions between music and the individual. The concepts of identity and the self have undergone some radical changes in psychological theory in recent years, to which we will return later in this chapter. The idea of the self as a kind of focus, or relatively unchanging core aspect of individuals' personalities, has given way to a much less static and more dynamic view of the self as something which is constantly being reconstructed and renegotiated according to the experiences, situations and other people with whom we interact in everyday life. Globalization and technological advance have led to rapid recent changes in many people's lifestyles, and our self-identities are changing correspondingly in ever more complex ways.

This book is about the role that music plays in this process, and we introduce the concept of *musical identities* as a crucial means of doing so. In this opening chapter, we shall attempt to answer some basic questions: what are musical identities, who has them and how do they form and develop? We tackle these questions from a social psychological perspective, as indeed do the majority of contributors to the book. The same questions are also of current interest in other disciplines: DeNora's (2000) sociological exploration of the role of music as a means of structuring everyday experience is a notable recent example. We have made an ambitious attempt to break new ground: our aim is to set out the territory and ask critical questions rather than necessarily to provide definitive answers.

The two-part structure of the book is based on the conceptual distinction between what we will call *identities in music* (IIM) and *music in identities* (MII). Part One, on IIM, deals with those aspects of musical identities that are socially defined within given cultural roles and musical categories. As we shall see, the ways in which young people do or do not define themselves as musicians, for example, and the role of specific influences such as the school and the family are central reference points for young people's self-concepts with respect to music. In the same way, the culturally defined features of musician, composer, performer, improviser or teacher are central to the identities of professional musicians.

Part Two, on MII, focuses on how we use music as a means or resource for developing other aspects of our individual identities. Our identities can be thought of as complex, hierarchical networks of inter-related constructs: some of these are overarching, superordinate constructs incorporating others which exist at a more subordinate level. For example, Bem (1981) proposed that 'gender schemas', namely our self-definitions as 'masculine' or 'feminine', are at the core of most of the other constructs we use to define ourselves, such that most of the new information we receive about people and their behaviour initially is coded and interpreted in terms of gender norms. This is one aspect of MII that is reviewed in this book, by Nicola Dibben, and we deal also with other aspects including national identity, youth identity and identity as a disabled person.

Four main sections follow this opening section of the chapter. In the first of these, we take a brief look at the development of music psychology over its relatively short history, and attempt to show how various theoretical and empirical developments lead naturally to the investigation of musical identities. We then look more closely at how people's self-concepts and identities have been defined and described within social psychology, and outline the main theoretical concepts that might be useful when we try to explain musical identities. The next section represents our attempt to define and explain the development of musical identities, looking at IIM and MII in turn. In the final section, we look ahead to the remaining contents of the book, and summarize the main orientation and contribution of each chapter.

Musical identity and the development of music psychology

There has been an explosive increase of interest in the psychological basis of musical thinking, behaviour and development over the last two decades or so which shows no sign of abating. Music psychology has very clear overlaps with a number of related disciplines such as cognitive science and computing, sociology, cultural studies, anthropology, education, medicine and health studies, acoustics, broadcasting, marketing and communication studies, as well as with music and musicology. The research is reported in journals in all of these fields, as well as in specialist music psychology journals such as *Music Perception, Musicae Scientiae* and *Psychology of Music*. The subdisciplines of cognitive, developmental and social music psychology are now clearly identifiable, and a brief historical outline of the theoretical and empirical developments which led to their emergence shows how the investigation of musical identities is a natural next step.

Psychometrics, acoustics and cognitive psychology

Before the 1980s, the discipline was characterized by a preponderance of psychometric and acoustical studies. Some well-known early texts such as Lundin's (1967) *An Objective Psychology of Music* and Shuter-Dyson and Gabriel's *The Psychology of Musical Ability* (1968, 1981) reflect this orientation very clearly, which can probably be traced right back to Seashore's (1938) *The Psychology of Music*. The main emphasis was on the objective measurement of acoustic abilities, and there was very little interest in the study of musical behaviour as such.

With the publication of two books, both entitled *The Psychology of Music*, by John Davies (1978) and Diana Deutsch (1982, 1999), a new era began which broadened the horizons of the discipline, and which had a strong grounding in cognitive psychology. The cognitive psychology of music deals with the internalized rules, strategies and operations which people employ in musical behaviour, and this early work included studies of the effects on listeners of tones, intervals and scales; of the perception of and memory for melody; and of the internal representation of harmony and larger scale aspects of musical structure (see Sloboda, 1985).

Although this tradition continues in contemporary research, some of the early research was criticized subsequently for its narrow focus on the minutiae of musical experience, for the artificiality of some of its experimental paradigms and 'laboratory' testing situations, for the unrepresentativeness of its participant groups and because many of the experimental stimuli employed bore very little relation to actual musical materials. Whilst these criticisms may still apply to some research studies, the cognitive psychology of music has now developed to include much more complex and ecologically valid questions about musical behaviour and understanding, including such issues as musical expressiveness and performance; the emotional effects of music; creativity in composition and improvisation; and practical issues for musicians such as sight reading and practice techniques.

The investigation of these issues needs to draw on theories and techniques which go well beyond the cognitive paradigms of the 1980s, however, such that these no longer hold centre stage in contemporary music psychology. Twenty years or so later, it is clear that the discipline as a whole has diversified into various subdisciplines. Alongside the contemporary cognitive psychology of music (e.g. DeLiège and Sloboda, 1997), whose scope has broadened considerably, we can clearly identify the developmental psychology of music (see, for example, Hargreaves, 1986; DeLiège and Sloboda, 1996) and the social psychology of music (see, for example, Hargreaves and North, 1997), and it is easy to foresee similar developments in other clinical and applied areas.

Social psychology

In the broadest sense, the music psychologist's job is to investigate the multifaceted ways in which we engage with music—creating, performing, listening, appraising—and to try to explain the mechanisms underlying its powerful influence on our behaviour. This necessarily means that musical behaviour must be investigated in all of the social and cultural contexts in which it naturally occurs. In a recent attempt to characterize the discipline, Hargreaves and North (1997) suggested that 'psychologists have neglected the social dimension, and that a social psychology of music ought to include the effects of the immediate social environment as well as the impact of broader-based cultural norms. The social psychologist's role is thus to investigate the effects of particular listening and performing/composing situations, as well as those of cultural standards and norms which the historian and the musicologist might investigate' (p. 5).

The social psychology of music is less easy to characterize than the developmental or cognitive subdisciplines since it is less clearly based on a circumscribed set of functionally related phenomena, or on age-related patterns of behaviour. However, its potential scope is delineated by Hargreaves and North (1997), who draw on Doise's (1986) distinction between four types of explanation or 'levels of analysis' in social psychological research. The highest of these are the social-positional and the ideological levels, which deal with the effects of broad institutional or group membership and cultural statements of belief, or norms, respectively. Within music psychology, these might include studies of the effects of social class, educational institutions or the media on musical behaviour. The other two levels of explanation are more microscopic, localized or situation-specific; these are the inter-individual and the intra-individual levels, respectively. The former includes the analysis of small group effects, such as those of conformity or leadership in musical behaviour, and the latter deals with the specific mechanisms with which individuals engage with their musical environments, which might include aspects of individual differences such as gender, age or personality.

The social psychological approach argues for a far greater emphasis on the study of musical behaviour in everyday life situations than in the laboratory and the classroom, and indeed to widen the sphere of investigation beyond specific, formal 'musical' situations such as the concert hall or the practice studio. Another aspect of this argument concerns the *functions* that music fulfils in people's everyday lives. 'What is music for?' is a central question for the social psychology of music, and it has also been discussed in anthropology and sociology (e.g. Merriam, 1964) as well as from an evolutionary point of view (Cross, 2001). From the psychologist's perspective, the functions of music fall into three broad domains, namely the *cognitive*, the *emotional* and the *social*.

Our contention, along with Hargreaves and North (1997), is that music psychology as a whole has placed a disproportionate emphasis on the first two of these domains, and that the social functions of music in the lives of individuals have been seriously neglected. Because music is essentially a social activity—it is something we do along with and for others, either as listeners or as co-creators—there is a strong argument that the social functions of music subsume the cognitive and emotional functions in certain respects.

The research evidence suggests that the social functions of music are manifested in three principal ways for the individual, namely in the management of *interpersonal relationships*, *mood* and *self-identity* (see review by Hargreaves and North, 1999a). First, people use music as a means of developing and negotiating interpersonal relationships. One's musical preferences can define which social groups one does and does not belong to, and this is particularly clear in the case of teenage music preferences (see Tarrant *et al.*, Chapter 8). Secondly, an increasing body of evidence shows that people use music as a means of regulating their mood, and that this is mediated by the immediate social environment in which listening takes place. This can explain patterns of musical taste and preference which are linked with specific listening situations and social circumstances (see, for example, North and Hargreaves, 2000).

The third area forms the central rationale for this book. We suggest that one of the primary social functions of music lies in establishing and developing an individual's sense of identity, and that the concept of *musical identity* enables us to look at the widespread and varied interactions between music and the individual.

Developmental psychology

The central subject matter of the developmental psychology of music is the description and explanation of the patterns of age-related changes that occur across the life span in various aspects of musical behaviour. Several specific models and theories of musical development have been proposed (see, for example, reviews by Hargreaves and Zimmerman, 1992; Swanwick and Runfola, 2002), and an impressive body of evidence is accumulating about the course of normative musical development, as well as about the specific effects of musical training and education. This rapidly growing body of research and theory has the potential to illuminate the ways in which musical identities develop across the life span, although this issue has not been raised as such in the discipline so far.

One of the most striking features of the recent developmental literature is the study of infant musicality, which is beginning to show how biological and social influences jointly shape musical development. Papoušek (1996) relates early musicality to the development of speech and communication. He suggests that 'speech, as a uniquely human form of communication, represents an unusually effective means of biological adaptation' (p. 38). Early musicality is seen as an integral part of early speech and language, and thus also presumably possesses adaptive significance. Speech-related and musical sounds are partly learnt in the infant's social environment, and Papoušek and Papoušek (1982) have demonstrated how parents scaffold the infant's vocal behaviour towards different levels of expertise, and towards the acquisition of emotional meanings.

Parents reinforce the musical aspects of early vocalizations, and also sing songs and lullabies. Gradually, vocal/musical play gives rise to speech and words on the one hand, and to more specific musical activities such as imitation and improvising on the other, so that singing develops as another sphere of activity in its own right. Early musicality thus encapsulates the interaction between biological predispositions and the social world: the development of babies' sense of their environment is inherently social.

Colwyn Trevarthen (1999, and Chapter 2 in this volume) has developed this idea into a theory of a basic motivation for musicality which he sees as providing the origins of later forms of musical expression and artistic creation. He proposes that 'communicative musicality' is the dynamic sympathetic state of an individual that allows co-ordinated companionship to arise. He considers that music communicates with young babies because it engages with what he calls an 'intrinsic motive pulse' (IMP) which is generated within the brain. This comprises a rhythmic time sense, which is able to detect regularities in musical elements, a sensitivity towards the acoustic elements of the qualities of the human voice, and the ability to perceive 'narrative' structures in vocal or musical performances.

In proposing his theory, Trevarthen uses the term 'communicative musicality' to characterize the broad features of early interaction and development, and this goes well beyond music itself. Early interactions between parent and child develop into 'narratives' of mutually constructed meaning, which are characterized by their intersubjectivity. Investigations of talk, singing and other rhythmic games with infants show that the general features of interactive musicality are displayed in the anticipatory movements and emotions which develop between infants and their caregivers. These early interactions can be seen as forming the foundations of musical self-identity: early musical identities are based on learning one's own position and role in relation to the reactions and communications of the other people around, and they are subject to constant development, renegotiation and change.

There is also a much more specific sense in which the musicality of early infant behaviour has been described, however. Sandra Trehub and her colleagues, for example (see Trehub et al., 1997), have been interested in the biological predispositions which infants bring to *listening*. Their extensive programme of research has shown that young babies are precocious in their sensitivity to rhythms, to melodic contours, to simple frequency ratios such as octaves and even to some aspects of harmony, in ways which previously were thought impossible. It appears that they possess strong biological predispositions to respond to the musical features of the sounds they encounter, although cross-cultural studies will need to investigate the relationship between these predispositions and particular tonal systems.

In the broader field of developmental psychology as a whole, there can be little doubt that the main theoretical trend over the last two decades or so has been the investigation of specific social and cultural influences in more detail and depth: this has influenced the course of empirical research as well as the development of developmental theory. The essence of what has become known as the socio-cultural approach within developmental psychology is the notion that the accumulation of knowledge can only be explained within its physical and cultural context: that we must think in terms of *situated cognition* (see, for example, Butterworth, 1992).

The interest in situated cognition introduced the idea of learning as 'cultural practice', and an interest in the 'ecology' of children's learning (e.g. Crook, 2000). This has led to an emphasis on the interactions between the teacher and the learner and between pairs or groups of learners rather than on the child as an individual learner, as was the case in the past. Children are seen as taking on social practices and cultural rules as active partners in the process of what Rogoff (1990) calls 'guided participation': individual development is based on a developing and accumulative series of shared social understandings. This is the essence of the socio-cultural perspective on development, and is now so widely accepted that the discipline of social developmental psychology, or developmental social psychology, which is based on this perspective, might be said to have emerged (see, for example, Durkin, 1995).

We suggest that the study of the development of musical identity is best approached from this theoretical point of view. Children's development of musical identities, which have their origins in biological predispositions towards musicality, are shaped by the individual groups and social institutions that they encounter in their everyday lives. These form an integral part of those identities rather than merely providing the framework or context within which they develop, and this perspective enables us to explain identities in music (IIM) as well as music in identities (MII).

This approach also puts a new perspective on the investigation of individual differences in musical behaviour: issues such as age, gender and personality differences have been studied largely within the psychometric perspective. However, such lines of research are conducted 'from the outside': they do not deal with people's *experience* of the features which define them as individuals. The concept of musical identity takes us a stage further in enabling us to understand the individual's musical behaviour 'from the inside': to explain some of the processes and mechanisms by which individuals monitor and conceptualize their own musical development. This represents a significant advance for the social and developmental psychology of music, and is the central task of this book.

Concepts of self and identity in social psychology

The notion of identity has long been a topic of interest within psychology, although it has been addressed in many different ways and from some very different theoretical perspectives. As early as 1890, William James, one of the founders of psychology, was perhaps the first theorist to try and understand the self—which he called 'the most puzzling puzzle with which psychology has to deal'. In the century of research and writing since then, this puzzle has stimulated a good deal of effort to explain, 'unpack' and, most recently, challenge the meanings of self and identity.

Self-concept, self-esteem and self-identity

There is a good deal of current research on different aspects of the self and its development, and it might be useful to start by clarifying some of the current terminology in this field. We might say that the *self-system* is made up of a number of *self-concepts*, or *self-images*, which are the different ways in which we see ourselves. These self-concepts can be context- or situation-specific (e.g. how I see myself as being able to cope under stress, or in an emergency), or domain-related (e.g. how I see myself as a linguist, or a musician). *Self-identity* is the overall view that we have of ourselves in which these different self-concepts are integrated, although the ways in which individuals accomplish this remain a central and unresolved theoretical question. *Self-esteem* is the evaluative component of the self, and has both cognitive and emotional aspects: how worthy we think, and feel we are.

Self-image and self-esteem have received most of the research attention. The development of different components of self-image in childhood and adolescence has received particular attention. The self-image includes aspects of personality style, appearance and the social roles that we play. Those components relating to the specific domain of music, for example, might include 'saxophonist', 'jazz fan' or 'music teacher'—all of which are instances of what we have termed identities in music (IIM). Harter (1999) has suggested that these domain-specific self-images typically become integrated into a generalized self-concept at around the age of 8 years, although the existence of such a 'core' self-concept or self-identity is itself problematic.

The self-image develops by a process of monitoring our own behaviour, and making social comparisons. We constantly compare ourselves with others, so that particular situations and social groups exert a powerful influence on what we do and what we say. We also compare our behaviour with what we expect ourselves to do on the basis of our self-image, which is built up from past experience, and with what we would like to do, i.e. with our ideal self-image. Rogers (1961) suggested that when these comparisons give rise to incongruity (between either ideal self and self-image, or between self-image and actual behaviour), psychological distress can be the result. An accomplished musician with classical western training may be disturbed to be asked to improvise in informal situations, for example. Equally, someone whose ideal self is built on their ability to improvise may feel embarrassed about their ignorance of musical theory, or their inability to read a score.

The psychological distress experienced by such discrepancies is often felt in terms of lowered self-esteem—the other factor which has received a good deal of psychological research attention in the last century. Self-esteem can involve overall evaluations of ourselves, e.g. as a musician, or of very specific aspects of our self-image, such as our aptitude as a piano improviser. The factors that influence self-esteem and its development have been studied extensively, and one of the key findings is the importance of the influence that other people can have on an individual's sense of worth.

This influence of other people's views can be felt partly through the indirect process of comparing ourselves and our behaviour with similar others to obtain a sense of our relative effectiveness and worth, even when those others may be unaware of their effect on us. It can also operate more directly, however, when others comment directly on our abilities, appearance and general behaviour. Such judgements are particularly influential when they are made by significant others—for a child, this would mean parents and siblings primarily, but could also include teachers. Family and school contexts can therefore be crucially important for a child's developing sense of self and particularly for their self-esteem. Some striking evidence for this in the case of what we might call musical self-esteem is presented in Chapters 3, 4 and 5 of this book.

Theories of self and identity

William James' (1890) distinction between two components of identity, the 'I' and the 'me', has had a long-lasting impact. The 'me' is that part of our identity which can be observed and known, whilst the 'I' is that part that is able to reflect on the 'me', i.e. which has subjectivity and is the knower. The 'I' therefore constituted the 'real' and unchanging self for James, whereas the 'me' was seen as subject to change since it is composed of social categories. James identified four aspects of the 'me': the spiritual self, the material self, the social self and the bodily self, all of which were seen as plural in that they come in different forms.

This view has been at the heart of the later theories which were influenced by the work of the influential neo-Freudian psychoanalyst Erik Erikson, who coined the term 'ego identity' (see, for example, Kroger, 1993). The concept of a reflexive 'I' influenced by social encounters is also to be found in the theories of Cooley (1902), who wrote of the 'looking glass self' in which we gain our identities partly by seeing reflections of what other people think of us. It is also a central part of the work of the sociologist and social philosopher George Herbert Mead (1934), who made a distinction between the personal and the social aspects of self in describing the 'I' and the 'me'. Mead saw language as the supreme symbolic system for communicating and for negotiating inter-actions, in that it allows people to carry on 'internal conversations' with themselves and to anticipate the responses of other 'actors'. This was the essence of 'symbolic inter-actionism', which pre-figured social constructionist theory.

Another account of the development and maintenance of self-esteem and the role played by others is social identity theory, which was developed by Henri Tajfel and colleagues (e.g. Tajfel, 1978). This proposes that individuals have a fundamental motivation to develop and maintain a high level of self-esteem, and that this is estab-lished through identification with groups of people who have a positive image, since social identity and personal identity are conceptually distinct, yet inextricably linked. Individuals attempt to maximize the differences between their own group (the in-group) and others (out-groups) on those dimensions that favour the in-group. They maintain a positive social identity by boosting the value of the in-group's attributes in compari-son with members of out-groups. For adolescents striving to establish their identities and to increase their self-esteem, identifying with particular genres of music which they rate highly (e.g. 'intelligent drum'n'bass') and distancing themselves from less valued genres (e.g. 'pop') allows them to establish favourable social and personal identities (see Tarrant et al., Chapter 8).

In many ways, these psychological questions about the self are very much in keeping with the 'common sense' perspective on identity that those of us in the Western world assume to be typical and a pervasive experience, i.e. we experience our selves as being self-contained, internally coherent, different in important ways from others around us, and relatively stable and consistent over our lifetimes. Psychologists in the main have also taken this view of individuals, and their research has focused on investigating the typical range of differences between people in self-esteem and other aspects of self-concept, and what sets of personality traits might account for the key dimensions underlying these differences.

However, social constructionist approaches within psychology diverge from this in suggesting that the self cannot be characterized in this way. Instead, they suggest that it is formed and developed continuously through conversation and interaction with others. In other words, we are not just influenced by others, but are in effect made up of interactions with others—we are ultimately social and not personal beings. Social constructionist ideas have diverse origins in a number of disciplines and, although there are many social constructionist perspectives, all of them clearly diverge from those of James, Erikson and Tajfel, in which the 'personal' and 'social' aspects of the self are differentiated.

The beginnings of this approach may perhaps be traced to Mead's (1934) emphasis on the interplay between self and society: that we cannot develop an understanding of one without the other, and that this is achieved through interaction with others. We play with a range of social roles in order to understand the self from the perspective of others in different roles (a development of Cooley's 'looking glass self'). Language is seen as vital to this process as it allows people to reflect on their own behaviour as well as that of others, and to come to a reflexive understanding of their selves as a result. Others have built on Mead's ideas in the social constructionist tradition, and their view of the self is well expressed by Bahktin (1981):

I am conscious of myself and become myself only while revealing myself for another, through another, and with the help of another . . . every internal experience ends up on the boundary . . . 'To be' means to communicate . . . 'To be' means to be for the other; and through him, for oneself. Man has no internal sovereign territory; he is all and always on the boundary (p. 287).

Social constructionist theories suggest that people have many identities, each of which is created in interaction with other people, rather than having a single, core identity. These identities can be contradictory; for example, a musician can be a 'different person' on stage than when in solitary rehearsals, and be different again when engaged in each of a number of non-musical activities. In social constructionist terms, identities are also always evolving and shifting—each interaction can lead to new constructions.

Language plays a central role in social constructionist accounts of developing identities, and Western theories of the psychology of the self have perhaps clung for so long to the view of a single unitary self because most of the Western languages include words such as 'I' and 'me' which imply that a consistent personal agent exists which underlies our actions. In the language of some other more collectivist cultures, such as Japan, the self is referenced very differently, and is signified by many more words, depending on the other participants in the interaction. Bruner (1990) suggests that we 'make ourselves' and our identities through our autobiographical narratives—the stories about ourselves that we tell others and indeed ourselves. This is perhaps one reason why we have a subjective feeling of having a core identity—a relatively unchanging sense of self that has a history—rather than the shifting and multiple identities of the constructionists' account. We construct particular narratives for ourselves as they fit our Western ideas of what people 'are'.

As we said at the very start of this chapter, music is a fundamental channel of communication, and we argue that it can act as a medium through which people can construct new identities and shift existing ones in the same way as spoken language. The continual construction and reconstruction of the self through autobiographical narratives can occur in music as well as in language, and Gergen's (1994) definition of meaningful discourse aptly describes some of the properties of musical communication:

Meaningful language is the product of social interdependence. It requires the co-ordinated actions of at least two persons, and until there is mutual agreement on the meaningful character of words, they fail to constitute language. If we follow this line of argument to its ineluctable conclusion, we find that it is not the mind of the single individual that provides whatever certitude we possess, but relationships of interdependency.... We may rightfully replace Descartes's dictum ('Cogito ergo sum') with 'communicamus ergo sum.' We communicate, therefore I am (p. viii).

There is an obvious parallel between this process and Trevarthen's notion of 'communicative musicality', which we discussed earlier. The early interactions and narratives which are constructed between babies and their caregivers display inherently musical features, but also exist in other activities such as linguistic play and physical movement, as well as in musical activities themselves. These can be seen as the origins of musical identities, which are therefore not individual but mutual constructions, as Gergen suggests.

Conceptualizing musical identities

We have now set the scene for our discussion of musical identities, and have made some basic conceptual distinctions. Is it true to say that everyone has a musical identity? Very few people claim to have no interest in or liking for any aspect of music whatsoever. Most people have strong musical likes and dislikes regardless of their level of musical expertise: even those who might proudly (and erroneously) describe themselves as being 'tone deaf' are likely to have clear-cut preferences. Individual patterns of preference, described in the literature as 'musical taste', can be an integral part of one's self-concept, and this is particularly clear in adolescence. Musical taste has been shown to be related to age, level of musical training and aspects of cognitive style and personality, and the notions of 'taste cultures' and 'taste publics' have been proposed to explain how social groups might have distinctive patterns of preferences and values (see Hargreaves, 1986; Kemp, 1996).

However, we have already pointed out that people's musical likes and dislikes vary according to their moods, the time of day, their social situation and many other circumstances which are constantly changing. The complexity of these reactions and their relationship to other aspects of everyday life are apparent in an increasing body of recent research (e.g. North and Hargreaves, 2000; Sloboda et al., 2001). In other words, music can have short-term, transitory effects as well as a more deep-seated influence on our beliefs and behaviour. It is perhaps useful to think of a continuum of the levels at which we engage with different kinds of music in different situations. The background music that is playing in a store or restaurant may engage us at such a low level that we are unaware of it: yet even this can been shown to have a strong influence, for example, on our spending behaviour (see, for example, North et al., 1998). This is at the opposite end of the 'engagement' continuum from the 'peak experiences' which people report, showing that music can produce extremely strong emotional and physical reactions (see, for example, Gabrielsson and Lindström, 1993).

In between these two extremes, most of us listen to music at varying levels of engage-ment to regulate our moods in different contexts, and whilst involved in different activ-ities. It seems reasonable to suggest that our broad patterns of preference, and indeed even our transitory likes and dislikes, form part of our musical identities: presumably those that exist at higher levels of engagement are more integral to those identities. Many people regard themselves as fans, amateur critics or 'buffs' within styles and genres that particularly interest them, and can indeed be just as knowledgeable as professional critics within these specific domains. The complexity and ever-changing nature of this process is readily apparent, and it is in this sense that aspects of our musical identities constantly are being reconstructed.

Although tastes and preferences in listening form part of the musical identities of most people, they may nevertheless play a minor or insignificant role for others. As we pointed out earlier, self-systems are made up of a number of different self-concepts, some of which are domain-specific: the importance of the domain of music will vary considerably in the self-identities of different individuals. This variation is very likely to depend on the level of specialist interest or professional training in music. Professional performers or composers are likely to be so highly involved that they see most aspects of their lives in relation to music: in Chapter 6, Jane Davidson suggests that professional solo performers take on additional 'performance identities' alongside their everyday identities. The musical activities of these individuals are at the core of their identities, and this perhaps represents the most clear-cut form of the first of the two broad areas of musical identity that we have delineated, and which we now go on to explore in more detail.

Identities in music (IIM)

These are defined by social and cultural roles within music, and might be categorized in a number of different ways. They might be derived from broad, *generic* distinctions within musical activities: we could speculate that the culturally defined roles of the composer, the performer, the improviser or the teacher are central to the self-definitions of professional or skilled musicians. Cook (1998) has discussed some of the relation-ships between these generic roles in terms of the question of *authenticity*, suggesting that they embody outmoded and hierarchical value systems which derive from 19th century European 'classical' music, and which can be traced back to Beethoven. This view of musical authenticity implies that its creators exist on a higher plane than its reproducers, or performers, which in turn implies that music is something which exists 'out there', in a sense independently of those activities which bring it to life.

Cook argues that this is inappropriate for contemporary musical experience:

There is, in short, a nexus of interrelated assumptions built into the basic language we use of music: that musicianship is the preserve of appropriately qualified specialists; that innovation (research and design) is central to musical culture; that the key personnel in musical culture are the composers who generate what might be termed the core product; that performers are in essence no more than middlemen...and that listeners are consumers, playing an essentially passive role in the cultural process...in truth none of these things are natural; they are all human constructions, products of culture, and accordingly they vary from time to time and from place to place (p. 17).

We agree, and the ways in which humans view themselves in relation to these culturally defined roles are at the heart of our concept of identities in music. Most creators are not solitary figures whose inspiration comes from some mysterious and unconscious muse, but hard-working professionals whose work is constrained by the everyday demands of working with others. Similarly, listeners are not passive consumers, but active partners in a cultural process who use music to fulfil different functions according to different social contexts and locations.

One body of research with an obvious bearing on the question of musical identity is that which has attempted to investigate the personality characteristics of specialists in different areas of musical activity. This has been reviewed painstakingly and expertly by Kemp (1996), who has himself conducted a good deal of the empirical research in the field. Kemp suggests that musicians as a whole have certain distinctive characteristics, such as introversion, anxiety and pathemia (sensitivity and imagination), and goes on to draw finer distinctions between the particular personality profiles of composers, music teachers, instrumental performers, and so on.

The notion of the 'musical personality' raises several obvious questions. Are people with certain personality predispositions drawn to certain instruments or activities, or does taking part in these activities give rise to the development of those personality traits? Another central issue in personality theory is the 'person–situation' debate: can personality traits predict our behaviour across different situations, or is the situational variation so great that it swamps any meaningful consistent individual differences in behaviour? In some ways, these issues run parallel to those we raised earlier about the nature of the self: do we construct 'core' self-concepts which are relatively unchanging across different situations and interactions, or do we adopt different selves in different contexts? This is not the place to try and answer these big questions, and traditional personality theory has some obvious limitations in dealing with these issues. For now, we will simply note that musical personalities and musical identities are closely inter-woven, and that our own emphasis is upon the way that both of these are constructed in relation to other people and different situations.

Alongside these *generic* distinctions, we might also propose that *specific* identities in music exist, which derive from special interest groups. Two obvious groupings might be those relating to particular musical instruments and those relating to particular musical genres. In the case of *instruments*, Kemp's (1996) review of the research literature on professional orchestral players suggests that orchestral string, brass, percussion and woodwind players have distinctive personality profiles, as have keyboard players, singers and conductors, and indeed that these may be reinforced by the stereotypical views that groups of professional players might have of each other. This leads to the obvious speculation that specific musical identities might exist in relation to particular instruments, although the theoretical implications of this idea must remain a question for the future.

As far as musical *genres* are concerned, Kemp's review also touches on particular aspects of the lifestyle and personalities of professional musicians in what he calls 'popular' fields, such as pop, rock, jazz and commercial session work. This is an interesting though undeveloped research area, and the role of genres in musical identity is much more clearly apparent in the notion of 'taste publics', which we mentioned earlier.

These are social groups which exhibit distinctive musical style preferences such as for jazz, country and western, folk, classical, or for subgroups within these broad genres. Defining taxonomies or classifications of these styles is no easy task, not least because the categories themselves change rapidly, particularly in pop music (see Hargreaves and North, 1999b).

In summary, we are suggesting that identities in music might be based on generic distinctions between broad categories of musical activity, as well as on specific distinctions which cut across these categories, in particular *instruments* and *genres*. This is of course extremely rough and ready, and musicologists and others could refine our argument considerably. Nevertheless, it serves as the starting point for our basic argument that 'identities in music' are based on social categories and cultural musical practices.

The development of these identities in childhood, which typically emerge at around the age of 7 years, is based initially on specific activities within music. Alexandra Lamont's research, which she describes in Chapter 3, provides a particularly clear example of the way in which children's self-definitions as 'musician' or 'non-musician' are based on activities within the school curriculum. She found that taking formal instrumental lessons was the critical factor in the self-description as musician. Half of the children she studied described themselves as 'non-musicians' because they did not have this formal tuition even though they did play instruments within general class musical activities.

If children's identities within music are grounded in social contexts, it seems even more likely that their 'musical self-esteem' has a similar origin. Reynolds (1992) has reviewed the literature on what she calls the 'self-concept of musical ability', which is how children see their ability in relation to others. She also reviews some psychometric tests which have been formulated to measure these levels of musical self-esteem. The crucial point is that children's self-ratings of musical ability determine the likelihood of their pursuing further activities in music, which in turn provide the opportunities for any progress and development that might take place. To define oneself as a 'non-musician' at an early stage may preclude such developments irrespective of the child's actual level of potential ability.

The mechanisms of the process by which children's musical self-perceptions determine levels of motivation, and thence actual development and achievement, are elaborated by Susan O'Neill in Chapter 5. O'Neill draws on Dweck's (1999) account of 'self-theories', which incorporate the distinction between 'entity theorists'—those who believe their abilities are fixed and innate—and 'incremental theorists', who believe that their abilities can be changed through practice and effort. People might implicitly hold entity theories about their abilities in some fields (e.g. sport), and incremental theories about those in others (e.g. music). O'Neill provides a convincing account of the ways in which children's motivations to be successful in musical activities are dependent on these processes of self-perception: those with what she calls 'mastery-oriented' strategies of motivation are more likely to persist despite instances of failure, for example, and to pursue new challenges.

Music in identities (MII)

The second part of the book deals with how we use music as a means of, or as a resource for, developing other aspects of our personal identities, including gender identity;

youth identity; national identity; and disability and identity. We suggested earlier that people's levels of engagement with music can vary from having virtually no investment to very high levels of commitment, and that these levels may vary markedly between active and passive participation in different individuals. In a similar way, music plays a greater or lesser role in other aspects of people's identities. The musical preferences of many 13-year-olds are a vital part of their overall identities, as Mark Tarrant and colleagues clearly demonstrate in Chapter 8, whereas they may play an incidental role in the self-concepts of others.

In order to explain the role of music in developing identities, we can draw on psychological theories of identity and of self-esteem, and three clear trends can be identified in the developmental literature. First, generalized aspects of the self-concept become increasingly differentiated with age. Whilst younger children might generalize being good at one activity to various others, an understanding emerges in middle childhood that they are good at some things but not at others (Harter, 1999): musical abilities may well therefore begin to be differentiated from others at around this age. Secondly, there seems to be a general shift away from an emphasis on physical characteristics and activities in early childhood, such as sporting or musical interests, and towards more psychological judgements involving feelings and emotions, such as how and why one participates in those activities (Damon and Hart, 1988).

This developing focus on psychological characteristics provides the origin of the mechanisms of self-perception that we described earlier, with its corresponding impact on children's motivation and ability in different activities. These mechanisms reflect the third main trend in the development of self-identity, namely that children's self-concepts become increasingly based on comparisons with others in middle childhood through to adolescence. Their own achievements and attitudes, for example in musical activities, become based on comparisons with their peers. Once again, the message is clear: children's identities, including musical identities, are constructed and reconstructed by making comparisons with other people, and this continues into adult life.

Plan of the book

The previous section represents our attempt to deal head on with the question posed in the title of this opening chapter. This is an ambitious undertaking which raises more questions than it answers; but we hope that others may be inspired to pursue some of those questions. The chapters in the rest of the book make a start on different aspects of the enterprise.

Chapter 2, by Colwyn Trevarthen, provides an account of the origins of musicality in infancy which highlights the communicative power of music, and which thereby illuminates not only the origins of musical identities, but also some of the processes which govern their development. Because this provides a general theoretical underpinning for the book as a whole, the chapter appears before the two main sections of the book. Trevarthen elaborates upon his assertion that we are all musical: that every human being has a biological and social guarantee of musicality. This is not a vague utopian ideal, but rather a conclusion drawn by an increasing number of academic researchers interested in developing our knowledge of the psychological foundations of music listening and performance (e.g. Hodges, 1996; MacDonald and Miell, 2000). Trevarthen's chapter emphasizes that music is central in babies' lives, and demonstrates the fundamental role that it plays in developing parent–child bonding. His ideas have wide-ranging implications for many issues in the developmental, social and therapeutic aspects of music psychology.

In Chapter 3, Alexandra Lamont discusses empirical research in discussing how the structuring of musical activities within the school environment has a significant influence upon a child's developing musical identity. One of the most illuminating aspects of her chapter is her reflection on the impact that instrumental music tuition provided by peripatetic teachers can have in this respect. She demonstrates that children in school who have no such instrumental music provision are more likely to see themselves as musicians, presumably through their involvement in general class musical activities, than children in schools in which individuals are taken out of class lessons to receive specialist tuition. This chapter has particular educational relevance: if children do not view themselves as musical, it will be difficult if not impossible for them to develop musically, as performers at least.

In Chapter 4, Sophia Borthwick and Jane Davidson discuss the influences that family interactions can exert upon a child's developing musical identity. This chapter utilizes script theory to highlight how certain key features of daily family interactions can have a significant impact on children's developing sense of musical identity. They trace the influence of parents and siblings, noting in particular how parents' perceptions of each child's musicality can affect the interactions of all the siblings in a family. One particularly interesting finding is that the parents involved in the study were very keen for their children to develop advanced musical skills, and viewed music as one of the most important activities in which their children were engaged. At the same time, however, these parents were not keen for their children to become professional musicians, and this *double bind* situation often perplexed the children.

Susan O'Neill, in presenting data from her in-depth interviews with young musicians in Chapter 5, also highlights the fluid and constantly evolving nature of musical identities. She explores the contradictions and complexities involved in adopting the label of 'musician', and uses social constructionist theory to illuminate the delicate interplay that exists between social perceptions of and personal beliefs about musicality. For example, her interviews with four young female musicians reveal that issues such as public performances and friends' expectations of how a musician should behave influence how these young people feel about themselves as musicians.

The final chapter in Part One, by Jane Davidson, introduces the notion of a 'performer identity'. She investigates the identity of the professional adult performer, and the intrinsically social nature of musical performance. The stereotype of composers who lock themselves away in solitude, wrestling with their creativity to produce original works of genius, has very little basis in reality, since a growing body of research highlights the social features of musical creativity: a musician's creative output is inextricably linked to a social and cultural milieu (Miell and MacDonald, 2000). Davidson highlights some key distinctions between the musical identities of individuals who see themselves as 'professional performers' and others who are also technically accomplished, but who see themselves as 'players but not performers'.

Part Two of the book (MII) looks at how music can influence and channel many non-musical aspects of identity: at the impact of music on our sense of who we are. In Chapter 7, for example, Nicola Dibben discusses some central and sometimes controversial issues concerning gender identity and music. Her review shows that boys' and girls' own gender development can influence their musical perceptions: girls often see themselves as good singers, whereas boys have more confidence in composition, for example. This gender distinction exists not only in musical performance, but also in musical taste: preferences for specific styles seem to influence and be influenced by our constantly evolving gender identity.

Mark Tarrant and his colleagues investigate young people's musical identities from the perspective of Social Identity Theory in Chapter 8. The distinction between in-groups and out-groups is central to this approach, and their research highlights the ways in which identification with musical styles affects adolescents' identification with these groups. This research shows that the music we choose signals many other non-musical aspects about ourselves, and that young people use their liking of particular forms of music to ally themselves with members of their peer group. Tarrant *et al.* note that music can act as a powerful badge of identity for adolescents, perhaps more than any other aspects of their lives, and that as such it represents a fundamental influence on their identities.

In Chapter 9, Göran Folkestad explores the relationship between national identity and music from a number of different perspectives. He provides examples that demonstrate how our sense of belonging to a nation can be communicated through music, noting that national anthems and the educational environment in which children learn about music are both very influential in developing and sustaining our national identities. Folkestad also discusses the influence of globalized popular music on people's concepts of national identity. Has the growth of popular music which does not recognize national boundaries diminished our identification with music from our own country, and what are the implications of this for music education? Folkestad provides some thought-provoking answers to these questions which should generate further interest in this topical yet neglected area.

The final two chapters of the book focus on the therapeutic applications of music, and the ways in which musical participation that has explicit therapeutic and/or educational objectives might influence our sense of self. The relationship between musical participation and an individual's psychological well-being is of increasing interest to researchers and practitioners working this area. Of particular interest are the precise connections between the educational, therapeutic, clinical and musical aspects of this type of work (MacDonald, O'Donnell *et al.*, 1999; Ockleford, 2000), and Chapters 10 and 11 contribute towards the dialogue which is needed between researchers and clinicians. Both chapters discuss how musical participation can help develop an individual's sense of ability in music, and feelings of ownership of a creative product, and this highlights some of the parallels that can exist between therapeutic and educational music interventions.

In Chapter 10, two of us (Raymond MacDonald and Dorothy Miell) focus on the work of a music company that specializes in working with people who have special needs. The chapter discusses both the musical and psychological developments that can result from musical participation, and then considers how specific observed developments in communication and musical ability can in turn influence the identities of those involved in musical activities.

In the final chapter of the book, Wendy Magee discusses a music therapy intervention. She carried out in-depth interviews exploring the music therapy experiences of her clients and presents here the detailed analysis of one case study of a client with multiple sclerosis, a chronic and progressive neurological disability. Magee highlights a number of key changes in self-concept that appeared to arise as result of the clinical improvisations that took place during the music therapy sessions. In particular, she demonstrates how music therapy gives opportunities for interactions that help to reduce the feelings of hopelessness and isolation that often accompany severe illness.

In this opening chapter, we have tried to develop and map out what 'musical identities' might be, drawing largely on research in the social and developmental psychology of music. The concept of identity is important because it enables us to understand individuals' musical development 'from the inside' whilst clearly locating identity as an emergent feature of our fundamentally social worlds. It provides us with a way of conceptualizing the interaction between biological and social influences, and provides continuity between our explanations of infant, child and adult behaviour. Studying the ways in which people perceive themselves in relation to music has the potential to explain some phenomena of musical behaviour and experience that might otherwise be inaccessible. This is an important undertaking, particularly at a time when the nature of musical experience itself is changing so rapidly in the globalized world.

References

Bahktin, M. (1981). Discourse in the novel. In M. Holquist (ed.), *The Dialogic Imagination*, (pp. 259–422) (translated by C. Emerson and M. Holquist). Austin, TX: University of Texas Press.

Bem, S.L. (1981). Gender schema theory: a cognitive account of sex typing. *Psychological Review*, 88, 354–364.

Bruner, J. (1990). *Acts of Meaning*. Cambridge, MA: Harvard University Press.

Butterworth, G. (1992). Context and cognition in models of cognitive growth. In P. Light and G. Butterworth (ed.), *Context and Cognition: Ways of Learning and Knowing*, (pp. 1–13). Hillsdale, NJ: Lawrence Erlbaum.

Cook, N. (1998). *Music: A Very Short Introduction*. Oxford: Oxford University Press.

Cooley, C.H. (1902). *Human Nature and Social Order*. New York: Shocken.

Crook, C. (2000). Motivation and the ecology of collaborative learning. In R. Joiner, K. Littleton, D. Faulkner and D.E. Miell (ed.), *Rethinking Collaborative Learning*, (pp. 161–178). London: Free Association Books.

Cross, I.C. (2001). Music, mind and evolution. *Psychology of Music*, 29, 95–102.

Damon, W. and Hart, D. (1988). *Self-understanding in Childhood and Adolescence*. Cambridge: Cambridge University Press.

Davies, J.B. (1978). *The Psychology of Music*. London: Hutchinson.

DeLiège, I. and Sloboda, J.A. (ed.) (1996). *Musical Beginnings: Origins and Development of Musical Competence*. Oxford: Oxford University Press.

DeLiège, I. and Sloboda, J.A. (ed.) (1997). *Perception and Cognition of Music.* Hove, UK: Psychology Press.

DeNora, T. (2000). *Music in Everyday Life.* Cambridge: Cambridge University Press.

Deutsch, D. (ed.) (1982). *The Psychology of Music.* New York: Academic Press.

Deutsch, D. (ed.) (1999). *The Psychology of Music,* 2nd edn. San Diego: Academic Press.

Doise, W. (1986). *Levels of Explanation in Social Psychology.* Cambridge: Cambridge University Press.

Durkin, K. (1995). *Developmental Social Psychology.* Oxford: Basil Blackwell.

Dweck, C.S. (1999). *Self-theories: Their Role in Motivation, Personality and Development.* Hove, UK: Psychology Press.

Gabrielsson, A. and Lindström, S. (1993). On strong experiences of music. *Jahrbuch der Deutschen Gesellschaft für Musikpsychologie,* **10,** 114–125.

Gergen, K. (1994). *Toward Transformation in Social Knowledge,* 2nd edn. London: Sage.

Hargreaves, D.J. (1986). *The Developmental Psychology of Music.* Cambridge: Cambridge University Press.

Hargreaves, D.J. and North, A.C. (ed.) (1997). *The Social Psychology of Music.* Oxford: Oxford University Press.

Hargreaves, D.J. and North, A.C. (1999a). The functions of music in everyday life: redefining the social in music psychology. *Psychology of Music,* **27,** 71–83.

Hargreaves, D.J. and North, A.C. (1999b). Developing concepts of musical style. *Musicae Scientiae,* **3,** 193–216.

Hargreaves, D.J. and Zimmerman, M. (1992). Developmental theories of music learning. In R. Colwell (ed.), *Handbook for Research in Music Teaching and Learning,* (pp. 377–391). New York: Schirmer/Macmillan.

Harter, S. (1999). *The Construction of the Self: A Developmental Perspective.* New York: Guilford Press.

Hodges, D.A. (ed.) (1996). *Handbook of Music Psychology.* Missouri: MMB Music.

James, W. (1890). *The Principles of Psychology,* Vol. 1. New York: Holt.

Kemp. A.E. (1996). *The Musical Temperament: Psychology and Personality of Musicians.* Oxford: Oxford University Press.

Kroger, J. (1993). *Identity in Adolescence: The Balance Between Self and Other,* 2nd edn. London: Routledge.

Lundin, R.W. (1967). *An Objective Psychology of Music,* 2nd edn. New York: Ronald.

MacDonald, R.A.R and Miell, D.E. (2000). Creativity and music education: the impact of social variables. *International Journal of Music Education,* **36,** 58–68.

MacDonald, R.A.R., O'Donnell, P.J. and Davies, J.B. (1999). Structured music workshops for individuals with learning difficulty: an empirical investigation. *Journal of Applied Research in Intellectual Disabilities,* **12,** 225–241.

Mead, G.H. (1934). *Mind, Self and Society.* Chicago: University of Chicago Press.

Merriam, A.P. (1964). *The Anthropology of Music.* Chicago: Northwestern University Press.

Miell, D.E. and MacDonald, R.A.R. (2000). Children's creative collaborations: the importance of friendship when working together on a musical composition. *Social Development,* **9,** 348–369.

North, A.C. and Hargreaves, D.J. (2000). Musical preferences during and after relaxation and exercise. *American Journal of Psychology,* **113,** 43–67.

North, A.C., Hargreaves, D.J. and McKendrick, J. (1998). The effects of music on atmosphere and purchase intentions in a cafeteria. *Journal of Applied Social Psychology*, **28**, 2254–2273.

Ockelford, A. (2000). Music in the education of children with severe or profound difficulties: issues in current UK provision, a new conceptual framework and proposals for research. *Psychology of Music*, **28**, 197–218.

Papoušek, H. (1996). Musicality in infancy research: biological and cultural origins of early musicality. In I. DeLiège and J.A. Sloboda (ed.), *Musical Beginnings: Origins and Development of Musical Competence*, pp. 37–55. Oxford: Oxford University Press.

Papoušek, H. and Papoušek, M. (1982). Integration into the social world: survey of research. In P.M. Stratton (ed.), *Psychology of the Human Newborn*, (pp. 367–390). London: John Wiley.

Reynolds, J.W. (1992). Music education and student self-concept: a review and synthesis of the literature. Unpublished Masters' thesis, University of South Florida.

Rogers, C.L. (1961). *On Becoming a Person*. Boston: Houghton Mifflin.

Rogoff, B. (1990). *Apprenticeship in Thinking: Cognitive Development in Social Context*. New York: Oxford University Press.

Seashore, C.E. (1938). *Psychology of Music*. New York: Dover.

Shuter, R. (1968). *The Psychology of Musical Ability*. London: Methuen.

Shuter-Dyson, R and Gabriel, C. (1981). *The Psychology of Musical Ability*, 2nd edn. London: Methuen.

Sloboda, J.A. (1985). *The Musical Mind: The Cognitive Psychology of Music*. Oxford: Oxford University Press.

Sloboda, J.A., O'Neill, S.A. and Ivaldi, A. (2001). Functions of music in everyday life: an exploratory study using the Experience Sampling Method. *Musicae Scientiae*, **5**, 9–32.

Swanwick, K. and Runfola, M. (2002). Developmental characteristics of learners. In R. Colwell (ed.), *Second Handbook of Research on Music Teaching and Learning*. Oxford: Oxford University Press.

Tajfel, H. (ed.) (1978). *Differentiation Between Social Groups: Studies in the Social Psychology of Intergroup Relations*. London: Academic Press.

Trehub, S., Schellenberg, E. and Hill, D. (1997). The origins of music perception and cognition: a developmental perspective. In I. DeLiège and J.A. Sloboda (ed.), *Perception and Cognition of Music*, pp. 103–128. Hove, UK: Psychology Press.

Trevarthen, C. (1999). Musicality and the intrinsic motive pulse: evidence from human psychobiology and infant communication. *Musicae Scientiae, Special Issue (1999–2000)*, 155–215.

CHAPTER 2

ORIGINS OF MUSICAL IDENTITY: EVIDENCE FROM INFANCY FOR MUSICAL SOCIAL AWARENESS

COLWYN TREVARTHEN

Because music is an outward sign of human communication, and communication can be achieved with or without audible or visible signals, the inner meaning of a piece of music can sometimes be grasped intuitively. In this case, its structure need not be understood nor need its style be familiar to the listener. But if we are to understand fully its outward form as well as its inner meaning, and particularly the relationship between the two, we cannot study independently any of these things, because all three are interrelated. The function of music is to enhance in some way the quality of individual experience and human relationships; its structures are reflections of patterns of human relations, and the value of a piece of music is inseparable from its value as an expression of human experience.

The common factor is therefore the experience of the individual in society. If the functions, structure, and value of music can all be related to patterns of individual and social experience, we have the groundwork for a theory of music making that can be applied universally. (Blacking, 1969/1995, p. 31)

Introduction: what is musical about infants, and what has it got to do with social identity?

This chapter accepts the challenge that Blacking so elegantly offers psychology in his theory of music as a natural ability—'an outward sign of human communication' that achieves meaning or function in its social uses. Like language, music must be learned. Like language, again, this learning is eagerly anticipated by the sensibilities and expressive initiatives of a child—by the impulse and pleasure of communication. I take evidence from infancy for motives of musicality, the 'inner meaning' of music. I believe we see in infants innate psychological foundations of both musical behaviour and musical awareness that are unique to human beings. A baby's selective orientation to musical sounds, critical discrimination of musical features of sound, and vocal and gestural responses that are timed and expressed to contribute to a joint musical game confirm that music, which is clearly a cultural achievement of human society, has strong roots in human nature.

A theory of the motives of 'musicality' has been formulated to explain the intrinsic features of human movement that provide the origin for musical forms of expression and artistic creation, and for the perceptual and cognitive appreciation of musical patterns (Trevarthen, 1999). 'Communicative musicality', in this general sense, is the dynamic sympathetic state of a human person that allows co-ordinated companionship to arise (Malloch, 1999). Clearly, the expression of 'music' is to be understood in the sense of the ancient Greek word, μουσικη (musiké), i.e. inclusive of all temporal arts—theatre, dance, poetry, as well as what we know as 'music'. Musicality manifests its fundamental features in the ways that infants behave in interaction with the expressions of motive forces in other human beings.

Early musicality has a powerful role in building memories. It marks with emotional signatures the identity of persons and ritual events. After very few months, an infant can 'make music', and seems to have found a proud performer's personality. Taken with the infant's clear preferences for particular companions, this musical 'showing off' looks like the beginnings of his or her social identity as a member of a group—a group with known habits, celebratory experiences and acting skills that are valued for the bonds that they represent and reinforce. Cultivation of intrinsic musicality is a way of declaring allegiance with a friend or a social band. A newborn knows its mother by the tone and inflections of her voice. When a 6-month-old smiles with recognition of a favourite song, and bounces with the beat, it is like knowing his or her name, displaying a social 'me' within the family's affectionate pleasure of sharing.

In 1982, I called a seminar in Edinburgh with John Blacking on the theme 'Are Infants Musical?' Blacking had published his book *How Musical is Man?* (Blacking, 1979), and an ethnomusical study of Venda children's education in the 'affective culture' of their society through non-verbal communication in dance and music (Blacking, 1988; Bohlman and Nettl, 1995). We met at an anthropological conference on children and their induction into culture—the organizers said it was, 'an effort to focus attention on the neglected theme of how children actually acquire the cultures in which they are socialised.' (Jahoda and Lewis, 1988, p. ix). This is still a confused issue in psychology, but there have been important advances, and perhaps most dramatically in relation to how infants appreciate what seem like products of musical culture long before they can speak, let alone sing 'in tune' or play the piano. New evidence on the place of affect in intelligence (Damasio, 1999; Freeman, 2000), and on how emotions regulate brain development, cognition and learning, makes the infant's sensitivity to expressions in musical form more comprehensible. Musicality may be at the source of the ability to be socialized in the human way.

Blacking asked if dance, music and other artistic activities are not, 'essential forms of knowledge which are necessary not only for a balanced personality but also for the development of cognitive capacities.' (Blacking, 1988, p. 91). In arguing the case for 'affective culture', he said, 'Passion is as important in scientific endeavour as is compassion in artistic vision.' (Blacking, 1988, p. 93). The ways in which infants present themselves as performers and masters of creative acts indicates that one of the principal outcomes of affective understanding with others is the development of a secure recognized and valued 'identity'—being somebody, placed in the world with others as a 'knower' and 'doer', 'making sense' of oneself. Again, to quote Blacking on the Venda, 'Pleasing others and pleasing oneself in musical performance were two inter-related aspects of the same activity. Self-actualisation included social service, and vice versa. Dance and music-making provided Venda people with experiential evidence of their system of ideas about self and other, their concept of intelligence and of the soul, and the balance that must exist between personal power and corporate power.' (Blacking, 1988, p. 111). We can see infant 'musicality' as the manifestation of essential motives for human sympathetic understanding.

Blacking was, not surprisingly, ready to see musicality in displays of mutual interest in videos of infants playing with their mothers, and especially in their reactions to mothers' songs and rhythmic chanting, and their participation in musical games. We agreed about the relationship between the infant's evident pleasure in mothers' melodies and cultivated, socially situated musical performances. The role of learning was undecided. Blacking says, 'If tone stress and ideal motion in music portray nervous tension and motor impulse and so stimulate emotional experience, it is because people have learnt to make the connections.' (Blacking, 1988, p. 108). I see the connections as provided, as a foundation, by the intersubjectively attuned motives that the baby is born with.

In the 1970s and 1980s, psychologists and developmental linguists found fascinating evidence of musical talents in babies (Trehub, 1990; Fernald, 1992; Fassbender, 1996; Papoušek, 1996; Trehub et al., 1997; Dissanayake, 1999). Hitherto unsuspected musical listening skills were proved for infants as young as 4 months. Fernald characterized mothers' speech to infants as carrying a 'melodic' message. The expressive dimensions of 'motherese', or 'infant-directed speech' were similar across all languages. DeCasper and Spence (1986; Fifer and Moon, 1995) proved that learning the indexical features of a mother's voice could begin before birth. The Papoušeks described the 'intuitive parenting' mode of vocal communication with infants in musical terms, stressing the modulation of affect provided by parental tones and rhythms (Papoušek and Papoušek, 1981). A diary study of their daughter documented the infant's enjoyment of nursery songs, and her private practice of acquired musical forms. From the early 1970s, Daniel Stern, Beatrice Beebe and colleagues have studied the 'co-ordinated interpersonal timing', melodic forms and choreography of parent–infant communication (Beebe et al., 1985; Stern, 1985, 2000). The concept of 'attunement', by which Stern describes how the parent picks up on infant expressions reflecting their beat, emphasis and intonation, encapsulates his strong musical sensibility (Stern et al., 1985). I find in his identification of 'dynamic affects' with the 'narrative envelopes' composed in a mother's play with her infant (Stern , 1999) an essential explanation for the development of creative companionship between them. The narratives of feeling and intending that parent and infant share are essential preparation for the joint attending and co-operative performance of tasks which ushers the child into what the linguist Halliday (1975) called 'acts of meaning'. Play with the 'formats' of baby games leads to 'child's talk' (Bruner, 1983), and the rhythms and vowels of infantile vocal exchanges pave the 'path to language' (Locke, 1993).

Spectrographic representations of the rhythms and melodies of mothers' vocalizations demonstrate that not only baby songs, but also playful conversational 'baby talk' have regular rhythmic features, and that infants can sometimes nicely time their simple coos and squeals so that they take part in a joint performance (Malloch, 1999; Trevarthen, 1999; Trevarthen et al., 1999). Scottish mothers and Nigerian mothers have similar time sense—and the same beat and phrasing appears in examples of aborigine

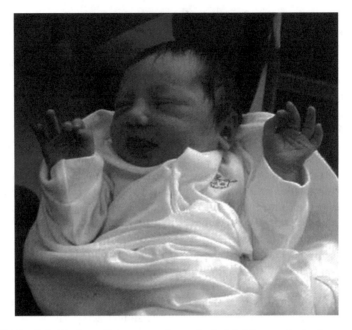

Figure 2.1 Why does baby Maria, newborn, seem to be conducting? Is it because her body expresses, with affecting delicacy, one acute moment in her rhythmic sense of passing time?

music made with didgeridoo and rhythm sticks. I identified these as features of 'inter-subjective motor control' (Trevarthen, 1986). Microanalyses of videos showed that the complex and highly integrated 'proto-conversations' with 2- to 3-month-olds were mediated by efficient use of vocal, facial and gestural expressions of both baby and mother.

In 1994, Christina Papaeliou, a post-graduate student from Greece studying prosody in mothers' speech to 1-year-olds, and an accomplished pianist, collaborated with me in a review of 'The infancy of music'. We stated the theory as follows:

Study of the expressive dancing gestures and aesthetic sensitivities of infants can be used to find basic motives of human communication, and to explore the passions that regulate mind–mind links of human 'intersubjectivity'. We believe that musicians can help us obtain a rich and accurate account of how momentary emotions are communicated with infants, how they are transformed into 'emotional narratives' in which meaningful memories can crystallised, and how these 'narratives' contribute to the development of structures in language and thought. Infants are surprisingly adept at musical forms of play. They join in song and dance with adult companions long before they can talk. (Papaeliou and Trevarthen, 1994, p. 19)

Our work made a major advance 3 years ago when, as a direct consequence of joint seminars between the Departments of Psychology and Music, I met Stephen Malloch, a post-graduate candidate in Music, who was applying computing techniques developed with Murray Campbell in the Acoustics Laboratory of the Department of Physics to study a composers use of timbre in an orchestral piece. He offered to apply his software to the mother's voice (Malloch *et al.*, 1997). With funds granted by the Leverhulme Foundation, Stephen and I began a 2-year investigation of our corpus of audio recordings, which resulted in the formulation of his theory of 'communicative musicality' to explain the regulation of pulse, vocal quality and narrative form in mothers' utterances to infants 1–6 months of age (Malloch, 1999).

Primary intersubjectivity, and knowing others with musicality

Research on infants' active contributions to vocal and gestural games reveals an intrinsic sensitivity to 'time in the mind' (Wittmann and Pöppel, 1999), rhythmic hierarchies of motor impulse in bodily expression and the emotive values of harmonic and melodic parameters in the voice. It is now evident that expressive signals of the whole body, but especially of face, voice and hands, are coherent in a single subjective or 'embodied' time and space from birth. While the infant's knowledge and skills are at their most rudimentary, a vitality of action with awareness is already there. The baby is an affectively charged human subject from the start (Stern, 1985, 2000; Reddy et al., 1997; Kitamura and Burnham, 1998; Trevarthen, 1998, 1999).

Vision, hearing and touch are equivalent senses for the capture and appreciation of the fundamental 'amodal' motor impulses and emotions in another human subject. The baby has 'innate intersubjectivity' with his or her whole being. Demonstrations of newborn infants' imitations of expression, and their responses to reciprocated imitations or 'attunements' of a partner in proto-conversational play, which caught psychologists by surprise (Kugiumutzakis, 1999), can leave no doubt that what Adam Smith (1759) called a 'natural sympathy' in us, for feelings that 'move' others, is a human birthright. Both intuitive musicality in parents' expressions—the features of 'motherese' and the patterns of dynamic emotion used to engage with and regulate emotions with infants—and the remarkable range of discriminations and preferences infants show for features of vocal or instrumental sound have been brought home to psychologists and developmental linguists as nothing short of a revelation.

These endowments are clearly relevant to the process that enables a human child to become proficient in appreciation and production of cultivated forms of music, as well as many other culturally significant behaviours. The innate communicative talent that shows itself in an infant's playful sharing of 'proto-conversations', songs and action games is what gives vitality and value to cultivated products of music, poetry and dance in their endless complexity and diversity (Dissanayake, 2000). Mary Catherine Bateson (1979) realized this when, in defining proto-conversation, she gave it the twin roles of an innate foundation for language and the origin of 'ritual healing practices'. She was an anthropologist, so she knew the universal importance of rhythmic rituals in creating or healing social bonds.

Music communicates with the very young human being because it engages with a fundamental intrinsic motive pulse (IMP) generated in the human brain (Trevarthen, 1999). This comprises: (1) a rhythmic time sense (that detects syllables, the beat, phrases and longer elements); (2) sensitivity for the 'sentic forms' (Clynes, 1973) or temporal variation in intensity, pitch and timbre of voices and in instrumental sounds that mimic the human voice; and (3) a perception of 'narrative' in the emotional development of the melodic line, which supports anticipation of repeating harmonies, phrases and emotional forms in a vocal or musical performance. Music, as it changes, evokes motive universals in the human experience of moving, the unfolding of purposeful projects and their dramatic cycles of emotional expectation and consummation. It has the capacity to give emotional companionship, and to heal, because it supports intrinsic, neurobiologically founded needs for qualities of human communication that are organized with musicality, 'in time' with the mind (Trevarthen and Malloch, 2000).

Evidently music satisfies processes that effect regulation of moving, feeling and cognition. The rational side of human consciousness is powerfully channelled and communicated by core activities of neural systems that often show their activity in audible expressions, and these may take rhythmic and emotive narrative forms that we recognize as music.

It now seems grotesque how infants' psychological talents and initiatives have been so misrepresented and misperceived in research that claims the utmost scientific rigour. The medical and scientific account of infant intelligence and its motives has grounded itself in the assumption that the 'biological' process by which the human body and brain are formed before birth could not possibly equip the infant with the consciousness, intentions and feelings of a socially competent human mind. Now, however, with the evidence we possess, we must view differently the whole process of being human, and becoming a member of society. The direction of influence seems to have been switched. 'Socialization' of a biological infant makes less sense than generation of society by an innate drive for co-operative awareness that is uniquely human in its origins and development (Bråten, 1992). A child is born 'socializing' its life with others. 'Education' in culture is truly a 'leading out' of a willing and active candidate (Bruner, 1996; Rogoff, 1998).

The biology and pre-history of communicative sympathy and group solidarity

Social psychology and anthropology are understandably reluctant to acknowledge the 'biological' foundation of complex human social life. Medical and psychological science have so reduced human nature to a physical systems level that the sources of motivation and conscious awareness are remote and difficult to comprehend. However, the comparative science of behaviour, as pioneered by Charles Darwin, shows that animate life is elaborately social in its essence. By studying the intersubjective foundations of joint action and co-operative awareness in infancy, we can perceive the crucial role of emotional impulses in the learning of culture (Bråten, 1992; Trevarthen, 1987, 1990, 1994).

Sensitivity to the rhythm and direction of movement in other individuals is the natural regulator of social life for even very simple animals. In all highly evolved social species, detection of movement, sensing the future intended action and monitoring the orientation of attending to stimuli in other individuals are all of vital importance. They determine the outcome in courtship and mating, in transactions between parent and offspring, leader and followers, contestants for leadership, predator and prey, etc. The socially clever species play as youngsters with the signalling of motives and experience, practising the risks and pleasures of convivial fighting, hide-and-seek and teasing with mock aggression and exaggerated emotions (Bekoff and Byers, 1998).

The foundations of all psychological co-operation or intersubjectivity are to be found in a sense of movement and in detection of the generation of qualities of movement in other bodies. It is in 'future sense', the anticipatory, generative mental image of a movement and of its likely sensory consequences that the parameters of intersubjective communication are defined. In the brains of socially co-operative species, 'motor images', and the operation of the IMP, create and elaborate both intelligible forms of expression and the choreographic parameters by which they may be perceived. The same three aspects of Malloch's 'communicative musicality' apply.

First, the timing or *pulse* of movements and the rhythms of their succession give data on the intentions and emotional energy of the moving subject as they are being created, on the system of coupled oscillators of neurobiological 'clocks' that govern initiation and co-ordination of movement in different body parts. Then, the dynamic *quality* of each movement—its force, coherence, economy, modulation or harmony— conveys the subject's confidence and determination, as well as single-mindedness and concessions or sincerity in confiding to social partners. Finally, the progress of movements over longer stretches of time, their grouping in phrases and longer cycles, give a *narrative* message concerning the anticipated course and outcome of action, what it is trying to achieve in the end (Malloch, 1999). All three, pulse, quality and narrative, but especially the narrative, give memorable information on which future collaborations and relationships may be built. A narrative also identifies the narrator and the occasion to which the narrative refers by its particular expressive 'signature' and syntactic course, and the repetition of distinctive phrases or cycles of expressed energy (Stern, 1999).

Neuro-ethologists show that social signalling has evolved from self-regulatory autonomic or visceral motor activity, making possible progressively more intimate engagement of an individual with the inner state and changing anticipations of social partners (Wallin, 1991; Porges, 1997; Panksepp, 1998; Damasio, 1999). Self-regulation evolves into group regulation. In vertebrates, movements of respiration have been important since fish developed awareness of the modulations of respiration in their con-specifics. Siamese fish signal their intentions in combat with elaborate rhythmic displays of their highly coloured gill covers, which flush with passion. In birds and mammals, exhalations of air in calls and songs carry intimate data on excitement, changing atten-tion, determination, vigour and many other nuances of motives. They also can give a sign of the individual's identity, status and sometimes details of personal experience, and may be broadcast over distances when the maker of the sounds is far out of sight. Thus a vervet sentry monkey up a tree can signal in a call which species of predator is threatening the safety of the family, where they should look and where seek escape.

Signalling of identity of the individual or the group by vocal calls, or even by elaborate song, has a long evolutionary past. Björn Merker (1999) conceives synchronous chorus-ing as a device for generating family bonds or group solidarity, as well as for advertising territorial or home ownership, calling aid to defend a territory or announcing the discovery of a source of food to be shared. Chimpanzees show features of synchronized group vocal-izing and communal 'dancing' that share elements with human celebration of musicality. Merker hypothesizes that early hominids must have danced and sung in this way to enhance the feelings of family or community.

I have proposed that a new sense of the body in movement has come with evolution of humans, consequent upon the liberation of head, arms and hands for free rhythmic action by bipedal walking and the upright stance (Trevarthen, 1999). Observing people gesturing, talking, looking about, carrying or handling objects while they walk, and comparing this with the versatile manipulations and communicative acts of seated group in animated conversation, I see a level of polyrhythmia in motor co-ordination not reached by other species. Combined with intense involvement in extended messages of verbal and non-verbal kind, and all the temporal arts in which the body becomes narrator, it seems as if we display a freedom in syntax of motive impulses and a flow of anticipated elaborations of experience that has no equal. All humans revel in a freedom of gestural action that is intensely shared. As Marc Turner has shown us, the whole of our consciousness and life together is made of story-telling (Turner, 1996).

Ethnographic and anthropological studies of music grapple with these universals of human vitality and its communication, and attempt to reconcile them with the endless diversity of musics and other systems of action and belief that define cultures and give place to different roles in their societies. A theory of the innate sources of value and standards of quality in intersubjective understanding between human beings in social groups is needed. Study of music and the other creative arts can give indications of how impulses for cultural learning arose, how shared consciousness of invented actions and created understandings, with their emotions, became necessary for a child's imaginative play (Dissanayake, 2000). It can clarify how teachers should explain a completely arbitrary way of behaving so the young can learn (Erickson, 1996). Ian Cross (1999) has suggested as much when he proposes that in our evolution, 'music was the most important thing we ever did.'

Archaeology, too, can offer some instruction on pre-historic human needs, and what was made of them in what has been a very short period of evolutionary time. The approach has to be more than cognitive—more than concerned with problem-solving modules of intelligence, and hypothetical levels of intellectual development according to Piagetian stages of object representation. As with contemporary human minds, the minds of our distant ancestors were not simply rational devices for categorization of perceptions or strategic processing of instrumental tasks. From the beginnings of scientific study of pre-historic artefacts and human remains, it has been clear that aesthetic and mythic forces are integral to the management of a human view of the world. These forces come from the impulses to act and create with anticipation, from dynamic evaluations of experience in action and from memories of exciting contingencies of acting in the natural world. They must also have depended on an enriched sense of being in intelligent company and sharing an affective culture (Dissanayake, 1999). Neanderthals collected and transported over long distances stones with attractive fossils in them. May they not have shown them, and with pride?

I believe that Merlin Donald (1991, 1999) has made an important conceptual advance by his thesis that before hominids acquired the semantic power of words, and the rational abstractions that words facilitate, messages of significance to life and relationships were transmitted by the dance and song of 'mimesis', in embodied rhythmic narratives of experienced events turned into allegories of body posturing and stepping, gesticulations of the hands, facial expressions of eyes and mouth, and modulated cries of the voice. The important addition Donald makes to cognitive theory is that he defines a form of story-making that is embodied and performed in regulated rhythmic time, that conveys narrative in transitions of feeling. In this, he agrees with Blacking's insistence on the vital role of an 'affective culture'.

Both theories harmonized well with Damasio's neuropsychological model of the mind in which body-related emotions and cognitions derive from one vital source that is in the coherently wired-up brain and that takes its organization from the anticipated effects of the body moving to pick up experience (Damasio, 1999). The psychobiology of narrative experience is given a firm foundation in subhuman minds by research on the neuro-humoral foundations of animal feelings and their regulatory role over conscious awareness, in the individual and in social relationships. Walter Freeman (2000) explains how emotions frame cognitions in an active/pragmatic and social mind. The developmental neurology of human emotional experience and its emotive communication is steadily rebuilding our view of how rational intentions and conscious perceptions come about, challenging the abstract, disembodied, static and linear structural analysis of cognitive science, with its logical algorithms for perception, thought, memory and language, offering a model of mind that has time and feelings about events, and is in the body, moving it.

Self-presentation in human infants

Important changes occur in the communication between infants and adults in the first year, at the end of which infants are capable of purposeful co-operation with the directions of interest and goals of purposeful movement displayed by companions in their movements. At every stage, a sensitivity to the timing and emotional and emotive quality of bodily expressions is crucial (Nadel *et al.*, 1999). Infants seek to engage with the intelligence and feelings of 'subjectivity' in their parents, and infant's expressions of pleasure or annoyance, of interest, excitement or rejection have immediate effect on how adults respond. A 'mutual attunement' of 'dynamic narrative envelopes' of expression carries them into intimate companionship, rich in memories of actions and experiences understood together.

By the middle of the first year, an infant will normally have attained a level of confidence and playful or comical exuberance which is readily perceived as 'self-conscious'—displaying Gregory Bateson's 'metacommunication', or communication about communication (Bateson, 1956). Play with expressive movement, affectively experienced, is acutely sensitive to the reactions of others. Humorous teasing provokes the infant to laughter and coyness. Subtle signs of self–other awareness are seen well before this. Reflections from the social world are affecting, even for a young baby. Reddy (2000) has documented coy smiling at a mirror image in 3-month-olds. We trace in the development of self-awareness a transformation of intrinsic motives to share consciousness and purposeful actions with others that were evident at birth (Reddy *et al.*, 1997; Trevarthen, 1990, 1998, 2001).

The playful 'showing off' so characteristic of a 6-month-old is sensitive to the familiarity or strangeness of the other person. It is not so much that the infant has an emotional attachment in the sense of an emotionally charged *dependence* on a caregiver, but the self-display depends on the quality of regard of a known 'friend' who knows how to play, and how to enjoy it. It is the quality of assured mutual *friendship* that counts. By 5 or 6 months, infants have favourite games and they quickly recognize songs or recorded music often heard—stopping to listen, smiling in recognition, then bouncing with the

(a)

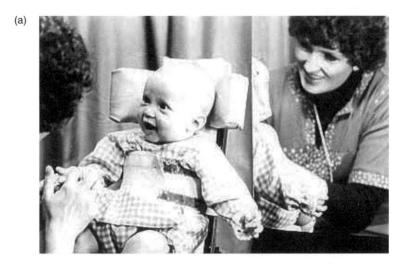

(b)

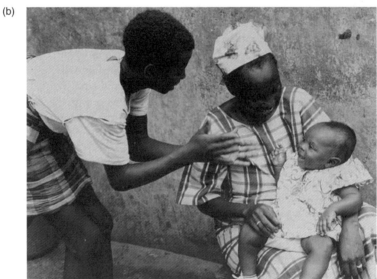

Figure 2.2 (a) Leanne, 23 weeks, in Edinburgh, is enthralled and delighted when her mother begins to sing 'Round and round the garden', stroking her hand in time to the song. (b) Oyabanji, 27 weeks, playing a clapping song with his mother's sister. (Photo by John and Penelope Hubley, Lagos, April 1978.)

tune (Mazokopaki, 2000). A strange place can dampen this interest and enthusiasm; and a strange person is regarded with very evident mistrust, even sadness and fear. I am convinced that the 'stranger fear' noted for 7-month-olds is a fear of seeming foolish with a person who cannot comprehend. It is a direct and strongly felt emotion—one of the 'complex' or 'relational' emotions, expression of which makes the infant seem a sophisticated social being long before language, and before any system of beliefs or explicit 'theory of mind' (Draghi-Lorenz *et al.*, 2001).

The work and play of cultural learning

The young child, like Sinbad, is anticipating companionship in adventure, and the discovery of infinitely varied customs and inventions. Only one side of the human spirit is revealed by the systematic development of the infant's investigative curiosity—the creative 'scientific' examination of reality (Piaget, 1953). Practice and exploration as a single actor and thinker increases what the individual knows and can do. It complements the need to socialize—the inner drive towards a co-operative intelligence, sympathetic to what others experience and do. It is by *communicating* that the cultural conventions and the meanings, of interests, actions and words in the adult society, are eagerly assimilated by a child (Trevarthen, 1988).

We defined a crucial development in our infant subjects in the last few months of the first year, which led them to seek instruction in the ways familiar companions know the world, and in the skills they develop to deal with it (Trevarthen and Hubley, 1978). We called it the beginning of 'co-operative awareness', or 'person–person–object understanding'. Having already shown an aptitude for picking up ritual performances in action games and baby songs, the 1-year-old has no trouble mimicking mannerisms and styles of self-presentation. Clowning comes naturally, provided the audience is appreciative. All the world becomes a stage (Trevarthen, 1990).

No reductive vision of how cognitive processes are built up by a child's rational investigation of the properties of objects can explain the imaginative creativity and

Figure 2.3 Abegbendro, 11 months, a Nigerian musician, asks for, gets and shows off his rattle, and plays piano with his mother. (Photos by John and Penelope Hubley, Lagos, April, 1978.)

imitative vitality of a toddler's play with manners, clothes, roles and artistic celebrations of the family and society in which he or she lives (Trevarthen and Logotheti, 1987). Learning a culture does not begin as a purely cognitive process; it is intuitively imparted and intuitively taken up, and, as Blacking insisted, it is full of emotion. It realizes a need in human relating, and it is charged with creativity and the pleasure of discovery or invention. Whatever the complexity of social, technical, linguistic or musical 'products' of human learning in society—whatever the 'things' we see as culture—all are outcomes of a 'process' of collaborative and creative learning. The art is in the doing, and the sharing. Cultural reality is a process, not a thing, and its growth force is human motivation.

The development of appreciation for music in infants through sharing of socio-dramatic games indicates that the creation of memorable forms of action and vocal expression is a fundamental need of human companionship and group experience. The manifestations of 'pride' associated with sharing musical pleasure, or of 'shame' when it is found that the enjoyment is not shared or is miscomprehended, appear in the first year, long before language is learned. This is evidence for primary motives of 'mimesis' and celebration of rituals that motivate 'cultural learning', and for emotions that evaluate success in expressing oneself and gaining approval from admired company. These precocious signs of a socio-cultural self of the infant in the intimacy of the family may give us a pointer to the origin and function of a sense of 'musical identity' in the 'mass intimacy' of an adult 'public', where recognition of pieces and genre of music can be harnessed to powerful emotions of sympathy or antipathy.

Especially interesting is comparison with the search for identity in adolescence through communal celebrations of dance and sharing of musical fashions. It is known that the psychological abilities for recognition of the indexical features of facial appearance, vocal qualities and language are enhanced at two periods of life, in toddlers and in early adolescence. In these periods, the brain, and perhaps particularly the right cerebral hemisphere, seems most actively seeking for formative experiences that enable new relationships to be formed and new habits gained. The essential creative dynamism of early musical communication will lead to the idea that identities are made to be negotiated and preferences and allegiances are naturally dynamic or 'alive' in the service of collaborative experience.

Social risks; loss of place and self

The induction of an individual into a family, community, school or society creates loyalties and expectations of understanding that can also provoke disorganization of identity and self-expression if the support is lost. Maya Gratier (1999) has made a fascinating pilot study of the effects of loss of 'belonging' in immigrant mothers on their ability to offer sympathetic communication with their infants. Using methods based on Malloch's analysis, she compared mothers of three groups, Indians in India, Indian immigrants in Paris, and French in Paris, in their conversations and singing with infants in the first year. Finding that the immigrant mothers, who were confronted with a foreign language, foreign social conventions and unfamiliar conceptions of infant care, were less harmonious in their interactions with their infants and less consistent in their vocal rhythms, Gratier draws on literature that reports that social alienation can diminish

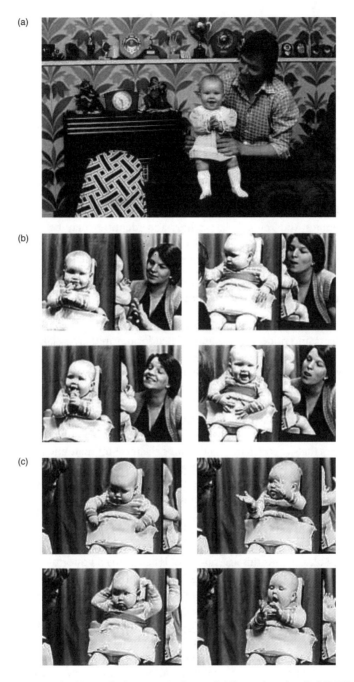

Figure 2.4 Emma, 6 months. (a) Proudly demonstrating how to do 'Clappa-clappa handies' (CCH). (b) Playing with her mother in the laboratory, showing CCH with happiness and pride. (c) Trying to communicate with a stranger, she shows him CCH, but he doesn't understand. Emma is ashamed.

a sense of self-worth and undermine spontaneous expression of feelings. The immigrant mothers were less responsive and less lively in response to their infants, but were not necessarily depressed. Their relatively unsympathetic reactions to their babies' behaviours had effects on the infants' communication, of a kind that might influence the child's development. She describes the effects of social uncertainty as a loss of 'communicative musicality'. Research on maternal post-natal depression has shown both similar effects on the 'musicality' of mothers' vocal expression to their infants and that there can be lasting effects on infants' psychological development (Robb, 1999). Evidently the human mind has needs for communication of feelings in companionship that go beyond the direct protection and emotional regulations of 'attachment' (Trevarthen, 2001).

Socialization of a child is acceptance of a human person who is seeking to share socially familiar and valued ways of understanding and interpreting the world. The customs that differ between cultures are ways of meeting this intrinsic human need for a definition of meanings and roles. Relationships and identities may be arbitrary in their particular features, but the motivation that gives them value is common to all human beings, and many of its dynamic regulations are the same in all societies.

Conclusions: from musical games in the family to a musical self in society

Our human relations are risky, playful, compassionate or antagonized with fear and anger. We take pleasure and pride in being appreciated for our initiatives skills and knowledge, and in helping others achieve success in what they try to do or know. We resent or despise those who would deny us the capacity to do things for ourselves or to understand commonly agreed meanings. We count as friends those who have similar enthusiasms and values, and mistrust and criticize those whose actions and beliefs are incomprehensible to us. Our identity is our place in a collaborative awareness of the world and what to do in it (Barnes, 2000). We gain this identity and keep it alive by celebrating the actions, feelings and experiences that we can share—and among the most intimate and powerful of things to share are the ritualized patterns of art, and especially the temporal arts, of which music, song and dance can be the most spontaneous and sincere (Dissanayake, 1999, 2000).

It is remarkable how much of this human need for companionship in expressive habits is evident in infancy, even in the first half year, when the practical purposes of collaboration are not grasped, when the baby is only interested in sharing the art of being with a familiar player who 'knows the score', who performs and 'competes' in the game with generosity and pleasure. At this age, an infant is exhibiting a powerful and growing sense of self, a self-consciousness that is intensely aware of the regard of others, and therefore a moral self; not an isolated, intending, object-conceiving and problem-solving ego. The festive participation a baby finds in a parent's lively singing and dancing is the pleasure of improvising intimacy. It leaves lasting echoes and images, and will be sought after many times in the future. It makes a foundation for building common understanding.

Practical cognitive interest in what the familiar companion knows and uses, what a mother intends with the objects and conventional gestures and utterances she shows and offers to share, grows in the infant's mind. In the next year, as the toddler practises first words in imaginative imitation of others' statements and begins to weave speech into elaborate mimetic narratives in imaginative role-play, we can see that the whole edifice of human cultural understanding would never take off without this foundation.

So, to gain the freedom of the knowledge of a society and its culture, we must commit ourselves to a place, a role, and one that recognizes the allegiance that fellow role players have in the act. This role in fellowship begins as a music-like composition, an improvised song or dance of companionship with someone we trust, whom we admire, and who admires us.

I have not attempted to consider what is required to achieve a high level of cultivated musical skill, in singing or instrumental playing. I am not qualified to do that. However, what I hear from teachers of advanced musicianship does not seem to contradict the impressions gained from less formal learning of early childhood. I understand that a high quality of artistic expression is linked to a sense of embodied emotion, that 'playing' difficult music needs a sense of grace and spontaneity, as well as a tempered pride in mastery. If joy in sharing is displaced by obedience to an instructive authority, or moulding by rules of conformity, talent can be lost. If the spirit of musicality is free and appreciated, it will grow. I note the poise and 'maturity' of high achievers in the Young Musicians of the Year competition, and it seems that the satisfaction that they feel in what they do is not so far removed from what a 6-month-old can display when responding with joy to a request to show 'Clappa-clappa-handies'.

References

Barnes, B. (2000). *Understanding Agency: Social Theory and Responsible Action.* Beverley Hills: Sage.

Bateson, G. (1956). The message 'This is play'. In B. Schaffer (ed.), *Group Processes.* New York: Josiah Macy Foundation. [Republished in Bateson, G. (1973) *Steps to an Ecology of Mind.* Frogmore, St Albans, UK: Paladin.]

Bateson, M.C. (1979). The epigenesis of conversational interaction: A personal account of research development. In M. Bullowa (ed.), *Before speech: The beginning of human communication*, pp. 63–77. London: Cambridge University Press.

Beebe, B., Jaffe, J., Feldstein, S., Mays, K. and Alson, D. (1985). Inter-personal timing: the application of an adult dialogue model to mother–infant vocal and kinesic interactions. In F.M. Field and N. Fox (ed.), *Social Perception in Infants*, pp. 249–268. Norwood, NJ: Ablex.

Bekoff, M. and Byers, J.A. (1998). *Animal Play: Evolutionary, Comparative and Ecological Approaches.* New York: Cambridge University Press.

Blacking, J. (1969). The value of music in human experience. *The 1969 Yearbook of the International Folk Music Council.* [Republished in Bohlman and Nettl (1995) as Chapter 1, Expressing human experience through music.]

Blacking, J. (1979). *How Musical is Man?* London: Faber.

Blacking, J. (1988). Dance and music in Venda children's cognitive development. In G. Jahoda and I.M. Lewis (ed.), *Acquiring Culture: Cross Cultural Studies in Child Development*, pp. 91–112. Beckenham, UK: Croom Helm.

Bohlman, P. and Nettl, B. (ed.) (1995). *Music, Culture and Experience: Selected Papers of John Blacking.* Chicago: University of Chicago Press.

Bråten, S. (1992). The virtual other in infants' minds and social feelings. In A.H. Wold (ed.), *The Dialogical Alternative (Festschrift for Ragnar Rommetveit)*, pp. 77–97. Oslo: Scandanavian University Press/Oxford: Oxford University Press.

Bruner, J.S. (1983). *Child's talk: Learning to use language.* New York: Norton.

Bruner, J.S. (1996). *The Culture of Education.* Cambridge, MA: Harvard University Press.

Clynes, M. (1973). Sentics: Biocybernetics of Emotion Communication. *Annals of the New York Academy of Science*, **220**.

Clynes, M. (1983). Expressive microstructure in music, linked to living qualities. In. J. Sundberg (ed.), *Studies in music performance*. Publication No. 19. Stockholm: Royal Swedish Academy of Music.

Cross, I. (1999). Is music the most important thing we ever did? Music, development and evolution. In Suk Won-Yi (ed.), *Music, Mind and Science*, pp. 10–29. Seoul: Seoul National University Press.

Damasio, A.R. (1999). *The Feeling of What Happens: Body, Emotion and the Making of Consciousness*. London: Heinemann.

DeCasper, A.J. and Spence, M.J. (1986). Prenatal maternal speech influences newborns' perception of speech sounds. *Infant Behavior and Development*, **9**, 133–150.

Dissanayake, E. (1999). Antecedents of the temporal arts in early mother–infant interaction. In N. Wallin and B. Merker (ed.), *The Origins of Music*. Cambridge, MA: MIT Press.

Dissanayake, E. (2000). *Art and Intimacy: How the Arts Began*. Seattle: University of Washington Press.

Donald, M. (1991). *Origins of the Modern Mind: Three Stages in the Evolution of Culture and Cognition*. Cambridge, MA: Harvard University Press.

Donald, M. (1999). Preconditions for the evolution of protolanguages. In M.C. Corballis and S.E.G. Lea (eds.), *The descent of mind: Psychological perspectives on hominid evolution*, pp. 138–154. Oxford: Oxford University Press.

Draghi-Lorenz, R., Reddy, V. and Costall, A. (2001). Re-thinking the development of 'non-basic' emotions: a critical review of existing theories. *Developmental Review*, **21**(3), 263–304.

Erickson, F. (1996). Going for the zone: social and cognitive ecology of teacher–student interaction in classroom conversations. In D. Hicks (ed.), *Discourse, Learning and Schooling*, pp. 29–62. New York: Cambridge University Press.

Fassbender, C. (1996). Infants' auditory sensitivity towards acoustic parameters of speech and music. In I. Deliège and J. Sloboda (eds.), *Musical Beginnings: Origins and Development of Musical Competence*, pp. 56–87. Oxford: Oxford University Press.

Fernald, A. (1992). Meaningful melodies in mothers' speech to infants. In Papoušek, H., Jürgens, U. and Papoušek, M. (ed.), *Nonverbal Vocal Communication: Comparative and Developmental Aspects*, pp. 262–282. Cambridge: Cambridge University Press/Paris: Editions de la Maison des Sciences de l'Homme.

Fifer, W.P. and Moon, C.M. (1995). The effects of fetal experience with sound. In J.-P. Lecanuet, W.P. Fifer, N.A. Krasnegor and W.P. Smotherman (ed.), *Fetal Development: A Psychobiological Perspective*, pp. 351–366. Hillsdale, NJ: Erlbaum.

Freeman, W.J. (2000). Emotion is essential to all intentional behaviors. In M. Turner and I. Granic (ed.), *Emotion, Development, and Self-organisation: Dynamic Systems Approaches to Emotional Development*, pp. 209–235. Cambridge: Cambridge University Press.

Gratier, M. (1999). Expressions of belonging: the effect of acculturation on the rhythm and harmony of mother–infant vocal interaction. *Musicae Scientiae, Special Issue (1999–2000)*, 93–122.

Halliday, M.A.K. (1975). *Learning How to Mean: Explorations in the Development of Language*. London: Edward Arnold.

Jahoda, G. and Lewis, I.M. (ed.). *Acquiring Culture: Cross Cultural Studies in Child Development*, pp. 37–90. Beckenham, UK: Croom Helm.

Kitamura, C. and Burnham, D. (1998). The infant's response to maternal vocal affect. In C. Rovee-Collier, L.P. Lipsitt and H. Hayne (ed.), *Advances in Infancy Research*, Vol. 12, pp. 221–236. Stamford, CT: Ablex.

Kugiumutzakis, G. (1999). Genesis and development of early infant mimesis to facial and vocal models. In J. Nadel and G. Butterworth (ed.), *Imitation in Infancy*, pp. 127–185. Cambridge: Cambridge University Press.

Locke, J.L. (1993). *The Child's Path to Spoken Language*. Cambridge, MA: Harvard University Press.

Malloch, S. (1999). Mothers and infants and communicative musicality. *Musicae Scientiae, Special Issue (1999–2000)*, 29–57.

Malloch, S., Sharp, D., Campbell, D.M., Campbell, A.M. and Trevarthen, C. (1997). Measuring the human voice: analysing pitch, timing, loudness and voice quality in mother/infant communication. *Proceedings of the Institute of Acoustics*, **19**, 495–500.

Mazokopaki, K. (2000). Subjective and intersubjective appreciation of music by infants. Presentation in Poster-Workshop: *Tracking the IMP: Studies of the intrinsic motive pulse in an infant's feeling for musical forms*. ICIS 2000–International Conference on Infant Studies, Brighton, UK, July, 2000.

Merker, B. (1999). Synchronous chorusing and the origins of music. In "Rhythms, musical narrative, and the origins of human communication." *Musicae Scientiae, Special Issue, 1999–2000*, pp. 59–73. Liège: European Society for the Cognitive Sciences of Music.

Nadel, J., Carchon, I., Kervella, C., Marcelli, D. and Réserbat-Plantey, D. (1999). Expectancies for social contingency in 2-month-olds. *Developmental Science*, 2, 164–173.

Panksepp, J. (1998). *Affective neuroscience, The foundations of human and animal emotion*. New York, Oxford University Press.

Papaeliou, C. and Trevarthen, C. (1994). The Infancy of Music. *Musical Praxis*, 1(2), 19–33. Faculty of Music, The University of Edinburgh.

Papoušek, H. (1996). Musicality in infancy research: biological and cultural origins of early musicality. In I. Deliège and J. Sloboda (ed.), *Musical Beginnings: Origins and Development of Musical Competence*, pp. 37–55. Oxford: Oxford University Press.

Papoušek, M. and Papoušek, H. (1981). Musical elements in the infant's vocalization: their significance for communication, cognition, and creativity. *Advances in Infancy Research*, 1, 163–224.

Piaget, J. (1953). *The Origins of Intelligence in Children*. London: Routledge and Kegan Paul.

Porges, S.W. (1997). Emotion: an evolutionary by-product of the neural regulation of the autonomic nervous system. *Annals of the New York Academy of Sciences*, 807, 62–78.

Reddy, V. (2000). Coyness in early infancy. *Developmental Science*, 3, 186–192.

Reddy, V., Hay, D., Murray, L. and Trevarthen, C. (1997). Communication in infancy: mutual regulation of affect and attention. In G. Bremner, A. Slater and G. Butterworth (ed.), *Infant Development: Recent Advances*, pp. 247–274. Hove, UK: Psychology Press.

Robb, L. (1999). Emotional musicality in mother–infant vocal affect, and an acoustic study of postnatal depression. *Musicae Scientiae, Special Issue (1999–2000)*, 123–151.

Rogoff, B. (1998). Cognition as a collaborative process. In D. Kuhn and R.S. Siegler (ed.), *Handbook of Child Psychology, Volume 2: Cognition, Perception and Language*, pp. 679–744. New York: Wiley.

Smith, A. (1759). *The Theory of Moral Sentiments*. Glasgow, 6th edn. 1790 (D.D. Raphael and A.L. Macfie, General editors. Oxford: Clarendon, 1976; Reprint, Indianapolis: Liberty Fund, 1984).

Stern, D.N. (1985). *The Interpersonal World of the Infant: A View from Psychoanalysis and Development Psychology*. Basic Books, New York.

Stern, D.N. (1999). Vitality contours: the temporal contour of feelings as a basic unit for constructing the infant's social experience. In Rochat, P. (ed.), *Early Social Cognition: Understanding Others in the First Months of Life*, pp. 67–90. Mahwah, NJ: Erlbaum.

Stern, D.N. (2000). *The Interpersonal World of the Infant: A View from Psychoanalysis and Development Psychology*, 2nd edn. Basic Books, New York.

Stern, D.N., Hofer, L., Haft, W. and Dore, J. (1985). Affect attunement: the sharing of feeling states between mother and infant by means of inter-modal fluency. In F.M. Field and N. Fox (ed.), *Social Perception in Infants*, pp. 249–268. Norwood, NJ: Ablex.

Trehub, S.E. (1990). The perception of musical patterns by human infants: the provision of similar patterns by their parents. In M.A. Berkley and W.C. Stebbins (ed.), *Comparative Perception; Vol. 1, Mechanisms*, pp. 429–459. New York: Wiley.

Trehub, S.E., Schellenberg, G. and Hill, D. (1997). The origins of music perception and cognition: a developmental perspective. In I. Deliège and J.A. Sloboda (eds.), *Perception and Cognition of Music*, pp. 103–128. Hove: Psychology Press.

Trevarthen, C. (1986). Development of intersubjective motor control in infants. In M.G. Wade and H.T.A. Whiting (ed.), *Motor Development in Children: Aspects of Coordination and Control*, pp. 209–261. Dordrecht: Martinus Nijhof.

Trevarthen, C. (1987). Sharing makes sense: intersubjectivity and the making of an infant's meaning. In R. Steele and T. Threadgold (ed.), *Language Topics: Essays in Honour of Michael Halliday*, Vol. 1, pp. 177–199. Amsterdam: John Benjamins.

Trevarthen, C. (1988). Universal cooperative motives: how infants begin to know the language and skills of culture of their parents. In G. Jahoda and I.M. Lewis (ed.), *Acquiring Culture: Cross Cultural Studies in Child Development*, pp. 37–90. Beckenham, UK: Croom Helm.

Trevarthen, C. (1990). Signs before speech. In T.A. Sebeok and J. Umiker-Sebeok (ed.), *The Semiotic Web, 1989*, pp. 689–755. Berlin: Mouton de Gruyter.

Trevarthen, C. (1994). Infant semiosis. In W. Noth (ed.), *Origins of Semiosis*, pp. 219–252. Berlin: Mouton de Gruyter.

Trevarthen, C. (1998). The concept and foundations of infant intersubjectivity. In S. Bråten, (ed.), *Intersubjective Communication and Emotion in Early Ontogeny*, pp. 15–46. Cambridge: Cambridge University Press.

Trevarthen, C. (1999). Musicality and the intrinsic motive pulse: evidence from human psycho-biology and infant communication. *Musicae Scientiae, Special Issue (1999–2000)*, 157–213.

Trevarthen, C. (2001). Intrinsic motives for companionship in understanding: their origin, development and significance for infant mental health. *International Journal of Infant Mental Health*, 22, 95–131.

Trevarthen, C. and Hubley, P. (1978). Secondary intersubjectivity: confidence, confiding and acts of meaning in the first year. In A. Lock (ed.), *Action, Gesture and Symbol: The Emergence of Language*, pp. 183–229. London: Academic Press.

Trevarthen, C. and Logotheti, K. (1987). First symbols and the nature of human knowledge. In J. Montangero, A. Tryphon and S. Dionnet (ed.), *Symbolisme et Connaissance/ Symbolism and Knowledge*, pp. 65–92. Geneva: Jean Piaget Archives Fondation .

Trevarthen, C., Kokkinaki, T. and Fiamenghi, G.A. Jr (1999). What infants' imitations communicate: with mothers, with fathers and with peers. In J. Nadel and G. Butterworth (ed.), *Imitation in Infancy*, pp. 127–185. Cambridge: Cambridge University Press.

Trevarthen, C. and Malloch, S. (2000). The dance of wellbeing: Defining the musical therapeutic effect. *The Nordic Journal of Music Therapy*, 9(2), 3–17.

Turner, M. (1996). *The literary mind: The origins of thought and language*. New York/Oxford: Oxford University Press.

Wallin, N. (1991). *Biomusicology: Neurophysiological, Neuropsychological, and Evolutionary Perspectives on the Origins and Purposes of Music*. New York: Pendragon Press.

Wittman, M. and Pöppel, E. (1999). Temporal mechanisms of the brain as fundamentals of communication—with special reference to music perception and performance. *Musicae Scientiae, Special Issue (1999–2000)*, 13–28.

PART I

DEVELOPING MUSICAL IDENTITIES

CHAPTER 3

MUSICAL IDENTITIES AND THE SCHOOL ENVIRONMENT

ALEXANDRA LAMONT

Overview

This chapter focuses on children's developing musical identities and the ways in which these relate to the experiences that children have at school in terms of music. I begin by considering what we mean by musical identities and how they might develop, drawing on social psychological and socio-cultural approaches such as Bronfenbrenner's (1979) ecological model of development. The perspectives of policy and practice concerning children's involvement with music in England and Wales are reviewed. Research evidence is then presented to illustrate how children's perceived musical identities develop over time and under different conditions. Studies are reviewed of children's attitudes towards music in relation to their actual experiences with musical activities, both in and outside school. These focus on their level of engagement with music in terms of practical activities, formal instrumental tuition, and group and individual performance, and also explore their attitudes towards music, sport and school in general. Some of the factors leading to the development of positive and negative musical identities are identified, and their implications traced out.

Identities in development

How does a child's identity develop? Two important topics need to be considered when thinking about identity: first, *self understanding*, or how we understand and define ourselves as individuals; and secondly, *self–other understanding*, or how we understand, define and relate to others. Children's development of self understanding and of self–other understanding seems to progress in parallel. For example, at the same point that babies are able to recognize their own reflections in a mirror (about 18 months), they also begin to recognize, and remember, other people in terms of their physical features (Lewis and Brooks-Gunn, 1979).

In early childhood, children's understandings of self and others are characterized by an emphasis on physical, observable features, are inconsistent over time, and are global or generalized. A 4-year-old girl who is good at physical games, for example, is likely to generalize this personal identity to every aspect of her self understanding. She may not have a very accurate understanding of her own abilities, as younger children tend to overestimate what they can do (Harter, 1999). Later in middle childhood, children begin to understand that their identities may be more flexible, yet based on internal and consistent features. The same child at the age of 8 years will appreciate that she may be good at sport but poor at formal academic skills, for example, but that these character-istics remain relatively stable over time (Ruble, 1987). In children's self-descriptions, physical characteristics decline in salience between the ages of 6 and 13 years, whilst social, psychological and activity-related characteristics become more important. Social characteristics in particular dominate at this stage (Damon and Hart, 1988), as children compare their own achievements and attitudes with those of their peers in both self and self–other understanding. Finally, in adolescence, internalized psychological features of self and others achieve a greater prominence (Hart *et al.*, 1993).

We can also separate out the influence of *personal identity*, or our individual and idiosyncratic characteristics, and of *social identity*, which is based on social and par-ticularly group characteristics. Social identity theory explains how interpersonal beha-viour (prioritizing individual characteristics, or the personal identity) and intergroup behaviour (prioritizing group membership, or the social identity) are interrelated in self-categorization (Tajfel and Turner, 1979; see also Tarrant *et al.*, Chapter 8). The developmental progression outlined above suggests that personal identity may be more salient in earlier childhood, whilst social identity becomes more influential in the processes of group comparison (Festinger, 1954) that children begin to engage in during middle childhood and particularly in adolescence, in terms of shaping children's understanding of themselves and of others.

The development of identity will thus be crucially shaped by the circumstances that children grow up in (cf. Ellemers *et al.*, 1999). One useful way of understanding these *contextual* influences is Bronfenbrenner's (1979) ecological model (Figure 3.1). The smallest inner circles represent the *microsystems* that children are directly involved in, such as the home or the school. Within each of these microsystems, the individual child is engaged in social processes of negotiation of meaning. The next circle represents the

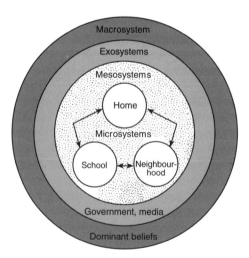

Figure 3.1 Bronfenbrenner's ecological model: contexts of development.

mesosystems, which reflect the relationships between microsystems. There may be differences in the processes operating at home and at school, for instance, which will create conflicts in children's lives. The outer levels reflect wider influences on individual children from contexts in which they are not directly involved. The *exosystems* incorporate influences such as government policy and the media. A government policy on working mothers is not something that individual children participate in, but it can have an effect on their upbringing by involving child care from an early age. The *macrosystem* reflects the dominant beliefs of a particular culture, such as the belief in the value of education for all children from a given age, which again influence the course of development.

One change in Western children's lives that may have an important impact on identity occurs around the age of 4 or 5 years, when children begin to come into contact with many more children of the same age at nursery school and school. Before this, children's social identities are shaped largely by their family circumstances. They define themselves in relation to other people within the microsystem of the home, which tends to be a relatively restricted group of parents, siblings, relations and family friends. Perhaps since children are mostly surrounded by people who are more competent than themselves (older siblings and adults), social comparisons are not common in the early years. However, once children have a larger group of peers of similar ages and abilities, social comparisons become more prevalent within the microsystem of the school, having an influence on both self- and self–other understanding (Higgins and Parsons, 1983). Similarly, changes in school systems such as the transition to secondary school are also likely to have similar effects on children's developing identities.

This brief summary of social psychological approaches shows us that identity is based on both personal idiosyncratic features and on social comparative features, and that self and self–other understanding seem to develop in parallel, with some major changes occurring around the age of 7 years (increases in comparative judgements, greater emphasis on social and psychological attributes) and in early adolescence (reduction in activity-related characteristics, increase in psychological comparisons). Personal features dominate younger children's more global identities, whilst social comparisons become more important in older children's more specialized identities, and are particularly influential in adolescence. Context is also an influential factor, and we can conceptualize this at many different levels of influence from the microsystem of the home to the macrosystem of a given society.

What might this mean for the development of a *musical* identity? Children should only be able to develop a specific identity as a musician at the stage when they can master the idea of a differentiated identity (around the age of 7 years). Earlier than this, children's personal identities should be influenced by other features of self understanding which do not relate specifically to music. Children's musical identities should be based initially on external and observable activities and experiences, and being a member of a group involved in music will be an important part of a musical identity. Moving through middle childhood, peer group comparisons will become increasingly important in children's musical identities, whilst attitudes and feelings towards music will come to dominate adolescents' musical identities. The contexts of children's development should also play a role in shaping their musical identities.

In this chapter, I begin by considering the wider level of the exosystem and explore the current government policy regarding music in school in England and Wales, before investigating the effects of this on the microsystem of school as a specific social context which shapes children's musical identities. The chapter also includes some consideration of the mesosystem—how school and home interact. The specific influence of the home environment is taken up in more detail by Borthwick and Davidson (Chapter 4).

Musical identities in policy

Music can change the way children feel, think, and act . . . Music enables children to define themselves in relation to others, their friends, colleagues, social networks and to the cultures in which they live . . . The teaching of music . . . introduces pupils to different forms of music making and response, both individual and communal, developing a sense of group identity and togetherness (QCA, 1999, p. 162).

This quotation from the Qualifications and Curriculum Authority (QCA) for England and Wales is part of the justification for the current National Curriculum programme for music. The National Curriculum, introduced in England and Wales in 1988, was intended to provide a commonality of educational experience for all children within the state-regulated sector. The inclusion of music as a foundation subject within the Curriculum was seen as a radical step by the music education community, not only as a recognition of the importance of the subject area but also, more importantly, for the emphasis which was placed on musical *activity* (Durrant and Welch, 1995). Although composing was introduced into secondary schools in the 1970s and 1980s (e.g. Swanwick, 1979) and singing has long been a major component of music education alongside more passive 'music appreciation' (Plummeridge, 1991), what was new was the entitlement for *all* children to experience and benefit from more active forms of music making, intended to help them develop a deeper understanding of music and become musicians themselves to some degree.

The National Curriculum for Music assumes that all children are capable of taking part in and benefiting from music education (DES, 1992). The uniform programme of study also assumes that all children begin at the same starting point, and it embodies an implicit model of musical progression (cf. Durrant and Welch, 1995) which follows an age-related improvement in sophistication (DFE, 1995). In principle, the Curriculum should bring music to a wider range of children and make them all more 'musical' as they get older. However, running alongside this inclusive agenda, there are many less democratic forms of music-making that children encounter at school and beyond, such as optional extra-curricular music activities or formal instrumental tuition through the peripatetic teaching system. This relates more closely to the élite Western classical tradition and the 'real world' of music as a profession. Under pressure from the professional music community and researchers (e.g. NACCCE, 1999), current government policy ostensibly supports such activities (DCMS, 2000), and the QCA mention the importance of the 'extended curriculum' in providing optional extras for some pupils which relate more clearly to the professional world of music (QCA, 1999).

In terms of developing identity, children are expected to 'define themselves' through music, and to develop 'a sense of group identity and togetherness' through the experiences of music at school (QCA, 1999). This reflects the dual aspects of identity discussed at the start of this chapter. However, the extended curriculum and opportunities for children to engage in additional musical activities suggest a *hidden curriculum* that assumes that not all children will benefit from the same set of musical opportunities. This suggests that the contexts in which children experience music are not common to all and that we might expect more diversity in terms of children's developing musical identities.

Musical identities in practice

Research supports the assumption that everyone has the capacity to be 'musical' (e.g. Gardner, 1983; Sloboda, 1985; Trehub *et al.*, 1997), yet the notion that all children begin at the same starting point conflicts with the considerable differences that exist in children's interests, experiences and abilities in music (Pugh and Pugh, 1998, p. 20). In practice, there is a broad range of different kinds of musical experiences open to children, and these can have both positive and negative effects on the way that children approach music in and out of school (see also O'Neill and Boulton, 1996; Sloboda and Davidson, 1996; O'Neill and Sloboda, 1997; O'Neill, Chapter 5, this volume).

The conventional defining feature of a 'musician' centres on instrumental performance skills—whether one can play a musical instrument (Plummeridge, 1991; Glover, 1993). Indeed, in primary schools, where children are taught all subjects by their class teacher, the teaching profession demonstrated considerable resistance to the inclusion of music in the Curriculum, feeling that this was an area which could not be tackled by 'non-musician' teachers. Much recent music pedagogy literature has focused on addressing this problem (e.g. Glover, 1993). There is thus a contradiction between the expectations of children engaged in Curriculum school music activities and the definition of a 'musician' in adult life.

The School Curriculum and Assessment Authority (SCAA) reflects the same bipolar distinction between 'musician' and 'non-musician' in its guidance for assessing musical activities at school, as illustrated by the following examples:

Simon plays keyboard, piano, and a range of tuned percussion with confidence and control. He chooses from this wide range of instruments and is happy to experiment in order to get the exact sound he wants. He is a good ensemble player. He plays with confidence and fits his part with the other parts in a musically sensitive way ... Simon identifies conventions and utilises them in his own work ... He has a real understanding of how music works and is extremely interested in a vast range of music. ... He has an excellent musical and expressive vocabulary, which enables him to analyse and comment clearly on changes in character and mood and make connections between music and its context (SCAA, 1996, p. 37).

Teresa plays a range of classroom instruments, although she prefers the xylophone. She can perform with confidence, especially when she is given help by other members of the group and sufficient time to practise. However, her playing technique is basic. She tends to play relatively simple parts and does not make adjustments to reflect the effect or mood ... Whilst she has a musical vocabulary she often fails to recognise musical devices when listening to music ... She is able to make comparisons between stylistically similar music but her comments tend to stay at a simplistic level, referring to musical elements such as tempo and structure (SCAA, 1996, p. 23).

Many reasons underpin the wide differences between these two children in terms of their attitudes towards, engagement with, and officially judged abilities in music. On the basis of previous research, Simon's development into a 'musician' is likely to have resulted from a series of social and cultural factors including parental support, a sympathetic peer group with shared interests, formal music tuition and the associated social reinforcement from a music teacher, and hours of practice leading to intrinsic motivation to continue with such tuition (Sloboda and Davidson, 1996; Sloboda *et al.*, 1996; see also Borthwick and Davidson, Chapter 4). Teresa's parallel development into a 'non-musician' would have resulted from the absence of these factors, although children like her typically will engage with music in many complex ways outside the school environment. Listening to popular music, for example, is the primary leisure activity of adolescents in contemporary industrialized societies (Zillmann and Gan, 1997, p. 162). Such activity typically is not valued at school due to the gulf between what is considered and valued as 'music' at school and outside (Shepherd and Vulliamy, 1994).

Teachers hold different attitudes to pupils of different levels of achievement, across the range of school subjects (Mortimore *et al.*, 1988). Underpinned by the assessment procedures, music teachers also make distinctions between 'musical' and 'unmusical' children, often based on whether or not they are able to play musical instruments. The conventional definition of a musician has many resonances in the school classroom, since it is easy to observe and measure whether or not children are accomplished musical performers (Plummeridge, 1991, p. 82; Durrant and Welch, 1995, pp. 12–13). As well as providing the arena where the children's musical identities are formed, the school thus also plays a role in reinforcing differences in musical identity. To borrow arguments from the sociology of education, it is not the content of the overt curriculum but rather the *form* of schooling, or the messages transmitted as a result of its organization and practices, which is more powerful (Dale, 1977).

One obvious outcome of differences in musical experiences at school is seen when children select subjects to study in Key Stage 4 between the ages of 14 and 16 years for General Certificate of Secondary Education (GCSE) public examinations. Bray (2000) has shown that the proportion of secondary school pupils opting to take GCSE qualifications in music is stable but low, at about 6.8%. He argues that despite the good intentions of the mandatory part of the Curriculum programme, as soon as children have a choice they tend to choose other subjects over music. At this stage in children's lives, the 'professional' world of music seems to be dominating over the 'inclusive' elements of school music. Those pupils who are involved in extra-curricular school musical activities, as part of the extended curriculum, seem to be those most likely to opt to study music in Key Stage 4 (SCAA, 1997). Those pupils who have not had experiences beyond the classroom curriculum seem to have a different perception of school music, as they drop the subject as soon as they can (Spencer, 1993; Harland *et al.*, 2000). At this stage, the influence of the hidden curriculum is brought into the open.

This suggests that children's musical identities develop at school between the ages of 5 and 14 years, and that these will be shaped not by the Curriculum but by the traditional defining activities of 'professional' musicians. By age 14 years, children who do not participate in these activities do not consider music something worth studying or something that they are able to do, whilst children who do are likely to have developed a more positive musical identity. This corresponds with the decline in positive attitudes towards music during secondary school found by Ross (1995) and Harland *et al.* (2000). If, as we expect, children are using music as a means of defining themselves and forming group identities, this means that inevitably some children will form negative musical identities whilst others will form more positive musical identities. I now turn to some more recent studies of my own, focusing directly on how school shapes children's developing musical identities.

Developing musical identities

My own interest in musical identity began with an unexpected outcome of research I conducted in the mid-1990s into children's cognitive understandings of music (Lamont, 1998a,b). A large sample of over 1800 children aged between 5 and 16 years participated in a series of listening studies, where they judged the goodness of fit of final notes of short musical sequences. Previous studies had tended to classify participants as either 'musicians' or 'non-musicians' according to whether they played a musical instrument or not, and most commonly whether they had a certain level of formal musical training (e.g. Krumhansl and Shepard, 1979). When trying to explain how listening sensitivity might be developed in childhood, I wondered whether a more sensitive categorization of participants' musical experiences might be important. In particular, since children were engaged in an amount of musical activity at school as part of the Curriculum, the traditional labels of 'novices' and 'experts' were clearly inappropriate, since even the 'novices' had a certain degree of musical experience. So I asked the children a series of short questions about their musical backgrounds. These began with the following two questions (square brackets show verbal explanations of the questions which were read out to the children before they answered each question):

1. Do you have music lessons?

   [What this means is if you are learning to play a musical instrument with a special teacher. This can be either on your own or in a group, but it doesn't mean the music lessons you have in your class at school.]

2. Do you play a musical instrument?

   [What this means is whether you can play a musical instrument. You don't have to have lessons on it, and it doesn't matter how well you play it.]

These questions were intended to provide factual information about the children's practical experiences with music. However, the children's responses did not seem to be based on fact but rather influenced by their self-perceptions, as follows:

1. Almost half the children (48%) described themselves as 'non-musicians', saying that they did not have lessons and did not play a musical instrument. Class teachers often remarked that these children *did* participate in class musical activities as part of the Curriculum. Nonetheless, if children's responses were based on what they actually did, they should all have said that they played musical instruments.

2. A further 22% of the sample said they were not having lessons but did play instruments ('playing musicians'). This group seems to reflect a more developed musical

identity, although its causes are unclear. These children may have placed a greater weight on the kinds of musical activity they were involved in at school in the classroom, internalizing them as part of their self-description. It is also possible that these children actually did engage in more musical activities, in addition to class music lessons, than the 'non-musicians'.

3. Finally, 30% of the sample said that they were having music lessons and played musical instruments ('trained musicians'). This corresponds to the upper end of estimates indicated by previous surveys (e.g. ABRSM, 1994). All but one school studied provided opportunities for children to have formal music lessons at school, which is likely to be the main reason for this high proportion.

Children used these self-descriptions in different ways at different ages. Some simple differences between primary and secondary school are shown in Figure 3.2. Although the proportions of 'non-musicians' were similar between the two school types, more primary school children described themselves as 'playing musicians' than secondary school children, and more secondary school children said they were having music lessons than primary school children. In broad terms, this shows how children's musical identities change over time: although they have less formal musical experience, more of the younger children seem to have more positive musical identities than the older children.

Why should these differences in identity occur? One explanation is that the younger children were overestimating their own abilities, whilst the older children provided more accurate self-descriptions (cf. Harter, 1999). This did not emerge in the question about musical training, as only a small proportion of primary school children said that they had formal music lessons. They all seemed to recognize that 'having music lessons' was an activity involving commitment, skill and motivation (Ericsson *et al.*, 1993; O'Neill and Sloboda, 1997). 'Playing musical instruments' might have been seen as less

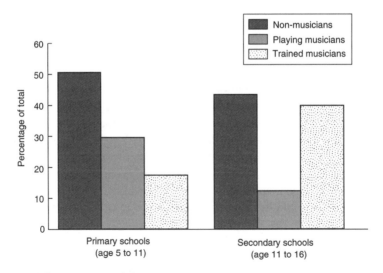

Figure 3.2 Age differences in musical identity.

skilled, and therefore something that more of the younger children felt they could do, regardless of their actual level of participation in this kind of activity.

Another possibility relates to age differences in identity. We would expect children younger than 7 years to base their self-descriptions on more personal aspects of their identities, whilst children older than 7 years should be making more group comparisons in forming their identities (cf. Damon and Hart, 1988). Looking at the figures year by year, the proportion of playing musicians remained relatively constant between the ages of 5 and 12 years, and then it dropped sharply. The proportion of non-musicians decreased as the number of trained musicians increased (beginning from age 7 and continuing gradually to age 16). This suggests that the observed differences in musical identity may be more influenced by the actual opportunities open to the children at different ages than by a shift from personal to social features of identity.

In schools in England and Wales, the opportunities for engaging in extra musical activity and provision of music lessons increase as children get older. Peripatetic instrumental teaching typically is provided for children aged 7–8 years and older and, in secondary schools, with specialist class music teachers, there are many more opportunities for extra-curricular structured musical activities such as choirs, orchestras and music lessons. This allows more children to become trained musicians, but it also results in fewer playing musicians and a far greater number of non-musicians. In contexts where there are more children (and adults) engaged in musical activities, those children who are *not* involved may feel the difference from the others becoming more marked, and this negative group comparison leads to them developing a more negative musical identity. In primary schools, conversely, where less extra-curricular music-making is taking place, children may be able to retain a more positive musical identity, due to a more positive group comparison.

I examined responses given by a subset of children in two different primary schools to explore these issues. The first school offered peripatetic teaching on a wide range of musical instruments, with class music lessons taught by general class teachers. The second school did not offer peripatetic teaching, and class music lessons were taught by a visiting specialist. As expected, fewer children in the second school were having formal music lessons. The proportions of children in the other two categories are more illuminating (Figure 3.3). The first school had a greater proportion of non-musicians and far fewer playing musicians than the second school, where only four children considered themselves to be 'non-musicians'. This confirms the notion that children's musical identities are shaped by group comparisons, even in the primary school.

Although older children are more likely to use social comparisons than younger children, the way in which this influences the development of musical identity seems to be associated with the kinds of opportunities open to the children, highlighting the importance of peer groups in shaping children's developing identities as musicians. As shown by the comparison of primary schools, the way in which music is delivered in the classroom (by a specialist or a generalist teacher) does not seem to be important, although this may have influenced the overall differences between primary and secondary school. These results also highlight the importance of school as the setting where group comparisons assume significance in children's developing identities. Importantly, different musical identities also have significant effects on children's cognitive understandings of music (see Lamont, 1998b). Children who described themselves as playing musicians

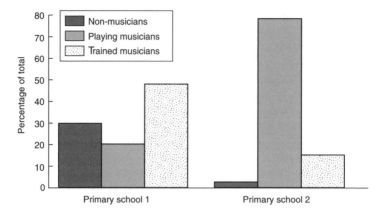

Figure 3.3 School differences in musical identity: primary school comparison.

performed at a consistently higher level than children who described themselves as non-musicians, emphasizing the importance of this area of enquiry.

Attitudes towards music and musical identities

Children's responses to the simple questions above appear to reflect an aspect of musical identity, yet the children's actual musical experiences beyond playing musical instruments or having music lessons were not known, nor did I have any information on children's attitudes towards school musical activities or details of the home musical environment. I next looked at these issues in research in collaboration with Mark Tarrant which was explicitly designed to explore questions of musical identity.

We carried out two studies to investigate the relationships between the National Curriculum for music, extra-curricular musical provision and take-up, school type, children's degree of identification with school music lessons and children's musical identities. We also studied the children's degree of identification with school in general, and their participation in and identification with sport and school physical education (PE) lessons. Although Harland *et al.* (2000) did not find any transfer effects of arts activity on other areas of children's academic life, other research has indicated that these effects can be considerable (e.g. Mahoney and Cairns, 1997; Jordan and Nettles, 2000). Sport and music share many features in children's lives: both are compulsory elements of the National Curriculum, but are also activities that children can choose to participate in both as an extra-curricular activity at school and in out of school contexts, in a group or alone, and are fiercely competitive fields in which to make a career.

The children were asked questions about themselves, their families and their activities in leisure time (music and sport), as well as the two key questions from the earlier studies: 'do you play a musical instrument?' and 'do you have music lessons?' The identification scales, developed from previous social identity theory research (Brown *et al.*, 1986; Hinkle *et al.*, 1989; Luhtanen and Crocker, 1992), consisted of statements such as 'I think this school is important' or 'music lessons have very little to do with how I feel about myself', and children were asked to indicate how much they agreed or disagreed with each statement on a five-point scale.

School transitions and identity

In music particularly, the transition from primary to secondary school (which takes place at age 11 years) has been found to be problematic in terms of the quality of teaching, as shown by official inspection reports (Mills, 1998). There is a considerable drop in standards of teaching in the first few years of secondary school in comparison with the relatively high standards attained in the last years of primary school. To focus on differences caused by changing school type, we first studied children in the last year of primary school (age 10–11 years) as well as the first 3 years of secondary school (age 11–14 years) (Tarrant and Lamont, unpublished data). The primary school was the feeder school for the secondary school, located in an area of socio-economic deprivation in the East of England. Both schools had very active extra-curricular music programmes, with visiting peripatetic teachers, school recorder groups, choirs and orchestras.

We analysed responses from 139 children (71 boys and 69 girls). Despite the relatively high levels of musical opportunities, only 11% of the sample said that they were having formal music lessons (13 girls and two boys). A further 19% said that they played musical instruments (21 girls and five boys), whilst 70% described themselves as non-musicians (34 girls and 63 boys). There were no marked age differences in the proportions of trained musicians, playing musicians and non-musicians, although the number of children describing themselves as trained musicians declined gradually from 15 to 5% between age 10 and 14 years. However, there was a clear gender bias in these self-descriptions: far more girls than boys described themselves as playing musicians, just as more girls than boys were having formal music lessons.

Why did these differences in self-description occur? Girls were more likely to describe themselves as musicians than boys, and older children were slightly less likely to be having formal music lessons. Armed with more information about the children themselves and their attitudes towards music, we found that nearly two-thirds of the playing musicians took part in extra-curricular musical activities of some kind (most often at school in the form of regular organized group activities), compared with only 4% of the non-musicians. There was little influence of the home environment, as the playing musicians did not come from more musically active families than the non-musicians. Children with more positive musical self-descriptions showed a stronger degree of identification with school music lessons than children with less positive musical self-descriptions. The more positive musical group also showed a higher identification with school in general, but there was no difference between groups in terms of identification with PE lessons.

Looking at these results over the 4-year age range, to explore whether school transition played a role in the results, we found that identification ratings for school in general and for music lessons both decreased gradually with age. The music identification ratings were significantly higher for children in the last year of primary school than for those in the second and third years of secondary school. (Identification ratings for PE lessons also dropped between primary and secondary schools but remained constant in the first 3 years of secondary school.)

These results support the earlier suggestion that children's self-descriptions as musicians reflect something of their musical identities. Participating in musical activities and gender are the most influential factors associated with a positive musical identity (as defined by responses to the self-description questions), whereas age and the home environment are not influential. A more positive musical identity is also associated with greater identification with class music lessons, yet we cannot establish any causality. Whether positive self-description as a musician leads to or results in stronger identification with class music, there is some transfer of these positive features to identification with school in general. This does not carry over into every aspect of school, as there is no influence on identification with PE lessons (although the more musical group included more girls than boys, and girls are known not to enjoy sport at school as much as boys; see Colley et al., 1994; Whitehead et al., 1997). Identification with music at school is seen to decline with age and with changing school type, but this does not seem to show a strong relationship with children's musical identities, which do not change with age or school type.

School comparisons and identity

We next explored the influence of the secondary school environment in more detail, in a second study comparing two different schools (Lamont and Tarrant, 2001). The first school had above-average levels of general academic achievement at GCSE examination level, and a well developed extra-curricular music programme with peripatetic instrumental teaching, whilst the second had below-average levels of GCSE examination passes and virtually no extra-curricular music provision. We focused on the 3 years from the start of secondary school to the end of the compulsory curriculum when pupils make GCSE subject choices (years 7–9, age 11–14 years), including two classes from every year group from both schools. In this study, we also asked the children how much they liked their music teachers.

Out of the 284 children sampled, we found a lower proportion of self-described non-musicians in this study at 60% (94 boys and 76 girls). Over a quarter of the sample described themselves as playing musicians (28 boys and 42 girls), whilst 13% had formal music lessons (15 boys and 23 girls). As shown in Figure 3.4, in the first school (where there were more musical opportunities), slightly more children had formal lessons than in the second school. The proportion of non-musicians was slightly higher in the first school than the second, whilst the proportion of playing musicians was greater in the second school than the first.

As well as the school differences, we also found a relationship between the self-descriptions, participation in extra-curricular musical activities, and the home musical environment. Only 6% of the non-musicians took part in extra musical activities, whilst nearly a third of the playing musicians did so. The playing and trained musicians were also more likely to come from homes where someone else also played a musical instrument. With age, we found a similar pattern of change in the self-descriptions as above: between year 7 and 9, non-musicians increased from 51 to 71%, playing musicians decreased from 30 to 20%, and trained musicians decreased from 19 to 9%. There were gender differences too: more boys described themselves as non-musicians than girls, whilst more girls described themselves as playing musicians or as having music lessons than boys. Both age and gender differences were more marked in the first school.

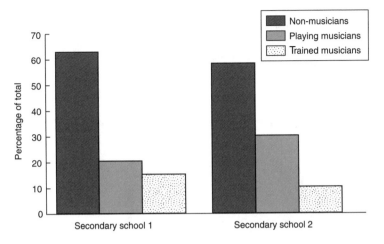

Figure 3.4 School differences in musical identity: secondary school comparison.

As before, children with more positive musical identities also showed higher levels of identification with their school music lessons, but we found no carry-over influences in terms of identification with school in general or with PE. There were some interesting school differences in the identification ratings. Children from the first school (with more musical opportunities) showed a *lower* overall level of identification with their school music lessons. Even though all the children's identification ratings with music lessons decreased with age, those from the oldest children in the second school were still higher than those from the youngest children in the first school. There were also marked gender differences. Girls showed much higher identification with music lessons than boys, whose low levels of identification did not change substantially over the 3 years studied. (This pattern of results was reversed for PE, where boys showed higher levels of identification than girls, although this decreased with age.) Despite all these findings, there were no differences in the children's degree of identification with their school in general between the two schools, with age or with gender.

We wondered whether identification with music lessons might be influenced by children's liking of the music teacher (who was not the same person for all the classes studied in the same school). Again, we found a difference between the two schools, with children from the first school showing a much lower level of teacher liking than those from the second. This was partly affected by age, as liking for the music teacher declined in the second school between years 7 and 9, whilst liking remained at the same low level for all children in the first school. There were also differences in teacher liking between the categories of musical self-description, and this again differed between the two schools (Figure 3.5). In the first school, playing musicians showed the highest level of liking for music teachers, whilst in the second school trained musicians showed the highest level of liking.

This study provides some firmer conclusions regarding the specific effects of different school contexts on children's musical identities. The school environment has a clear influence on children's self-descriptions as musicians: in more overtly musical contexts,

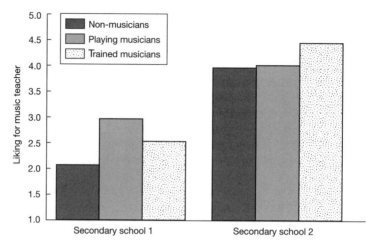

Figure 3.5 School differences in liking for music teachers: secondary school comparison.

more children have a negative musical identity (i.e. there is a greater proportion of non-musicians and fewer playing musicians), whilst in less overtly musical settings more children have a positive musical identity (i.e. more playing musicians and fewer non-musicians). Gender differences are also apparent, with a strong bias towards girls being more involved in music, in terms of both activities and their own musical identities. Very few of the non-musicians participated in any kind of extra musical activity, although self-description as a playing musician was not as strongly associated with extra musical activity as in the first study above. The home environment also plays a role in children's self-definitions and attitudes towards music at school. Finally, children's liking of their music teachers is also associated with higher levels of identification with music at school and with their emerging musical identities.

Discussion

The results of these studies shed some light on how children's musical identities develop in different contexts and at different stages of development, and have helped identify some key features of this process. First, there are several clear influences on musical identity which are external to the realm of the school. Girls are more likely to hold positive attitudes towards music and to develop more positive musical identities than boys. Children from homes where other people are involved in musical activities are also more likely to develop positive attitudes towards music. In addition, children from lower socio-economic backgrounds are less likely to develop positive attitudes towards music or to engage in musical activities, due perhaps to the lack of financial support that such activities require. Further research would be needed to explore this question of socio-economic status in more depth.

There are also age differences in children's musical identities. Younger children seem to be willing to describe themselves more positively in terms of music than older children. This can be related to developmental changes in the nature of identity itself: as noted earlier, older children are able to make more accurate estimations of what they can do, and are more likely to use group comparisons as the basis of defining their own and others' identities. These changes may explain why more secondary school children describe themselves as non-musicians. Yet some of the differences are also due to the *contexts* of development. Children of the same ages but in different contexts use these musical self-descriptions in different ways.

Turning to the specific influence of school as a context, the official curriculum (class music lessons in the National Curriculum) does not help every child develop a positive musical identity. Although all the children do play musical instruments as part of their school music lessons, only a small proportion of the children studied here say that they do so. Some of the children also take part in extra-curricular musical activities, either at school or outside. This seems to be one defining feature of a more positive musical identity, as very few of the 'non-musicians' take part in these activities. Yet between one- and two-thirds of the children who describe themselves as playing musicians at secondary school level do not take part in extra musical activities, indicating that there is more to children's musical identities than the activities they engage in.

Children in school contexts where there are less 'exclusive' and more 'inclusive' musical activities are more likely to demonstrate positive musical identities, as shown through self-description and identification with school music. In schools with a considerable amount of extra-curricular musical activity, if children do not or choose not to become involved in these activities, they are more likely to develop a negative musical identity. This is seen across the entire age range, from 5 to 16 years of age, suggesting that children are using social comparisons at younger ages than expected from previous research. As noted above, whilst the official school curriculum is in favour of inclusive musical activities, the hidden extended curriculum of extra-curricular musical activities seems to be more influential in shaping children's musical identities. Contradictions between official government policy (at the level of the exosystem) and the ways in which this is realized in individual schools (at the level of the microsystem) have an effect on children's understandings of the social structures open, or closed, to them, and the hidden messages are clearly received.

Children's degree of identification with their school music lessons also provides a different angle on musical identity. This seems to be closely related to the factors identified above of gender, home, school and involvement in musical activities (with school influences being the most important). However, where self-description remains the same, identification with music lessons is subject to a marked decline during the secondary school years. More research that focuses on identification with school music with younger age groups would help to clarify this issue. Children's degree of liking for their music teachers is also related to their musical identities. This measure may reflect the attitude towards music held by particular schools, since the children do not all have the same music teachers and yet there are marked differences between schools in terms of teacher liking. The evidence reviewed here suggests that peers have more influence than adults in defining children's musical identities, but studies of teacher liking with younger age groups would help clarify this issue.

Implications

Children with a positive musical identity, as shown by their self-descriptions, are those who engage in more extra-curricular musical activities, show more positive attitudes towards school music and like their music teachers. In some cases, this is also associated with a greater sense of identification with school in general. At present, the direction of this relationship cannot be established. However, irrespective of whether positive musical identities are the cause or the result of increased involvement with music, it would be beneficial for children to develop positive musical identities. Having a strong musical identity is clearly an important step on the way to becoming a more sophistic- ated 'musician', whether this be in the realm of listening and understanding or in more active forms of music-making.

As we have seen above, school is an important social context where messages about the value of music, and who music should be for, are transmitted effectively. It is important to recognize that children's musical identities are not simple reflections of the adult, or professional, distinction between musicians and non-musicians. Despite the contradiction between policy and practice outlined above, it is encouraging to see that some children who are not part of the extra-curricular musical life of the school are still defining themselves as musicians. Teachers, and the values they transmit within the classroom and beyond, also play a role in influencing children's attitudes towards music. This suggests that there is scope for school as a context for encouraging all children to develop a more positive musical identity.

The evidence points to a decline in positive musical identity and in degree of identi- fication with music lessons as children move through the first 3 years of secondary school (cf. Harland *et al.*, 2000). This decline is associated with a decrease in identifica- tion with school in general, and this period in children's school lives is often associated with a higher incidence of disciplinary problems and disaffection (DfEE, 2001; OFSTED, 2001). At least some of these issues are not unique to music but relate to more general difficulties with school in early adolescence. However, the decline in iden- tification with music occurs only gradually, and there may be scope for interventions to work with 'vulnerable' children as they move into secondary school to halt and even- tually reverse this decline. As noted earlier, primary school children seem to have more positive attitudes towards music, and their music teaching is often of a higher quality. The potential exists for continuing this trend into the secondary school period. Studies isolating this factor are needed to enable a causal relationship to be established.

Music clearly does enable children to define themselves in relation to others. How- ever, at present, classroom music helps *some* children to develop a sense of group identity and togetherness, but for other children the activities at school beyond the classroom lead them to develop a sense of group *difference*. There are other influences on children's musical identities outside the realm of the school, which could be used to identify 'at risk' children in terms of musical identity. Most notably these include boys, children from lower socio-economic groups and those with little musical activity at home, and those children in the early years of secondary school. Achieving the more pragmatic aims of music education as a route to an ever-increasing range of music- related careers will depend on whether children's musical identities can be encouraged to such an extent that they are motivated to continue with music beyond the compulsory stage. Yet we would want to encourage all children to develop a healthy musical identity as a step towards the less pragmatic aims of being able to enjoy and participate in music throughout their lives.

References

ABRSM (1994). *Making Music: The Associated Board Review of the Teaching, Learning and Playing of Musical Instruments in the United Kingdom*. London: Associated Board of the Royal Schools of Music.

Bray, D. (2000). An examination of GCSE music uptake rates. *British Journal of Music Education*, 17, 79–89.

Bronfenbrenner, U. (1979). *The Ecology of Human Development: Experiments by Nature and Design*. Cambridge, MA: Harvard University Press.

Brown, R., Condor, S., Mathews, A., Wade, G. and Williams, J. (1986). Explaining intergroup differentiation in an industrial organization. *Journal of Occupational Psychology*, 59, 273–286.

Colley, A., Comber, C. and Hargreaves, D.J. (1993). Gender effects in school subject preferences— a research note. *Educational Studies*, 20, 13–18.

Damon, W. and Hart, D. (1988). *Self understanding in Childhood and Adolescence*. Cambridge: Cambridge University Press.

Dale, R. (1977). Implications of the rediscovery of the hidden curriculum for the sociology of teaching. In D. Gleeson (ed.), *Identity and Structure: Issues in the Sociology of Education*, pp. 44–54. Driffield: Nafferton Books.

DCMS (2000). *Government Response to All Our Futures: Creativity, Culture and Education*. (14 January). London: Department for Culture, Media and Sport.

DES (1992). *Music in the National Curriculum (England)*. London: HMSO.

DFE (1995). *Music in the National Curriculum*. London: HMSO.

DfEE (2001). *Schools: Building on Success: Raising Standards, Promoting Diversity, Achieving Results*. Government Green Paper, February. London: HMSO.

Durrant, C. and Welch, G. (1995). *Making Sense of Music: Foundations for Music Education*. London: Cassell.

Ellemers, N., Spears, R. and Doosje, B. (1999). Introduction. In N. Ellemers, R. Spears and B. Doosje (ed.), *Social Identity*, pp. 1–5. Oxford: Blackwell.

Ericsson, K.A., Krampe, R.T. and Tesch-Römer, C. (1993). The role of deliberate practice in the acquisition of expert performance. *Psychological Review*, 100, 363–406.

Festinger, L. (1954). A theory of social comparison processes. *Human Relations*, 7, 117–140.

Gardner, H. (1983). *Frames of Mind: The Theory of Multiple Intelligences*. London: Heinemann.

Glover, J. (1993). Music in the National Curriculum. Performing, composing, listening and appraising. In J. Glover and S. Ward (ed.), *Teaching Music in the Primary School: A Guide for Primary Teachers*, pp. 46–66. London: Cassell.

Harland, J., Kinder, K., Lord, P., Stott, A., Schagen, I. and Haynes, J. (2000). *Arts Education in Secondary Schools: Effects and Effectiveness*. Slough, UK: National Foundation for Educational Research.

Hart, D., Fegley, S., Chan, Y.H., Mulvey, D. and Fischer, L. (1993). Judgments about personal identity in childhood and adolescence. *Social Development*, 2, 66–81.

Harter, S. (1999). *The Construction of the Self: A Developmental Perspective*. New York: Guilford Press.

Higgins, E.T. and Parsons, J.E. (1983). Stages as subcultures: social–cognitive development and the social life of the child. In E.T. Higgins, W.W. Hartup and D.N. Ruble (ed.), *Social Cognition and Social Development*, pp. 15–62. Cambridge: Cambridge University Press.

Hinkle, S. Taylor, L.A., Fox-Cardamone, L. and Crook, K.F. (1989). Intragroup identification and intergroup differentiation: a multicomponent approach. *British Journal of Social Psychology*, **28**, 305–317.

Jordan, W.J. and Nettles, S.M. (2000). How students invest their time outside of school: effects on school-related outcomes. *Social Psychology of Education*, **3**, 217–243.

Krumhansl, C.L. and Shepard, R.N. (1979). Quantification of the hierarchy of tonal functions within a diatonic context. *Journal of Experimental Psychology: Human Perception and Performance*, **5**, 579–594.

Lamont, A. (1998a). The development of cognitive representations of musical pitch. Unpublished doctoral dissertation, University of Cambridge.

Lamont, A. (1998b). Music, education, and the development of pitch perception: the role of context, age, and musical experience. *Psychology of Music*, **26**, 7–25.

Lamont, A. and Tarrant, M. (2001). Children's self-esteem, identification with and participation in music and sport. Paper presented at the *Xth European Conference of Developmental Psychology*, Uppsala, Sweden (August).

Lewis, M. and Brooks-Gunn, J. (1979). *Social Cognition and the Acquisition of Self*. New York: Plenum.

Luhtanen, R. and Crocker, J. (1992). A Collective Self-Esteem Scale-Self Evaluation of One's Social Identity. *Personality & Social Psychology Bulletin*, **18**(3), 302–318.

Mahoney, J.L. and Cairns, R.B. (1997). Do extracurricular activities protect against early school dropout? *Developmental Psychology*, **33**, 241–253.

Mills, J. (1998). Music. In OFSTED, *The Arts Inspected*. Oxford: Heinemann.

Mortimore, P., Sammons, P., Stoll, L., Lewis, D. and Ecob, R. (1988). *School Matters: The Junior Years*. Wells: Open Books.

NACCCE (1999). *All Our Futures: Creativity, Culture and Education*. London: National Advisory Committee on Creative and Cultural Education/DfEE.

OFSTED (2001). *1999–2000 Standards and Quality in Education: The Annual Report of Her Majesty's Chief Inspector for Schools*. London: HMSO.

O'Neill, S.A. and Boulton, M.J. (1996). Boys' and girls' preferences for musical instruments: a function of gender? *Psychology of Music*, **24**, 171–183.

O'Neill, S.A. and Sloboda, J.A. (1997). The effects of failure on children's ability to perform a musical test. *Psychology of Music*, **25**, 18–34.

Plummeridge, C. (1991). *Music Education in Theory and Practice*. London: The Falmer Press.

Pugh, A. and Pugh, L. (1998). *Music in the Early Years*. London: Routledge.

Ross, M. (1995). What's wrong with school music? *British Journal of Music Education*, **12**, 185–201.

Ruble, D.N. (1987). The acquisition of self-knowledge: a self-socialisation perspective. In N. Eisenberg (ed.), *Contemporary Topics in Developmental Psychology*, pp. 243–270. New York: Wiley.

QCA (1999). *The Review of the National Curriculum in England: The Consultation Materials*. London: Qualifications and Curriculum Authority.

SCAA (1996). *Consistency in Teacher Assessment: Exemplification of Standards, Music: Key Stage 3*. London: School Curriculum and Assessment Authority Publications.

SCAA (1997). *Arts, Humanities and Language in Key Stages 3 and 4.* London: School Curriculum and Assessment Authority Publications.

Shepherd, J. and Vulliamy, G. (1994). The struggle for culture: a sociological case study of the development of a national music curriculum. *British Journal of Sociology of Education*, 15, 27–40.

Sloboda, J.A. (1985). *The Musical Mind: The Cognitive Psychology of Music.* Oxford: Clarendon Press.

Sloboda, J.A. and Davidson, J.W. (1996). The young performing musician. In I. Deliège and J. Sloboda (ed.), *Musical Beginnings: Origins and Development of Musical Competence*, pp. 171–190. Oxford: Oxford University Press.

Sloboda, J.A., Davidson, J.W., Howe, M.J.A and Moore, D.G. (1996). The role of practice in the development of expert musical performance. *British Journal of Psychology*, 87, 287–309.

Spencer, P. (1993). GCSE Music: a survey of undergraduate opinion. *British Journal of Music Education*, 10, 73–84.

Tajfel, H. and Turner, J.C. (1979). An integrative theory of intergroup conflict. In W.G. Austin and S. Worschel (ed.), *The Social Psychology of Intergroup Relations*, pp. 33–47. Monterey, CA: Brooks/Cole.

Trehub, S.E., Schellenberg, E.G. and Hill, D. (1997). The origins of music perception and cognition: a developmental perspective. In I. Deliège and J. Sloboda (ed.), *Perception and Cognition of Music.* (pp. 103–128) Hove, UK: Psychology Press.

Whitehead, J., Evans, N.J. and Lee, M.J. (1997). Relative importance of success in sport and schoolwork. *Perceptual and Motor Skills*, 85, 599–606.

Zillmann, D. and Gan, S. (1997). Musical taste in adolescence. In D.J. Hargreaves and A.C. North (ed.), *The Social Psychology of Music*, pp. 161–187. Oxford: Oxford University Press.

CHAPTER 4

DEVELOPING A CHILD'S IDENTITY AS A MUSICIAN: A FAMILY 'SCRIPT' PERSPECTIVE

SOPHIA J. BORTHWICK AND JANE W. DAVIDSON

Introduction

Past research has shown that the beliefs held by one family member will influence the values, attitudes and behaviour of the others to the point that the identities of both children and parents seem 'shaped' by the interactions between them (Radford, 1990). Despite this, it is only recently that music psychology research has acknowledged that family members are key in determining a child's musical development (see Csikszentmihalyi *et al.*, 1997, who look at the role of parents in the development of musical ability of talented teenagers). Such work has suggested, however, that the influences to become a musician within the family are unidirectional and typically from one parent to the child. In general, the research fails to explore the potential influence of reciprocal family interactions on the development of a 'musician's identity'. By this term, we mean the way in which an individual comes to take on and accept the role—the label and behaviours—associated with being a 'musician'. Overall, the chapter looks at the many influencing factors within family life which seem to contribute towards a musical identity. The chapter begins by making a theoretical exploration of general family influences on the identity of the child as a musician. It then goes on to report some findings from a detailed investigation we undertook with 12 families in which at least one child was engaged in musical activity and was labelled as 'being a musician' within the family.

Theoretical contextualization

Script theory

According to 'script theory' (Byng-Hall, 1995, 1998), the patterns of relating and functioning within a family emerge out of those that have been established and then transmitted down the generations. They include the family's attitudes, taboos, expectations, myths, secrets, legacies and loaded issues with which children grow up, and represent the 'given' aspect of upbringing, the value framework which exists from the very beginning of the child's life as a result of, amongst other things, the parents' own childhood (Carter and McGoldrick, 1989). Byng-Hall stresses the critical role of transgenerational influence on stability and change in family patterns of behaviour.

Being used principally as a means of analysing family interactions in therapy contexts, Byng-Hall describes the use of the term 'script' thus:

For me the most compelling reason for using the term 'script' is that families understand it immediately. If they complain about how the same situation arises again and again, we are soon likely to find ourselves talking about scripts. Although I will probably have introduced the actual term 'script', it may soon be forgotten and a shared set of metaphors emerges in the discussion: old scripts, writing new scripts, and improvising, etc. (Byng-Hall, 1995, p. 23)

Byng-Hall uses metaphors, in particular that of a play on a stage, to represent family life. These encapsulate the rich variety of action and discussion which is present within familial interaction. Byng-Hall regards each family member as taking on a role for a time to support the scripted plot of family expectations (the 'family script'). The 'family cast' is flexible to the extent that changes in family role can be instituted over time. However, the script is defined to a degree by the combination of past experiences of previous generations and 'parenting scripts'.

Influences of key others

Script theory recognizes other influences, such as peers and teachers (see Byng-Hall, 1995), and some robust birth ordering effects also demonstrate that, within the family, siblings have powerful influences on one another according to their age and ordinal position, irrespective of the family script. Sulloway (1996), for instance, examined siblings in a number of domains and found a marked difference between first- and second-borns, with first-borns typically being higher achieving, more self-focused and confident and occupying positions of higher authority than their younger sibling. Additionally, the first-borns appear to strive for compensatory approval through spending more time with parents than their younger sibling, emulating parental values and accepting their authority more readily (see Dunn, 1993). In contrast, second-borns are reported to feel 'overshadowed' by the first-born since, taking part in the same metaphorical 'race' of life, the younger sibling is rarely able to surpass and conquer the elder sibling. Thus, in our study, we pay attention to the birth order effects as well as the parenting scripts.

Examining scripts in case study families

The data were obtained from a qualitative study of 12 families, in which both parents and children in each family accounted for their own musical development and tastes through semi-structured interviews. The families were recruited through a snowballing technique, with the first family introducing the researchers to the second family, and so on. This technique was adopted as a means of recruiting families from the same geographical area, where at least one child was in receipt of similar kinds of musical instruction. All members of 11 families were interviewed once, in contrast to the one family who was traced over a period of 18 months to make a detailed case study in order

Table 4.1 Family codes

Family code	Sibship size	Gender, age, instruments of children	Parents' musical backgrounds	Parents' occupations
LS	2	Boy, 10 (James) piano, cello, flute	John, piano (a)	Teacher
		Boy, 6 (Daniel) piano, violin	Helen, cello (p)	Professional Musician
A	2	Boy, 18 (Josh) piano, violin	Martin, piano, violin (p)	University music lecturer
		Boy, 15 (David) piano, violin	Ann, violin (a)	Violinist/teacher
B	3	Girl, 17 (Sue) violin	Robert, cello (p)	Architect
		Girl, 15 (Caroline) cello	Jane, piano (a)	Ex-family doctor, now professional pianist
		Girl, 11 (Frances) clarinet		
C	2	Boy, 14 (Theo) piano	Tim, no instrument	Vicar
		Girl, 11 (Karen) flute	Wendy, piano (b)	Clinical psychologist
D	2	Girl, 11 (Stacey) flute	Steve, piano (b)	Secondary science teacher
		Girl, 9 (Joanne) recorder	Carol, no instrument	Part-time shop
E	3	girl, 12 (Fay), flute	Mike, no instrument	Barrister
		Girl, 10 (Jessica) guitar	Sheila, no instrument	Runs own business
		Girl, 8 (Kayleigh), no instrument		
F	3	Boy, 13 (Charles), no instrument	Tony, guitar (p)	Estate agent
		Girl, 11 (Vanessa), clarinet	Heather, no instrument	Legal secretary
		Girl, 9 (Kim) violin		
G	3	Girl, 11 (Rachel) violin	Ben, violin, organ, piano (a)	Secondary music teacher
		Girl, 9 (Amy) harp and piano	Pauline, cello, piano (p)	Education officer
H	3	Boy, 18 (Jon) saxophone, bass, bass guitar and flute	Neil, no instrument	Photographer
		Boy, 16 (Chris) drums	Trish, no instrument	journalist
		Boy, 14 (Steve) piano		
I	2	Boy, 14 (Mark) violin and piano	Michael, violin (p)	Secondary drama teacher
		Boy, 10 (Dean) recorder	Liz, no instrument	Primary teacher
J	1	Girl, 17 (Charlotte) classical guitar	Jeff, piano (a)	Ex-vicar/primary teacher
K	1	Girl, 7 (Nicola) piano	Jack, piano (b)	Builder
			Jean, no instrument	Cleaner

Note: (a) = amateur; (p) = professional; (b) = beginner.

to attain breadth and depth of qualitative data. All families showed a commitment to Western art music but represented a range of working and middle class backgrounds. Table 4.1 gives more specific details of the families involved. Note that pseudonyms have been used to respect confidentiality.

Each interview was undertaken in a one-to-one setting with the first author. Each interview was then transcribed and examined to reveal common themes and to establish how each participant saw the 'family script' and each other. The interviews were subjected to 'Interpretative Phenomenological Analysis' (see Smith *et al.*, 1997, 1999) in which key themes were structured and ordered after they emerged from repeated readings of the data. The interpretations of the raw data were validated through an external audit by two independent parties.

The sections that follow present the themes produced as a result of the data analysis. To facilitate the discussion, quotations are used as illustrative evidence and the codes used to identify these quotes are presented in the Appendix on p. 78.

The transgenerational 'plot'

Our study revealed that all the parents in the study had been affected by 'scripts' during childhood within their respective families of origin. It seemed that the degree of importance given to music by members of their immediate and extended family influenced their decision to accord music a particular status and role, and this had a direct influence on their current family lifestyle. Many parents saw their own parents as key players in their children's current musical identity:

If their grandparents hadn't been into music then there wouldn't have been anything to pass down and they'd more than probably not be playing today. [B, F]

For some parents, musicianship was an inevitable part of continuing the family identity across the generations:

Naturally I think it was just assumed it would be something that they'd do [play an instrument]. There was never any question that there wouldn't be some music [in the children's lives]. [G, M]

This was particularly the case especially when past experience had been positive:

When I think of all the wonderful friendships I've got from music and all the fun times I had over the years, it's like nothing else. It just provides you with so much enjoyment I can't imagine my kids having lives without it. [A, F]

My father loved music very much and my mother was quite a serious pianist in her teens so I suppose I was well set up to learn and pass it onto my kids later on. [LS, F]

However, other parents' negative experiences within the family filled them with caution in scripting their own children's futures:

I'm going to be really wary with my kids. Mum's sister said her Dad pushed her so much that she never wanted to play again. [D, M]

I hated it. The grand piano was God and therefore we practised in the totally freezing cold because any heat might have damaged it. It was as though he [father] cared more about the instrument's welfare than ours. I couldn't do that to my children. [LS, M]

Other members of the extended family also played an influencing role. Indeed the current children were fully aware of their musical legacies and myths that fuelled family expectations:

Apparently my great uncle played the bassoon or something you know. Everyone said he was really very good. Nice to think he was in our family. I mean that's all the more reason why she could do well too, you know that sort of thing runs in families. [B, f]

Granny likes to listen to opera so I think I will too when I'm older. [LS, f2]

Thus, within each family, there were different influences coming to bear depending on the parents' own experiences. Overall, the data showed how two successive generations seemed inextricably linked by both the father's and the mother's desires to relive their favourable experiences and not repeat what they perceived as the mistakes of the past. Sometimes parents' experiences were contrasting, but where there was a very negative and a very positive former experience with music, it was always the positive one that was aimed at being replicated for the children. There was no evidence of men or women being more or less dominant in their influences on their children.

In essence, transgenerational influence was shown to hold whether original musical values were held or rejected. If retained, data showed that these parents had either experienced a critical level of personal satisfaction from their former musical exposure, or at least felt the need to retain the 'heirloom' of the collective musical identity of the wider family. Indeed, the urge to retain the familiar meant that despite an element of physical, emotional or financial upheaval, some parents were enthusiastic for music to retain its former status within their family irrespective of whether or not as children they had experienced high levels of satisfaction. For example, one mother insisted in involving her children in performance examinations despite having felt distraught herself at sitting them as a child. She argued that with hindsight, she felt that the musical examinations had been good for her, so therefore her children would also benefit.

Cramer (1997), a child psychiatrist with a special interest in parents' scripts, believes that script replication is driven by the desire to pass down family values from one generation to the next, irrespective of the effect they have caused in the past. This was supported in our study in the account of one father, John, who acknowledged the 'inevitability' of his sons learning musical instruments taught by their mother Helen (a professional cellist), despite John's own negative musical experiences with his own mother when he was as a child. For John, it was inevitable that each of his sons would learn an instrument, because, according to his family script, he felt that all musician parents teach their children to play. However, he believed that learning for them would be a far more positive experience than his own because he recognized that his wife Helen was a different person from his mother, and a much more accomplished musician.

Current daily influences

For all 12 families, there was a clear and united 'musical group identity' which served to bind all the members of the household together: music was for all to discuss, listen to and either play or supervise. There was a strong parental expectation for the children to be involved in musical activities. Only half the parents interviewed played instruments either as keen amateurs or professionals, with the other half of the sample of participants having no performing or learning experience. Those with musical skills were much more demanding of their children in the setting of goals for musical achievement in their children. The families with one or two parents seeing themselves as musicians expected their children to achieve a higher level of musical accomplishment and involvement than the families with parents who saw themselves as non-musicians. A recurring script featured where non-musician parents seemed to want to give their children the opportunities they had missed in their own childhood. Where only one parent was a musician, the non-musician parent was particularly keen for his/her child to acquire the musician status they regarded as desirable and possessed by their partner, particularly as many identified being a musician as something valued by the surrounding culture. All the musicians wanted to replicate their own musical scripts in the sense that they wanted their children to learn an instrument as a potential vehicle for personal gain in terms of emotional expression, pleasure and possibly a future career. There were also many indications that the musician parents wanted the opportunity for their children to experience greater musical achievements than they attained themselves.

Parents generally imposed practice regimes on their children to ensure that they practised their instruments daily. They allocated time 'slots' solely for playing. In one extreme case, priority was given to studying the musical instrument over and above social life and schoolwork. Indeed, the teenage son of the family concerned recalled how his mother was angry that he had spent so much of his time on a school assignment when she felt that his violin practice warranted more attention:

I've got all this homework upstairs and Mum thinks that some of it is pretty unnecessary, things like I do long projects and she says 'You don't need to do that, it's pointless. Why do fifteen pages?' and she says: 'That was absolutely pointless, you could have done that in a page. You could have been practising when you did that!' So I said, 'Well I'm going to get a good mark on this, I want to spend some time on it'. I got back late today. Well she'll ask if I've done it and I just say 'no' I have been doing some homework about an hour . . . Mum thinks practice first, homework afterwards, and things like that. Well if I don't do practice then I just get shouted at. If I don't do my homework, then I get a detention, and I have to stay back after school or something. [A, m2]

The educational environment described in the quotation could be paralleled with 'hothousing' techniques (see Warmsley and Margolis, 1987 for details) where children are directed towards achieving their maximum potential in a controlled and deliberate manner. Certainly in this single case of parental pressure, a competitive atmosphere was encouraged. Friction was evident between parents and siblings, with the parents indicating to us that they needed to find a balance between encouragement, force and potential rebellion. They saw the need for an optimum level of expectation to be set. As another mother commented:

It's just extremely difficult for us to know how much to push her really. She needs us to tell her to get on with it or I don't think it would get done. I mean if we don't tell her to get the flute out of the box, well, I suppose she wouldn't bother, it doesn't happen automatically. But saying that, it's hard to know how much to push really. I mean we're on a very fine line here, she could easily turn round and tell us where to go, and I'm very conscious of that the whole time. It's as if we have to keep her sweet or she won't do it [practice] and I'd be quite upset if she gave it all up so she knows we expect her to keep going. [C, M]

Parental expectations

The parents expected their children to conform to a strict daily routine. The children who proved themselves to be reliable in their practice activities were given jurisdiction over their use of time. We regarded this concession to be the result of parents marking a shift from their own externally imposed motivation to the child's development of intrinsic motivation for engaging with music. Unfortunately, however, the eldest child was usually the first to be given such comparative freedom and the result was to leave the younger children with some pangs of rivalry:

It's just so unfair. I get treated like the baby round here. I get told when to do the practice and he just is allowed to do it when it suits. How come they trust him and not me? Josh basically does what he wants and they don't say 'You haven't done enough practice' and he should be sort of working several hours more than I am every day, but, they don't nag him to do more, they just let him do what he wants. I'm always shouted at, 'You've got to do this, do that!' [A, m2]

One father, Jack, insisted on staying with his daughter during the interview and, whenever she was asked a question, he answered for her, perhaps revealing some evidence of attempts to control. For example, when Nicola was asked to list her favourite pieces of music, he responded immediately, and when she suggested some other easier pieces, he contradicted her saying that she could play much more difficult pieces than those. This evidence indicated some overexpectation on his part.

When Jack spoke of playing the piano, it was evident that he possessed only elementary formal knowledge and technical skill. He believed it was his duty to supervise Nicola's practice sessions both before and after school, in order for her to be able to advance in music to a level beyond his own achievements. He insisted upon the twice-daily regime as being the minimum required. It was apparent from the discourse he used that he did not want Nicola to suffer the deprivation of opportunity in his own background, and so believed it was his 'duty' to push her beyond the level set by her teacher, giving her 'extra work' to do. From Jack's comments, it seemed that Nicola accepted the practice regime, but Jack's dominance in the interview might suggest that the impetus for her participation was mainly his, not hers:

Yeah she's a good kid is our Nicola. She gets on with it [practise] when I tell her to. [K, F]

So we see that parental expectations shaped the way in which music was promoted in that family, and sometimes this led to a no-win situation.

Families were selected for interview on the criterion that one child was learning an instrument. Analysis revealed that in all cases, the parents put music first in their family's lives. We cannot be sure, however, that the snowballing technique used to contact these families may have created this commonality, acting as a bias in selecting families where music was a central construct. Despite the central importance of music in these families' daily lives, for reasons based on financial security, some of the parents were not keen on the idea of their children taking up performing professionally whereas others saw professional music as a clear objective. This seemed an ironic script especially given that the parents had transmitted strongly encouraging messages to put music at the forefront of their children's lives from the beginning of instrumental tuition. At the point of career decision making, some of the children were confused about their parents having encouraged them initially and then denying support for pursuing what they felt was an inevitable career step given the intensely musical environment of their childhood.

I don't understand it really. It just doesn't make sense. Mum and Dad have both gone on about practising every day for years, you know. They've made sure I'm in this and that orchestra, giving me lifts to my lessons and everything and telling me how important it is. But then when I do show an interest and mention to them that I might like to do it as a job when I'm older, well they get all funny about it and go on about it being nice as a hobby but just a hobby and nothing else. It's really confusing. I mean I thought it was really important to them. [B, f1]

This set of demands may be identified as a 'double bind' (see Bateson, 1979). This musical double bind was expressed in childhood, with classical music being regarded as a challenging intellectual skill, a gateway to good social encounters and, above all, a focal point for family sharing. In adulthood, however, it was only regarded as appropriate to continue to afford this music a status a pleasurable, social role. Parents worried that professional music was low in financial reward and professional credibility, and, therefore, making it a career focus was discouraged.

Parent–child coalitions

In 10 of the 12 families, interview data revealed a strong musical link that we interpreted to be a 'musician identification' between one parent and one child. This seemed to have a negative influence on some of the other relationships within the family: husband–wife, parent–child and sibling–sibling dyads. The pull seemed even greater when the child learned the same instrument as a parent. One mother, Helen, seemed to project her own musical identity as a professional cellist onto her eldest son. She assumed that he would achieve a level of musical success similar to her own over time. Helen believed that her eldest son had inherited her high-level musicality, evident in his ability to play in perfect time with her in cello duets:

I think the most impressive single thing he does is that if I play duets with him he plays absolutely together. I never have to say as you might expect to say to a child so young 'O well you got faster there, you mustn't rush there'. He plays completely together, I mean you know, perfectly... [LS, M]

With the case study family, throughout the interviews, Helen concentrated her praise of the elder son solely on this one ability. Typically, musicality is rated globally in terms of overall technical ability (there is a significant research literature in this domain; see Hallam, 1998) but, for Helen, the construct of synchrony provided evidence of a strong sense of shared identity and she regarded James as a musical projection of herself:

I think James, although completely sort of dozy and muddled headed, um is an artist. There's no doubt he's an artist. I think he has inherited a kind of poetic streak and also a kind of gift of mimicry too. I can see myself in him, in his playing. Yes I can definitely see him as having my, well I know enough about music to know that there are aspects of James' talent, which I think, are very real... [LS, M]

Over time, evidence emerged from interviews with James' younger brother Daniel and their Dad, John, that the Helen–James dyad resulted in other family members feeling excluded from the musical equation. It seems that Helen offered James far more attention, and this contributed to John feeling a sense of relational imbalance that he felt detracted from the marital relationship:

Well Helen plays with James a lot. We don't seem to play together as much as we used to and that's a big shame but that's life I suppose [laughs]. [LS, F]

However, the coalition process seemed a reciprocal one, as the son took on the musical mantel of his mother, and vice versa:

I want to be a real musician like Mum. You know she's really really good at it. I suppose Dad's good too but not like Mum is. So well I think to myself, yes, then I want to be like Mum not Dad. [LS, m1]

In our other data, parent–child coalitions seemed to affect the dynamics of the sibling relationships within the families. For example, in four families, the elder child joined forces with parents and adopted a surrogate parent role, applying additional pressure in order to make a younger sister or brother practise. This interactive pattern engendered considerable hostility and resentment on the part of the younger child, since it was seen as a betrayal of sibling allegiance:

She shouldn't do that you know. It makes me feel very angry that she, well she thinks she can just boss me around like Mum and Dad and tell me when to practise. I get cross, very very cross. I say, 'Who do you think you are? Whose side do you think you're on?' [F, f3]

I don't mind him trying to help me [practise] but I really do mind it a lot when she [speaking of the mum] tells me to get it out of it's case. I mean she's not my Mum she's my sister and I don't like her getting all bossy like that. [C, f2]

I told him to leave me alone. Dad can tell me [to practise] I suppose but he's [older brother] not going to. [LS, m2]

Parental dual identity

Some parents gave their children instrumental tuition themselves. These parents described teaching them as a great privilege, yet, at the same time, they were aware of the responsibility and element of risk which this entailed, especially in terms of defining the parent–teacher boundary:

I see teaching him as a huge responsibility. I mean how he plays to a large extent depends on what I've shown him doesn't it? And I guess that's quite a big thing really. Sometimes it seems pretty terrifying and I wonder how I'm still doing it [laughs]. [A, M]

For some children, the issue of their parent's dual role was particularly problematic. One younger son, Daniel, found it especially disquieting to relate to his mother as his mother and as his teacher simultaneously. For him, the two roles were not mutually compatible and he found difficulty in reconciling her two identities:

You see it's really weird, I mean she's mummy but then as well you see she's also my teacher, it makes me feel really strange—how can she really be my teacher as well? [LS, m2]

He was not prepared to conform and respect his mother's role like his elder brother did and, as a result, rebellion peppered his father's conversations about him:

Well Daniel is Daniel and therefore he does what he wants, so he learns when he feels like it . . . whatever we say. [LS, F]

Another child in the sample also displayed acute bitterness and resentment over having to adopt pupil status with his mother. He objected to what he saw was an artificial situation:

It's awful you know. She thinks she can boss me around in the lesson because she's my teacher but it's not fair, she never treats her real pupils like that. I have to be her son and her pupil. I hate it. [A, m2]

Certainly the mother supplied additional evidence of such tension:

Yes David argues like a lawyer all through the lesson. He tells me how he's going to bow and things like that . . . Often we have to stop to cool down. [A, M]

One mother constantly changed lesson times and, in her opinion, she taught in a more flexible way than an 'outsider' would be able to do. Indeed, the 'lessons' took on a very different format from what would usually be expected from a 'normal' teacher. Commitment to the lessons seemed compromised since the mother only taught the boys when she was 'free' and when she felt that they were feeling receptive. This aside, of course, the boys had access to a level of opportunity seldom found within a family setting with the benefit of having a professional musician and teacher on-site.

Directionality of musician influence

Although the data emphasized how children were shaped in their musical involvement and progress by the family environment, to a large extent it was clear that the children themselves also influenced the musical identity of their parents and siblings. Children's musical tastes had an impact on the other family members' listening patterns. For example, parents showed a willingness to find out about and become familiar with the musical genres enjoyed by their children, which were different from their own backgrounds. Vanessa's mother commented:

I like to keep a tag on what they're [the children] listening to. Often I'll ask them to bring their CDs down here [kitchen] and pop them on and I'll sing along. I've taken them to concerts at the Birmingham NEC. Went to a Boyzone one with them. It was great. Yeah it certainly keeps me young! [F, M]

Furthermore, some parents were inspired to learn to play themselves as a direct result of their children starting instrumental tuition. One mother recalls her sudden motivation to start guitar lessons after hearing her daughter play:

I used to listen to her strumming away upstairs until one evening I thought 'I can do that!' and do you know I phoned up this friend of mine who I knew gave lessons. My kids were so surprised to see me going along there. It was really funny. [E, M]

Also, younger siblings were influenced by their elder sibling's attitudes towards music and were willing to share music in the communal living areas of the home. Despite seeming to promote art music, many parents felt the need to emphasize that they were not dictating their children's identity but rather that their children were in some way influencing their own musical taste. Helen claimed:

I profoundly feel that they [James and Daniel] should listen to music you know in I hope a kind of voracious way, a kind of omnivorous way too. I mean James now has a CD player and a motley collection of compact discs of all types, you know, some which I would personally hate and most of which I would very much enjoy. I mean I'm basically omnivorous too. [LS, M]

Daniel's musical preferences in particular impacted upon his mother's listening tastes:

I'm just very aware that Daniel often influences the sort of music I may listen to. Actually I find myself laughing at that. There are some things he plays on his music system, which don't really seem me but then after a few times I start to want to listen myself. So yes he certainly um has an effect. It's odd isn't it? [LS, M]

On the other hand, sometimes influence seemed to be multidirectional. Non-musician parents recognized the value of music in their partners' lives in contrast to the lack of musical skill in their own and, as a consequence, showed aspirations for their children to become musicians to experience vicarious fulfilment:

I want our kids to be like Ann. Ann performs in all these orchestras, she plays quartets to get away from a day's teaching. I mean that shows us how much she enjoys it doesn't it? I wish I had that so they can have it instead I suppose. That will give me pleasure. [A, F]

Conflicting parent–child preferences

The parents did present, however, many mixed messages to their children in terms of the expectation of allegiance to different musical genres. For example, Caroline's father saw the necessity for his daughter to identify with her peers musically in order to be accepted in the longer term, with the consequence of having a regular diet of pop music. He felt the need to endorse wider musical tastes, yet, despite these remarks, Caroline knew that her parents' loyalty lay with art music irrespective of what was claimed publicly.

They *say* they want me to discover my own tastes [in music] and they like to tell their friends that, but in reality I *know* that's not the case as they only allow their sort of music on downstairs. It's like they say one thing but do another. [B, f1]

As a result, Caroline developed a current knowledge of the pop world to enable her to create the veneer of a 'normal' pre-pubescent girl, but she did not diminish her engagement with classical music. Her action gave her a certain freedom from the boundaries of her family's identity, yet the ability to exist within it simultaneously.

Birth order

Constellatory positioning within the family was a major factor in influencing the nature of family relationships and identity. The child's position within the family impacted upon interactions with other family members. All of the two-child families in this study labelled their first-born child as musically 'talented', even before onset of formal training:

We knew Theo was special as far as music was concerned, much more so than his sister. Maybe it was the way he used to get up and bounce up and down when music came on the telly or something. You know, I just thought, yeah, that kid's going to be really musical one day. I was excited for him. [C, M]

I knew from an early age that he was quite a good singer because when he was at Infants' School the music teacher said he had a lovely voice ... and it sort of followed and he's only been playing three years and he's come on leaps and bounds, far more than the others. He's so gifted. [I, M]

Many of the parents who made these judgements about their first-born children seemed to perceive their second-born child (irrespective of the age difference between the two siblings) as being much less able musically and inferior in terms of their musical potential:

Well Stacey always seemed to have something Joanne didn't have. From being a baby she was the one that liked either me or Steve to sing to her. She'd just gurgle away, sort of joining in sort of thing. I don't think um Joanne enjoyed that so much so I always thought Stacey was the musical baby. It was strange really but there we are. [D, F]

In line with parenting scripts (Byng-Hall, 1998), it seems that the parents constructed and corroborated their evidence for one child being a better musician than his/her sibling/s.

Well we both thought from the very beginning really that he's always been the more musical one, we knew that even when he used to sing in his cot as a baby [laughs]. You can just tell that sort of thing. [I, M]

From the time that he sat outside his tent with that harmonica when he was the littlest of boys, my husband said to me, he's got a gift for music that boy, and I have to say, I agreed. [H, M]

This preferential treatment shown by many of the parents was evident in the longitudinal study where James, the eldest, was regarded by both as the more musically able child from a very early age:

You see he [James] always has had a very special talent [for music], I realised how musical he was long before I started teaching him. [LS, M]

However, after observing the family for 18 months, there was little objective evidence of James being more talented in terms of level of performance than his brother after the age difference was taken into consideration. This seemed to indicate a predetermined script, the parents' construction of 'talent' appeared to be based on expectancy for the eldest child to occupy the 'musician' role. To accommodate the eldest siblings and their perceived talents, the younger siblings appeared to cope by re-labelling themselves out of the musician role.

Niche diversification

In the longitudinal case study family, strong evidence of 'niche diversification' (Sulloway, 1996) became apparent with Daniel the second-born, who seemed to be far more confident, adopting an 'artist' script rather than performing the script of a 'second class musician'. This 'niche carving' also occurred in the other two-sibling families. The parents defined their second-born child's different area of interest with confidence: 'sportswoman', 'architect', 'dancer' and even 'the family problem'.

These alternative 'niche' types were not necessarily positive, however, with Dean, aged 12, being labelled the 'problem' by his immediate family since he rejected his parents' offer to start instrumental lessons on the same instrument as his successful elder brother:

He [Dean] seems pretty determined he doesn't want to play a musical instrument. He doesn't want to do anything because other people can do it better than him. In fact it's a serious problem, we're actually considering psychological help. . . . [I, F]

It seems that this negative labelling may have arisen as a result of parents' failure to encourage appropriate diversification, and instead, pressure the second-born to follow the same musical path as the first-born in a bid to preserve sibling equality and success:

We thought he wanted to play the same instrument as his elder brother. It's strange, we can't tell why he's been so 'anti' when we thought if we gave him the same opportunity it would stop him being jealous. [I, M]

From our data, we argue that, when sibling differentiation occurs at the very beginning of instrumental tuition, when positive parental feedback can promote confidence in each of the siblings' musical abilities, it can be associated with a feeling of musical well-being and the perception of equal worth between siblings. For instance:

They all know that they're all good at their own thing. The children have always had different instruments and I don't think they've ever felt compared, we've just emphasised the difference from the start. It's seemed to work and they've felt good about themselves musically, which is important. [B, M]

Within this study, it seemed that the scarcity of resources within an expanding family often contributed toward creating an imbalance between siblings, especially if the second child forfeited formal tuition due to financial factors or time availability.

Intriguingly, even though the second-born children recognized their own relatively inferior musical skills by comparison with the elder sibling, none attributed this to anything other than having started learning their instrument later. However, they were aware of the perception their parents had of their relative standing from comments made during the practice sessions and in everyday life. One mother recalls:

Theo's really good . . . right from being a baby he just loved music. Theo in particular loves it and always wanted to play it, for him he gets enormous satisfaction from it. . . . Theo's the one that gets the distinctions. Theo can do anything, which is why in a way I suppose we encouraged her [younger sister] to choose a different instrument, although she still compares herself to him. I mean that's the problem with everything, I mean not just music, just everything. He has a higher level of achievement therefore she feels rubbish. In fact she's good at everything too I mean, but not to the same degree as Theo . . .   [C, M]

In Vanessa's family, sibling rivalry and resentment appeared to have been promoted by both the parents' praising Vanessa above her younger sister Kim and by making Vanessa a role model for Kim. Such patterns evoked significant levels of inter-sibling jealousy and made Kim aware of her inferiority:

No I'm not as good as Vanessa, she's always done better than me on the piano and everything [sighs]. He [father] thinks that too. But I'm okay [.] but she's really really good. It's just not fair. [F, f3]

We had little doubt that Vanessa was unaware of the situation:

Well I know they think I'm the musical one. They always ask me to play in front of gran when she comes to stay and go on about me being special and really encourage me. Sometimes I feel sorry for the others, they don't get all the encouragement they give me. [F, f2]

Interestingly, parents attributed the difference in sibling capability to global, stable, internal dimensions such as personality and physiological make up.

Personality

I think it's just a different attitude. She will sit for a while, and she'll learn something, but then she's often forgotten about it for quite a while and then she'll go back and learn a simple tune but she hasn't really got much further than that . . .   [G, M]

Well Theo's just more laid back about it [his playing] . . .   [C, F]

They're just different characters really, I mean if I'd said to Stacey 'Go and do your practice' for a couple of days, she'd go and do it. If I said the same to Joanne, we'd end up having a stand up row... [D, M]

Joanne's more of a wanderer, I think it's just her different attitude... [D, F]

Physical attributions

Josh's the one that's more successful whereas David's physically has got very flabby fingers you know, the co-ordination, it's all right, but it's not the same sort of really quick sort of responses like Josh. That's just something that's there and I mean there are personality factors as well... [A, M]

However, the parents did not seem to account for the superiority of the eldest child as the consequence of increased age, which led to them having accumulated a greater number of musical opportunities and more practice time.

From the evidence presented so far, we argue that it seems that many second-born children are 'scripted' by their parents to attain less musically than their elder brother or sister. The parents' underlying belief that their younger child lacks musical talent, or at least the same degree of talent as his/her elder sibling, appears to result in them failing to provide the younger sibling with similar resources to enable him/her to develop as a musician. Often this discrepancy between the siblings is justified in terms of the availability of financial resources:

Jon is the really talented one round here so it seemed to make sense for him to have the [instrumental] lessons 'specially since they cost an arm and a leg. [H, M]

Multiple sibship families

The data showed that none of the three-sibship families conformed to the pattern associated with the two-sibship families. Obviously, prior to the birth of the third child, the patterns of family behaviour may have been like those observed in the two-sibship families. However, all these families were interviewed at a single point in time, and so we had to observe them at that time. When looking at their behaviour, we saw that in all three-sibship families, each of the three children was identified as an individual with their own qualities. The parents focused on the idiosyncratic natures of each child, and perceived them as three unique beings occupying their own niches rather than being compared with one another:

I mean all our kids are so, well I suppose they're all so different, so you see competition isn't even an issue, yes they're all doing music, but I don't suppose they line themselves up against each other, I mean they enjoy different things... [H, M]

...there's no rivalry between the three of them, not at all. I mean, I expect Amy's motivation for beginning was because Rachel was doing something and she wanted to do it, but since then, they've done distinctly different things. But they enjoy playing in the school orchestra together. They'd done that the last two terms, and I think the older two have been quite proud of having the youngest member of the orchestra as well in the family, you know the three of them were involved... [G, M]

Often the close proximity of the children's ages meant that the three children had functioned as a fully interactive triad before the first child commenced his/her instrumental lessons. All the children from three-child families suffered far less inter-sibling comparison than those belonging to smaller families, despite having been single, two- and eventually three-sibship family units at some time in their lives. Reasons for this cannot be formulated from the current data. Dynamics which preceded the current family units were not examined in this study due to time constraints.

Rejecting family values

Even though some second-born children were encouraged to occupy alternative niches, 'musical' identity of the whole family was still considered important in all cases studied. Rejecting instrumental lessons as a result of disillusionment seemed too much to contemplate for most second-born children. The distinction between the musical status of the first- and second-born children in the families was particularly clear in the longitudinal study family. Their mother projected the roles of 'musician' and 'artist' onto the boys from early childhood. This gave little scope for role flexibility in the longer term:

I think Daniel's forte is art rather than music. He's definitely the family artist. Maybe he gets that from John's Mum. You saw the [picture of] mountaineers he brought back last week? Well quite honestly, even we were stunned. [LS, F]

Although Daniel's parents wanted him to find some enjoyment in music, they felt it unlikely in the long run that he would ever experience from his playing the same level of satisfaction as James would be likely to due to his higher level of ability:

I'd say that we'd love Daniel to enjoy his playing, but at the end of the day I can't see him getting as much satisfaction out of it as his elder brother. It's just not his main thing. [LS, F]

The flexibility of musical identity: rewriting the scripts

Thus far, family scripts have been shown as powerful influences in the development of the child's musical identity. However, as Byng-Hall himself acknowledged, flexibility in scripting is often necessary, even after a family has become firmly embedded in a par-ticular musical value system over a significant period. Indeed, in the families studied, the modification of parental expectations (i.e. the parenting script) and re-formation of the child's musical identity often resulted through life circumstances and unforeseen external factors affecting the family's development. Three examples are given here.

The first example we encountered was a divorce. Charlotte, the youngest daughter, became the channel through which the post-divorce relationship expressed a host of underlying anxieties. Charlotte became the victim of 'conflict detour' (see Muncie *et al.*, 1995) with her instrumental choice being the focus of interfamilial conflict. Jeff, the father explained:

Strange as it might sound, I know this [conflict] isn't about the sort of guitar she [Charlotte] plays. You see it's all about control and whether her mother is going to get the upper hand or not. Um you see to be honest it could have been about a whole host of other things, but she [Jeff's ex-wife] chose to focus it [the conflict] on which instrument she [Charlotte] is going to play because she [ex-wife] knows that's what matters to me. That's what hurts. [K, F]

Certainly, Charlotte understood that she was the metaphorical pawn here:

Well Mum prefers the electric [guitar] but Dad wants me to do the classical [guitar] so they're really at each other's throats over it. [K, f2]

Although Charlotte's father Jeff tried to compensate for the effect of the separation, much of the original parenting script was 'rewritten' since he no longer had regular visiting access to his daughters.

The second example of script change came as a result of chronic illness. In one family studied, the youngest daughter Frances had taken up the clarinet long before her diagnosis of a terminal illness. Before her illness, her parents' musical expectations for her had in no way matched the level of those they had voiced for her elder sister. Nonetheless, since music was given the central value in her family home, she had recognized the obligation to take instrumental examinations and 'succeed' in the accustomed way children from 'musical' families do. Certainly this family was rooted firmly in the lifestyle associated with a 'musical' family script: weekly private lessons, participation in local youth orchestras, attending local concerts for children, etc., and the expectation that over time they may audition for regionally and nationally based youth orchestras. However, after Frances' diagnosis, subsequent treatment and remissions, music took on a less performance-oriented position, and Frances' musical goals were radically re-framed by her parents in the light of the many restrictions brought about by her ill health. There was a key shift towards experiencing enjoyment, and even experiencing potential therapeutic benefits. Jane, their mother explained:

... Now, I just, well her I just want her to enjoy whatever she can as far as playing goes ... grades go by the board here ... it's a way of her expressing herself through all of this ... [B, M]

The third example of scripting change is a result of a common change which all families experience, the transition the child faces when moving from school to school. Of those families studied, one experienced the transfer to secondary education, and another the transfer from secondary to tertiary education. Lamont (Chapter 3, this volume) has investigated the role of the school environment on musical involvement and self-perception, and thus further insights into this issue can be achieved by reading the evidence in that chapter. In the context of our chapter, however, it is evident that the sudden increase in academic workload or changing living arrangements was instrumental in producing a dynamic change.

James, of the longitudinal study family, moved from primary to secondary school near the end of our investigation. His increased homework timetable meant that he was less available to practise and so his parents seemed to encourage Daniel (the younger son) more. Daniel entered a new phase of intense interest, increased motivation and, consequently, greater amounts of practice. He loved his parents' attention, and within a month seemed to show considerable enjoyment and increased self-confidence:

... well I'm actually doing really well now with both instruments. Uh I'm starting to get onto harder things, and I'm skipping grade one 'cause Mr Evans thinks I'm too clever for the exam. [LS, m2]

James, in contrast, fell into a fallow period for his music as he attempted to come to grips with all the other changes in his life at that time. His parents were understanding about this and didn't push him to continue with music as intensively as before. He explained:

I can't do all the practising I used to at the moment. Mum and Dad said just to let it go at the moment since I've moved schools. At least until I get everything sorted out. I don't know you see I've got such a lot to get through at the moment. It's just impossible. There's so much homework. It's not like it was in the Juniors. Still I suppose it means that Daniel's getting a bit of their attention. He seems to be happy enough with the way things are anyway! [LS, m1]

This turn of events actually helped to improve relations between the two siblings generally. Indeed, as soon as the siblings no longer attended the same school, the sense of competition between them diminished.

Conclusion

This chapter has shown how children's musical identities are influenced by a combination of relational factors, connected with how their parents regard them in the role of musician. We argued that the musical beliefs and experiences of the parents are of central importance here, as they shape the way in which the subsequent generation experience and value music for themselves within the family. In sum, the 'parenting script', i.e. the initial blueprint of expectation for musical development, is either 'amended' or 'replicated' in the next generation depending on the levels of musical satisfaction experienced by each parent during his/her childhood. Current and external factors also play a part in shaping the children's identity as 'musician', especially birth order and how the parents interact with their children according to the child's position within the family. Therefore, the child's musical identity is shaped primarily by the responses and values given by his/her immediate family.

All immediate family members play a shaping role, both children and adults alike, *irrespective of whether or not they learn musical instrument* themselves. Although it was common for those parents who played instruments themselves to provide technical support, others who could not play made no less an impact on musical development through their desire to encourage others to gain musically where they felt they had 'missed out'. We also demonstrated how long-held musical values belonging to specific family members can be adapted as a result of external factors impacting upon the family irrespective of the seemingly deterministic nature of the parents' goals. This is evidence for the fact that musical identity does not develop in isolation, is not static, but evolves as part of a multidirectional and reciprocal process.

Throughout this chapter, we have attempted to retain the essence of individual case studies, yet at the same time identify the complex relational patterns which occurred within the households as a result of music being held in high esteem as a core family value. So in contrast to families who chose to either reject or marginalize music in their lives, we have seen how, in families who adopt music as a core value, their views allow music to dictate and systematize the daily routine. Certainly, parental supervision was high on the agenda and, as a result, children were expected to progress at an 'appropriate' rate. These findings supported Sosniak's (1990) claim that a high level of musical attainment would be achieved if parent and child worked alongside each other and took on a unified musical identity together.

In sum then, this chapter has argued that familial expectations, some based on trans-generational influences, are highly powerful forces on family scripts with regard to the adoption and study of a musical instrument. However, despite our overwhelming evidence to suggest that these scripts have an element of determinism, it seems that certain external factors can always bring about consequences to family life which cannot fail to change expectations. This caveat is by no means meant to undermine the power of the script but, instead, it serves to point towards there being a 'ceiling' on its prescription, as shown in the case of family break-up or serious illness. This aside, our evidence has shown that the combination of the parents' family histories, emergent expectations, role allocations and current dynamic interactions within the household plays a central role in defining musical identity.

References

Bateson, G. (1979). *Mind and Nature*. New York: EP Dutton.

Byng-Hall, J. (1995). *Rewriting Family Scripts*, 1st edn., Vol. 1. London: Guilford.

Byng-Hall, J. (1998). Evolving ideas about marriage: the re-editing of family mythology. *Journal of Family Therapy*, **29**, 133–141.

Carter, B. and McGoldrick, M. (ed.) (1989). *The Changing Family Life Cycle: A Framework for Family Therapy*, 2nd edn. Boston: Allyn and Bacon.

Cramer, B. (1997). *The Scripts Parents Write and the Roles Babies Play*. New York: Aronson.

Csikszentmihalyi, M., Rathunde, K. and Whalen, S. (1997). *Talented Teenagers: The Roots of Success and Failure*. Cambridge: Cambridge University Press.

Dunn, J. (1993). *Young Children's Close Relationships*, Vol. 4. London: Sage.

Hallam, S. (1998). The predictors of achievement and dropout in instrumental tuition. *Psychology of Music*, **26**, 116–132.

Muncie, J., Wetherell, M., Dallos, R. and Cochrane, A. (ed.), (1995). *Understanding the Family*, 2nd edn. London: Sage.

Radford, J. (1990). *Child Prodigies and Exceptional Early Achievers*. London: Harvester Wheatsheaf.

Smith, J.A., Flowers, P. and Osborne, M. (1997). Interpretative phenomenological analysis and the psychology of health and illness. In L. Yardley (ed.), *Material Discourses of Health and Illness*, pp. 68–91. London: Routledge.

Smith, J.A., Jarman, M. and Osborne, M. (1999). Doing interpretative phenomenological analysis. In M. Murray and K. Chamberlain (ed.), *Theories and Methods*, pp. 218–240. London: Sage.

Sosniak, L.A. (1990). The tortoise, the hare, and the development of talent. In M.J.A. Howe (ed.), *Encouraging the Development of Exceptional Skills and Talents*. Leicester: British Psychological Society.

Sulloway, F.J. (1996). *Born to Rebel: Birth Order, Family Dynamics and Creative Lives*. London: Little, Brown and Company.

Warmsley, J. and Margolis, J. (1987). *Hot House People: Can we Create Super Human Beings?* London: Pan.

CHAPTER 5

THE SELF-IDENTITY OF YOUNG MUSICIANS

SUSAN A. O'NEILL

Introduction

What does it mean to be a young musician? In Western cultures, being a 'musician' is often equated with being able to play a musical instrument. However, there is growing criticism of this narrow conceptualization by researchers in such diverse fields as psychology, sociology, musicology, ethnomusicology, education, music analysis, aesthetics and cultural theory (see, for example, Cook, 1990; Trevarthen, 1999; DeNora, 2000). Although there is no agreed definition of what constitutes a musician, contemporary theorists from across these disciplines appear to agree on the need for the term to encompass more than the ability to demonstrate music performance skills. Despite this recognition, both popular and scientific discourses continue to distinguish between those who are musicians and those who are not. This distinction is particularly prominent and influential in childhood and adolescence (see also Lamont, Chapter 3, this volume). Young people come to understand the categories of musician/non-musician through the multifarious contextualizing, symbolic factors associated with the ways in which music is produced and distributed, as well as listened and responded to. As children and adolescents negotiate a sense of self and identity in relation to music, they respond in ways that sustain and perpetuate these differences. Once established, these categories appear resistant to change and disconfirmation, and, as I aim to demonstrate in the discussion which follows, they convey a constraining influence on young people's musical engagement and understanding of what it means to be a musician.

There is a long history of thinking in psychology and philosophy about the nature of human identity and the experience of a psychological self. James (1890) referred to the 'struggle with the pure principle of identity' as the 'most puzzling puzzle with which psychology has to deal' (p. 330). Despite the volumes of theoretical and empirical research devoted to the subject, we are still striving to achieve a clear understanding of the complex nature of self. The chapter begins with a review of traditional psychological approaches to the development of self. This is followed by an overview of research I have conducted into the role of children's self-perceptions in the development of musical performance skills. This research is based on the dominant framework in social psychology known as social cognition, and implications for identity theory and some of the key criticisms of this approach are discussed. The second part of the chapter considers post-modern and social constructionist approaches and reports findings from two recent studies where I adopted this theoretical framework to explore young musicians' construction of self and identity.

The development of a sense of self

Developmental theories of identity mainly focus on how individuals' thoughts about themselves develop and change (e.g. Montemayor and Eisen, 1977). For example, young children are likely to view themselves and their musical involvement in concrete terms: 'I play the piano', 'I take music lessons'. As we grow older, our concept of self in relation to music places less emphasis on physical characteristics and typical activities, and more on psychological characteristics (e.g. thoughts, feelings, motives) as well as social, moral and political judgements: 'I am an expressive performer', 'I think it is important to practice regularly', 'I am qualified to teach music'. Cooley (1902) argued that the development of self-consciousness and self-reflective awareness is dependent on our relationships with significant others and how we imagine we appear from their point of view. In other words, our self-perceptions develop through a perspective-taking process. Both Mead (1934) and Piaget (1936) extended these ideas by emphasizing that interpersonal communication, and in particular symbolic communication such as language, is essential for the emergence of self (see further Crossley, 2000). Language provides labels that enable a child to distinguish between itself and other people and things. Mead also argued that the development of self requires more than the ability to adopt the perspective of a particular other toward the self. It also requires an individual to adopt the perspective of an abstract, generalized other that represents the broader society and culture into which we are born (Durkin, 1995).

Research into the development of self has also been concerned with the change in children's self-evaluations as they grow older. Young children (aged 5–7 years) tend to have a simplistic global view of themselves, and tend to endorse a positive belief across all attributes. Older children begin to apply different beliefs to different domains and attributes, and exhibit a downward trend, with their self-evaluations becoming less positive (Ruble, 1994). This trend continues into early adolescence and is particularly prominent following the transition from primary to secondary school (Eccles *et al.*, 1993). Children's self-evaluations are related to the different self-theories they hold about the nature of ability (Dweck, 1999). So, for example, a child might hold an entity theory (a belief that one's ability is innate and fixed) in relation to musical activities, and an incremental theory (a belief that one's ability can improve through effort) toward sports activities. Dweck (1999) has also found that self-theories and goals can be manipulated experimentally, which suggests that a person can operate in both systems. This would mean that we might conceive of ourselves as a fixed object that is being judged at some times, and as a dynamic system whose aim is to grow at other times. Our beliefs about ourselves, in turn, influence both the goals we choose and pursue and our achievement behaviour in a variety of contexts (Dweck and Leggett, 1988; Elliott and Dweck, 1988). Within a social cognitive framework, the individual is viewed as a 'perceiver' or 'information processor' who learns and interprets information about the self through his or her interaction in social contexts (see, for example, Markus and

Nurius, 1987). This approach is particularly associated with motivational implications of the self, which I will discuss in the next section.

The role of children's self-perceptions in the development of music performance skills

Pintrich (1991) highlighted the need for identity and self constructs to be developed further within social–cognitive models of achievement motivation. However, few studies have examined the social–cognitive and affective components of children's motivation to engage in music. In this section, I will outline some of my research into children's self-perceptions in the development of music performance skills (see also O'Neill and McPherson, 2001). The findings indicate that children's self-beliefs (i.e. confidence in their ability) play a key role in their subsequent performance ability and evaluations of their performances over and above their actual ability. In other words, the pathway between the skills individuals *can* use and the skills they *actually display* in certain contexts is not direct but is mediated through their self-perceptions—and in particular their ability-related self-perceptions.

Dweck's (1986) social–cognitive model of achievement motivation proposes that children's adaptive and maladaptive motivational patterns influence their behaviour and achievement during difficulty or failure situations in predictable ways. Maladaptive 'helpless' patterns are associated with failure to establish reasonable valued goals, or to attain goals that are within one's reach. Thus, helpless children will avoid challenges, and show low persistence and performance deterioration in the face of failure. Conversely, children who display adaptive 'mastery-oriented' patterns tend to remain high in their persistence following failure and appear to enjoy exerting effort in the pursuit of task mastery. What is especially interesting about these two motivational patterns is that helpless children often are initially equal in ability to mastery-oriented children. Indeed, some of the brightest, most skilled children exhibit helpless behaviour.

Research in music lends support to these ideas. For example, O'Neill and Sloboda (1997) found that children who reported low confidence in their ability following failure on a musical test experienced more performance deterioration (helpless behaviour) than children who reported high post-failure confidence and displayed mastery-oriented behaviour. Interestingly, measures of children's actual ability to perform the test prior to failure did not predict their confidence levels following failure nor their subsequent behaviour. However, this does not rule out the possibility that exposure to frequent and repeated failure situations may well have devastating and far-reaching effects on the motivation and musical achievement of children who are vulnerable to the self-beliefs associated with helpless behaviour. This raises an important question. Since the performance of helpless children is often equivalent to that of mastery children prior to difficulty or failure, when do the long-term negative effects on performance achievement become apparent?

I addressed this question in a longitudinal study involving children during their first year of learning to play an instrument (O'Neill, 1997b). The overall aim of the study was to further our understanding of why some children succeed in the early stages of learning to play a musical instrument, while others, with seemingly equal levels of ability and potential, make little progress. The participants were 46 children (aged 6–10 years) who had received no formal instrumental music instruction prior to the beginning of the study. The children were interviewed individually and administered a variety of measures at two points in time: (1) prior to the first music lesson; and (2) after the first year of music lessons. Findings indicated that those children who displayed low confidence and helpless behaviour following failure on a problem-solving task which was administered prior to the first music lesson went on to show less progress after 1 year than those children who had demonstrated mastery behaviour before music lessons began. Once again, both groups of children did not differ on initial tests of musical ability or intelligence.

One explanation for the above finding is that the types of goals individuals pursue during achievement situations determine the motivational patterns associated with mastery and helpless behaviour. Helpless children evaluate achievement situations in terms of performance goals where the aim is to display their competence and avoid failure and negative judgements of their performance. In contrast, mastery children tend to choose learning goals which emphasize the need to increase their competence. As a result, mastery children tend to view failure as part of the learning process, rather than something to be avoided. According to Elliott and Dweck (1988), these goal orientations 'interact with confidence to set in motion a sequence of specific processes that influence, in turn, task choice, performance, and persistence' (p. 11). In other words, helpless and mastery children tend to pursue different goals, and these different goals create the framework within which they interpret and react to events.

Dweck (1999) has demonstrated that children's self-theories or beliefs about their ability are strong predictors of the goals they pursue and their motivational behaviour. In the case of musical performance skills, an individual might endorse an entity theory associated with the notion that people have only a certain amount of 'musical' ability and that some people have more musical ability than others. On the other hand, those who hold an incremental theory might believe that anyone can improve their musical ability through effort and practising musical skills. By the age of 8, children begin to distinguish between abilities in different domains and apply different self-theories to different domains (Bempechat *et al.*, 1991).

In a study with 172 children (aged 6–11 years), I found that children were far more likely to endorse an incremental (flexible) view about athletic ability than about musical and intellectual abilities (O'Neill, 1994). Also, children who had never played an instrument before were far more likely to endorse an entity (fixed) view of musical ability than children who were already involved in, or about to begin, instrumental training. These self-theories have important implications for the ways in which individuals make self-evaluations about their own and others' ability. For example, entity theorists are more likely to use outcome traits (e.g. grades, number of instruments played) as evidence in support of their judgement of abilities, whereas incremental theorists are more likely to focus on process traits (e.g. tries hard, practices, has lessons once a week). Dweck (1999) argues that her social–cognitive model of achievement motivation does not portray the self as one monolithic thing. Rather, it focuses on the self-beliefs and self-relevant goals that people develop, and these can be domain-specific, situation-sensitive and malleable over time. What is important, however, is that the model attempts to account for the cognitive, affective and behavioural processes that individuals engage in as they strive to create a sense of who they are through the validation or expansion of their attributes and competencies.

The majority of research on children's self-perceptions in music is focused on competence beliefs such as how good one is at an activity, expectancy beliefs about one's future performance or self-efficacy beliefs that one can produce the desired outcome. However, this approach fails to take into account the role of subjective values such as interest in, or enjoyment of, the activity; perceived importance of being good at, or involved in, the activity; perceived usefulness of the activity for short- and long-term goals; and the cost of engaging in the activity. Eccles and her colleagues integrated these constructs in their expectancy–value model of achievement motivation. Research has established that children's competence beliefs and values become established during the elementary school years (e.g. Stipek and Mac Iver, 1989; Wigfield, 1994). Children as young as 6 years of age can distinguish between their sense of competence for an activity and its value for them. Ability-related self-perceptions have also been found to vary across domains (Eccles *et al.*, 1993). Wigfield *et al.* (1997) demonstrated that even children with very little experience with instrumental music still differentiate between competence beliefs and subjective task values. However, there has been little research to indicate whether these two constructs relate differentially to aspects such as practice and achievement in music.

In order to examine these issues, I conducted a study with 60 young musicians (aged 12–16 years) who differed in their levels of performance achievement and were attending two different educational institutions (a specialist music school and a state secondary school) (O'Neill, 1999). Based on the Experience Sampling Method, first developed by Csikszentmihalyi (see further Csikszentmihalyi and LeFevre, 1989; Csikszentmihalyi *et al.*, 1993), the musicians were required to carry electronic pagers for a week and to complete a diary sheet which recorded their self-perceptions each time the pager beeped. This occurred once at random in every 2-hour period from 8 a.m. to 10 p.m. They also completed diary sheets each time they played their instruments. What was useful about this approach was that the data collected were concurrent with children's actual experience of music in the context of everyday life. It also enabled more detailed reporting of individual subjective experience, and interviews held at the end of the week with each participant were used to gain further understanding of how they viewed themselves in terms of their ability as musicians.

The results indicated that subjective task values were a significant predictor of the amount of time spent practising, uniquely explaining 10% of the variance in practice. Competence beliefs were not found to be associated with practice. In other words, it was the extent to which practice was considered important that contributed to the prediction of time spent practising and not the extent to which the young musicians felt successful and living up to their own and others' expectations. Another interesting finding was that 'highest' achievers at the specialist music school were far more likely to report that they found their peers at the school supportive. In fact, they were much happier at the music school than at their previous schools because they found themselves with more 'like-minded' peers. Supportive peers were also a feature in the accounts of the musicians from the state school. However, the 'average' achievers at the specialist school were far more likely to report being unhappy with what they perceived to be a competitive and non-supportive atmosphere at the school.

Eccles and her colleagues proposed that values are linked to more stable self-schema and identity constructs (Eccles, 1987; Eccles and Harold, 1992). In other words, when a task such as instrumental music practice provides the opportunity to demonstrate aspects of one's competence, it is likely to attain higher value in terms of importance. One interpretation is that the young musicians who rated importance of practice more highly engaged in more practice because it provided them with the opportunity to demonstrate their competence, thereby further reinforcing their motivation to practise in future. Additionally, how well a task relates to current or future goals can have positive value even if an individual is not particularly interested in the task for its own sake. Eccles *et al.* (1998) argue that 'students often take classes that they do not particularly enjoy but that they need to take to pursue other interests, to please their parents, or to be with their friends. In one sense then this component captures the more "extrinsic" reasons for engaging in a task' (p. 1029). However, the authors also refer to the possibility that these values may relate directly to individuals' internalized short- and long-term goals. Thus, it may be that the young musicians varied in their interpretation of the importance or value of practice. This may provide an explanation for why no differences in self-perceptions were found according to different levels of performance achievement. Although the young musicians in each of the achievement groups gave similar ratings for importance of practice, they may not have been interpreting 'importance' in the same way (e.g. they may have been more or less concerned with intrinsic or extrinsic issues).

Social–cognitive approaches to the study of self and identity are not immune to criticism. Based on 'realist' assumptions, researchers from this tradition purport the existence of concepts such as personality, attitudes and motivation and their associated characteristics as responsible for individuals' observable behaviour and social phenomena such as prejudice and delinquency. A central concern of social psychologists in understanding what it means to be a person is to examine individual differences in personality (for a detailed discussion of personality and musicians, see Kemp, 1996). Personality is viewed as a set of relatively stable traits or characteristics used to describe others and ourselves. Personality research has a long tradition in psychology, mainly concerned with the measurement of personality traits and exploring the relationship between personality factors and behaviour. However, this approach has been criticized extensively for its essentialism (i.e. the notion that there is a biologically determined 'essence' or nature that can explain individuals' actions or behaviour). For example, research has demonstrated that different behaviours are more likely to be a consequence of the particular situations individuals find themselves in, than any 'stable' aspects of their personality (Mischel, 1968).

Dweck (1999) argues that 'the social–cognitive approach has permitted researchers to begin to capture many of the processes that classic personality theories attempted to capture, but to do so in a way that is more differentiated, more specified, and more amenable to rigorous research' (p. 139). Indeed, this approach has provided valuable insights into the central role of identity and self-perceptions in motivation and development and the ways in which self-theories mediate and regulate behaviour. However, as Geertz (1979) pointed out, we need to be cautious in interpreting mainstream psychology's conceptualization of the self as a 'bounded, unique, more-or-less integrated motivational and cognitive universe, a dynamic centre of awareness, emotion, judgement and action, organised into a distinctive whole and set contrastingly against other such wholes and against a social and natural background' (p. 229). This conceptualization of the self must not be accepted uncritically as an objective understanding of such complex phenomena. Rather, research in this tradition offers one of many parts in what currently constitutes knowledge and thinking about the development of self and identity.

Another key criticism of research in this area is that it emphasizes the distinction between young musicians and non-musicians and perpetuates the notion that these labels are associated with whether or not individuals play a musical instrument. It is important to recognize that this distinction is not necessarily one that children and adolescents adopt for themselves. Lamont (Chapter 3, this volume) describes how children tend to refer to themselves as non-musicians (i.e. that they do not have lessons or play a musical instrument) even though a high proportion of them participate in music class at school where playing instruments is a feature of the music curriculum. Even among children who play instruments and have instrumental music lessons, they do not necessarily incorporate their engagement in this activity as part of their self-concept. This is often a result of the differences they observe between their own musical activities and those they associate with 'real' musicians in the adult world. However, there are other constraining influences on young people's ability to adopt a conception of self as a musician. For example, one of the young musicians I interviewed from the specialist music school told me 'I'm not really a musician because I'm shy and my teacher says you can't be a musician if you're shy'. This suggests that self-identity has more to do with an individual's purposes than the 'nature' of the thing itself. So, in the case of a 'musician', it might be viewed as a socially bestowed identity rather than something which can be defined by a predetermined set of characteristics. Social constructionists employ the concept of 'identity' in order to avoid essentialist connotations of a fixed self and emphasize that 'self' is an implicitly social concept. The following section examines this approach.

Post-modernism and the social construction of self

Post-modernism and the rise of critical social psychology resulted in a rigorous challenge to the assumptions of traditional psychological approaches to the study of individual identity. Existential phenomenologists such as Merleau-Ponty (1962), Heidegger (1962) and Schutz (1962), and more recently social constructionists such as Gergen and Davis (1985) and Harré (1983), have criticized the idea that knowledge about the self can exist in a 'pure', 'private' and 'subjective' form. Their conceptualization of subjective experience is something that is inextricably linked to the social world and the linguistic practices used to make sense of that world (Burr, 1995). Thus, a sense of self and identity is viewed as constructed out of the discourses which are culturally available to us and which we use when communicating with others (Harré and Gillett, 1994). According to Potter and Wetherall (1987), social constructionist approaches 'displace attention from the self-as-entity and focus it on the methods of constructing the self. That is, the question becomes not what is the true nature of the self, but how is the self talked about, how is it theorised in discourse?' (p. 102).

There are a number of dominant discourses that inform and shape our view and understanding of the world. Parker (1990) defines discourses as 'coherent systems of meaning'. He argues that some discourses are used to legitimize or reinforce existing social structures. As Crossley (2000) explains, 'alternative discourses compete with one another so that their specific vision of self, world and morality will be accepted and incorporated into dominant institutional and political structures through and by which power and influence are reproduced. It is in this sense that Parker argues that discourses have a material and almost "physical" presence because once created they proliferate within society' (p. 27). Harré (1998) argues that even when we begin to look at any skill, such as playing a musical instrument, we are immediately back in the social, linguistic realm.

In order to investigate how an individual's sense of self is displayed discursively, social constructionists most often employ discursive analytic approaches. The focus of the analysis is on examining the constructive processes the speaker uses within a particular discursive and social context (e.g. the ways in which young musicians assemble or construct their accounts), and the construction of meanings associated with individual identity and subjectivity. The following section provides an overview of two studies I have been involved in which adopted this theoretical framework to explore young musicians' construction of self and identity.

The self-identity of young musicians

This section describes two research studies that employed a social constructionist framework to examine the self-identity of young musicians. The first study examined the discourses that four adolescent female musicians (aged 17–18 years) used when describing what it means to them to be a musician (see further O'Neill *et al.*, 1999). Some of the themes and quotations from the interviews are provided below in order to illustrate this approach to furthering our understanding of the ways in which young musicians, and in this case female musicians in particular, construct a sense of self.

The study focused on young musicians who were considered by those who know them (parents, teachers, peers) to be talented musical performers. All of the girls had achieved the highest level on graded music examinations for at least one instrument. They were selected from four different secondary schools. Two semi-structured interviews were conducted with each girl at two points in time, approximately 4 weeks apart. The girls were asked to talk about their experiences of being a young musician. Their names have been changed to ensure anonymity.

We were interested in divergence and variety of information and adopted an emergent approach involving discursive analysis to investigate 'interpretative repertoires' and reflexive analysis to clarify assumptions made in relation to the findings. Interpretative repertoires refer to the linguistic resources (i.e. grammatical structures, metaphors, linguistic devices) that individuals use when constructing their accounts (see Potter *et al.*, 1990). They operate at a broad, semantic level and consist of patterns of explanations, evaluations and descriptions that are used to sustain social practices through conventionality and conformity with established cultural norms and values. These 'versions' of the world become established as 'real' and independent of the individual both in the immediacy of experience and over the longer term as part of a particular ideology. In our analysis, particular attention was given to variability (contradictions) and repetition in the accounts and the ways in which individuals justified themselves, apportioned blame, made excuses or created morally defensible positions. Additionally, we examined the accounts in terms of the 'subject positions' individuals adopted in relation to particular interpretative repertoires or the construction of self. Based on this approach, a number of themes were identified. Despite the fact that significant people in the girls' lives reassured them of their talent, for three of the girls, their discourses denoted a constraining influence on their self-identity as musicians.

Sarah is studying maths, French, physics and music A'levels. She plays the saxophone, flute and piano. Sarah does not want to continue music as a career, either in teaching or performing, but wishes to keep it as a hobby, with the possibility of private teaching later on. Sarah's response indicated that she was not comfortable with the 'musician' part of her in terms of the expectations it appears to create in others:

Interviewer: So what does it mean to you to be a musician?

Sarah: Um, just that I've got a talent. I mean when you go out a lot of the time everyone expects you to um, get up and have a sing song and be really good and, you know if you go to a karaoke they want you up there and singing. But it's not me. You won't catch me up there. But like the non-musicians have expectations of you and you just, you're just not their expectations and they can't understand that so . . . it's just not me, I just don't get up and do things in public. I hate playing and being in public.

The conflict that Sarah describes is complex and multifaceted, made up of a number of stated or implied dichotomous categories: talent versus 'normal', musician versus non-musician, public versus private, 'good' versus poor performance, personal versus social expectations, understanding and acceptance versus ignorance and alienation. The use of these categories implies a number of contradictions, which result from her moving between different types of categorization. For example, her friends' expectations of her to perform in public because she is a musician is denied in her statement 'its just not me'. Her response 'I hate playing and being in public' is also an example of the way in which she moves between her 'self' as someone who feels uncomfortable in social situations with the discomfort she also feels performing in public as a 'musician'. Her words also contradict the widely held belief that a 'musician' is someone who performs in public, thereby separating her 'self' from cultural norms and values about what it means to be a musician.

Helen is studying music, French and English A'levels. She has been playing the clarinet for 8 years and the piano since she was about 4 or 5 years old. She would like a career in music, probably teaching after attending university, although she would like a year out in between. For Helen, being a musician is both 'personal' and 'social'—something she equates with what she is 'like in life anyway':

Helen: I explain it as a warm feeling and just, satisfaction and um, enjoyment and being social as well because it gets you out [. . .]. I like being sociable and I like meeting new people and I like being with people but I also like being on my own as well which is when I am practising. So as long as I get a bit of both I'm ok. Well that's what I'm like in life anyway: I like being with people but I still need space to myself, you know time on my own.

Unlike Sarah, being a musician to Helen is connected with her construction of self as a person who is comfortable in both social and individual contexts. She sees music as providing both social and private, personal opportunities which reinforce her sense of self and enable her to feel a connection between these aspects of her identity.

Jane is studying English literature, music and business studies A'levels. She has been playing the violin for 13 years and the piano for 10 years. She would like to perform as a career, but before her first interview she auditioned for a music college and was unsuccessful in gaining a place. During her interview, members of the audition panel advised her to make a career change. Following this experience, Jane speaks about being a musician in the past tense, as if that part of her identity has changed (or is in a process of change). She appears to resolve this conflict (at least temporarily) by referring to her ability to use something else she is good at (English):

Jane: I'm glad I've had the opportunity to do it, I think that's my main appreciation of music and also that you know I've got, I've done English and I've got some sort of way of saying what things mean because you know that's all interconnected. [. . .] I don't think that I would ever be able to do it as a performer, but maybe as a music critic or something like that. You know, I think I could, I think I could do it, um because I've got quite a lot of ideas about what music means myself.

Jane's response illustrates the fluid and changing nature of identity. This was made even more apparent during the second interview 4 weeks later when she had auditioned for a different music college and been offered a place which she is excited about in terms of her future as a performing musician. At no point during her second interview did she mention English or the possibility of music journalism as a future career, which had featured prominently in her first interview. It also indicates the influence of powerful others (in this case those with the power to decide her future) in shaping her discourse and construction of self, revealing the nature of subjectivity and the relationship between discourse and reality.

Kath is studying history, music and information technology A'levels. She has played the viola for 11 years, percussion for 9 years, and studied voice for 2 years. Kath would like a career in music and wants to become a famous singer. Kath's sense of self is deeply embedded in the notion of being a musician:

Kath: I see myself as a musician. That's all I can see myself as. Um, I think a musician isn't something you kind of develop over time, its something you are and I don't think you can ever run away from that as some people, as I tried to do. But its, its something that's there at the beginning and although you can appreciate, learn to appreciate music and what have you, but you can never really become a musician, you can just learn to appreciate it that's what I think anyway, so . . .

Unlike the other girls, at no point in the interview does Kath make reference to how being a musician is related to other aspects of her 'self'. For Kath, being a musician is central to her construction of self: 'I see myself as a musician. That's all I can see myself as'. This implies that she has a special talent, which not only distinguishes her from non-musicians, it extends to others who are involved in music: 'You can never really become a musician'. It also illustrates the way in which she struggles after a core, unified identity. According to Burr (1995), 'calling upon images from the individualist, liberal humanism discourse in order to construct an account of oneself is likely to be quite successful, given the stronghold that this way of viewing human beings currently occupies in contemporary western societies. It stresses the person's individuality and uniqueness, and his or her need to make his or her own decisions about how he or she ought to live his or her life.' (p. 75). However, the success of discourses involving individualism are also limited in that they serve to emphasize further the 'common-sense' assumptions we make about what it means to be a musician. In other words, Kath constructs a sense of self that reaffirms societal and cultural norms and stereotypes.

It is necessary to acknowledge that there are other possibly equally valid ways of interpreting the girls' accounts. However, the aim of research within a social constructionist framework is not to search for 'truth' or 'facts'. Rather, the aim is to provide new insights and ways of understanding social phenomena, which can contribute to the development of new theoretical models and/or influence change among those the research aims to address. This was a key aim of another study I conducted recently with Yaroslav Senyshyn into the subjective experience of anxiety and music performance among undergraduate music students (see further Senyshyn and O'Neill, 2001).

This study involved individual, in-depth interviews with young musicians prior to and immediately following their final year music recitals. The recitals were a compulsory requirement of their degree. The students were asked to talk about their (1) reasons for choosing a performance option; (2) performance preparation; (3) expectations for the final performance; and (4) self-evaluations of their final performance. We found that for most of the young musicians, anxiety was viewed as an entity that was detrimental to performance, requiring the individual to take some form of action in order to prevent, avoid, control or eliminate its perceived negative effects. Anxiety was not only alienated or disassociated from their sense of self, it was seen to occupy a position of power relative to the individual, with the capacity to control their actions and responses both before and during the actual performance. The following quotations from the musicians' accounts illustrate this notion:

It's a great feeling when [the recital] is all going right, but you get these moments of anxiety when it's not going as right as it could do.

When I'm in the performance you kind of got this anxiety and awareness and I think that kind of adds something to the music but you've not got to let it spoil the music, which I think it can do.

Well if [the performance] is not going right you're not going to be aware of the fact that, well, it's just cos it's likely, maybe you're too nervous and it's out of your control.

The musicians' conceptualization of anxiety was not only in terms of a negative entity with the potential to 'spoil the music', but one in which anxiety was presented as dominant in the sense that the individual appears powerless to prevent it since 'it's out of your control'. The use of a particular discourse, which contains a particular organization of the self, can maintain power relations and patterns of domination and subordination. This was particularly evident in the musicians' accounts through the use of metaphor involving a 'battle' or 'fight' between the individual and his or her anxiety, in which anxiety was presented as the 'enemy' or 'opponent', for example:

I very much want to get over these nerves, I don't want them to bodge up my recital, its almost a slight battle with it, you know, I'm telling myself that I've got to deal with it because it will be so bad if I don't.

I want to go out there and I want to beat my nerves.

Hopefully nerves won't get the better of me.

The 'battle' metaphor serves to emphasize the musicians' experience of negative anxiety by imbuing it with the connotations and implications of the concept it is related to (e.g. control, power, tension and conflict). In particular, anxiety was presented as a separate entity which had 'control over' the individual or which the individual was 'struggling under'. The implication is that one or the other would emerge as the 'victor/victrix ludorum': the individual in the case of a successful performance, and anxiety in the case of failure. Jaynes (1979) argued that the most effective metaphor for making sense of subjective experience is metaphor itself. In other words, metaphorical representation of a personal world is not a direct copy or comparison, rather it is like map. He suggested that individuals have the capacity to use metaphor in order to represent experience and then act upon it and transform their experience by forming new ways of representing a phenomenon. However, not only can a metaphor illuminate a phenomenon by alerting an individual to its critical features, it can also serve to obscure them. For example, by associating anxiety with the notion of an enemy or opponent, the musicians were in fact reinforcing its negative implications, thereby limiting their potential to see positive ways of representing it.

Throughout the interviews with the undergraduate musicians, anxiety was associated with a feeling of uncontrollability and therefore uncertainty about the outcome of the performance. This presents a conflict with the individual's sense of agency or autonomy which only serves to perpetuate a perceived lack of control which in turn sustains and increases the individual's awareness of anxiety and its negative attributes. It also poses a dilemma. If it is considered necessary for the individual to evade or eliminate anxiety in order to achieve a successful performance, how is it possible to apportion blame or responsibility to 'anxiety' as separate from one's self should the performance not live up to the performer's expectations? This dilemma not only presents a conflict for the individual in that anxiety is viewed as distinct or disassociated from the performer's experiences, it also presents a conflict in terms of the performer's sense of identity as a 'musician' and what she considers her 'true' self to be. This conflict tends to be resolved by resorting to an assertion that the more experience you have of performing the less anxious you will be, as the following examples illustrate:

I think you can kind of diminish the nervousness and the anxiety that one does get, by experience.

Experience counts for a lot and I think you can kind of diminish the nervousness and the anxiety that one does get by experience.

Its something you build up and this year we've been doing lunch time concerts, and they've helped me out and there's only been two where I have been super nervous which is quite good for me, so I think its just experience.

An individual's understanding of successful performance in the past, present or future, is inextricably linked to the perceived amount of control she or he feels in terms of being able to evade negative anxiety, or overcome its negative manifestations. For the most part, the undergraduate music students perceived themselves to have relatively little experience of performing (compared with other students or professional musicians) and therefore perceived themselves as lacking the knowledge or skills necessary to control the negative effects of anxiety which would 'normally' be gained through experience. In this way, they were able to rationalize the possibility of failure as resulting from their lack of experience rather than their lack of ability as a performer, thereby protecting their sense of worth as a musician. This is particularly the case when one's goal is to achieve positive judgements of a performance and avoid negative judgements, not only by the audience but in the case of the music students their performance was part of a formal assessment which would influence their final degree result. The sense of security, protection or evasion of anxiety that is believed to be achieved through strategies aimed at gaining control can be interpreted not only in terms of an inauthentic existence that is temporary and fleeting (i.e. the nature of public performance suggests that no matter how many strategies the performer may rely on to overcome anxiety, she will nevertheless be confronted at some point with a sense of overwhelming anxiety whereby these strategies appear powerless to eliminate it), but also in terms of maintaining self-imposed restrictions on an individual's potential.

Social constructionism depicts the self as something that is fluid and constantly changing from situation to situation whilst embedded in social and cultural contexts. Gergen (1991) states that, 'social saturation brings with it a general loss in our assumptions of true and knowable selves. As we absorb multiple voices, we find "truth" relativised in our simultaneous consciousness of compelling alternatives. We come to be aware that each truth about ourselves is a construction of the moment, true only for a given time and within certain relationships' (p. 16). One of the problems with this notion, however, is that we feel ourselves to have a 'fixed' or core self. Burr (1995) argues that just by saying you have no 'fixed' self does not necessarily imply that the selves we construct are 'false'—rather we have a number of different selves which are all equally 'real'. Our experiences of ourselves are 'real' enough, and there is a sense in which we give the concept of self real existence in the way in which we live it and act it out in our encounters with each other. One explanation for the feelings of consistency or continuity is that memory allows us to look back on our behaviours and experiences. We therefore look for patterns and repetitions that provide us with the impression of continuity and coherence.

Although the above studies demonstrate the ways in which social constructionism provides a useful framework for understanding the self-identity of young musicians, there are an increasing number of researchers who argue that social constructionism needs to 'loosen its almost exclusive focus on language and discourse, and begin to include other vital issues' (Cromby and Nightingale, 1999, p. 1). Cromby and Nightingale outline several issues that are often neglected, including the possibilities and constraints of embodiment, materiality and power. I will now examine each of these in relation to the self-identity of young musicians.

Embodiment refers to the biological and physical presence of our bodies, which are a necessary pre-condition for subjectivity, emotion, language, thought and social interaction. Music performance requires 'real' physical activity and the body conveys not only expressive meaning (see further Davidson, Chapter 6, this volume), the gestures and facial expressions also convey messages about an individual's internal state (i.e. anxiety, confidence, emotion, etc.). Green (1997) describes how the body of a female singer during a performance is also an 'object' which conveys 'inherent' meanings of sexuality that become associated with the music itself. Research has established, in the case of young musicians, that gender associations about what is deemed appropriate musical activities for girls and boys to engage in is founded on their biological sex differences which are then socialized according to social norms (O'Neill, 1997a). Michael (1996, 1999) argues that realist notions such as the physical, or material object and constructionist notions, such as subjective interpretation are (albeit tacitly) contingent on each other in order to produce a meaningful account of a phenomenon. Another example of embodiment is the way in which physical changes as children grow can provide further opportunities for musical engagement (e.g. young string players growing enough to play full-sized instruments), thereby increasing their status and identity as musicians as mirrored in the adult world. On the other hand, the body may also have a constraining influence (e.g. those with disabilities are limited in their ability to take part in musical activities by the physical demands of traditional instruments), thereby reducing their status and identity as musicians (see related discussions by MacDonald and Miell, Chapter 10, and Magee, Chapter 11, this volume).

There are many other ways in which musical instruments as material objects shape and inform the social constructions and identity of young musicians. For example, the recorder is played frequently by children in schools and as such is often viewed as a child's instrument. This certainly affords opportunities since it is a small, light, inexpensive and relatively durable instrument that most children can learn to play and therefore gain experience of active music-making. On the other hand, this same simplistic design also constrains children's performance experiences and musical expression by the recorder's limited range, timbre, volume, articulation, repertoire, and so on. Also, by making the recorder available to all children in a classroom, it may increase socio-economic distinctions between those who can afford to own and play 'real' instruments (either at or outside school hours) and those who cannot. Finally, the widely held belief that the recorder is a 'toy' or not a 'real' instrument acts as a constraining influence on children's ability to view themselves as musicians since they do not associate it with instruments they see played in the adult world.

The inequalities mentioned above do not result merely from the presence or absence of material objects; they are part of a much wider issue to do with representations of power. Power is associated with institutions, government, large corporations and the media, and is often discussed in terms of capitalism and patriarchy. The ways in which young musicians are represented by these social structures can serve to support power inequalities while at the same time making them appear as fair or natural. Feminists and critical social psychologists have pointed out how accepted notions of the self are in accord with social structures and the roles considered appropriate within those structures. In other words, there is an ideological component to the ways in which we construct a sense of self. An example of this is how the role of music-making in child-hood is congruent with the 'natural' characteristics we stereotypically ascribe to children (e.g. innocent, naive, emotionally immature). Lovlie (1992) describes this as the 'romantic image of the child unfolding its innate abilities and talents towards a final ripening' (p. 120). These characteristics contrast dramatically with those we accept as necessary for an expressive (adult) musical performance. Children are also characterized as playful, creative and imaginative. This is congruent with the aims of classroom music education where children are encouraged to improvise and compose in ways which are more typical of 'experimenting with sound' than with the 'serious' intent we attribute to adults who improvise and compose. As such, there is an ideological component which acts as a constraining influence on children's forms of musical engagement.

Each of the above-mentioned issues (embodiment, materiality, power) have received far less attention by social constructionists, although the examples I have referred to (and there are many more) illustrate that they are deeply enmeshed in children's self-identity and beliefs about what it means to be a musician. The high cultural value we place on music is associated with its capacity to transcend the 'normal' mundane experience of our everyday lives. However, for young musicians in particular, it also has the ability to *construct* a reality that may not capture the expressive or authentic aspects of their musical experiences. As Nightingale and Cromby (1999) argue, 'the nature of our being is such that we are always embedded within historical and cultural processes, our embodied and material nature cannot be dismissed or explained away as a simple consequence of those processes, as merely epiphenomenal to language' (p. 223).

Conclusion

There is little doubt that social influences shape our lives (see further Giddens, 1991). These structures include institutions such as the family, education, the media and 'structures of power' (e.g. economical, political) which define social groups according to classifications such as gender, ethnicity and social class. Widdicombe and Wooffitt (1995) assert that society 'appears to have firmness or solidity comparable to objects in the material environment. Because of this, society seems external to us: we live *in* [original emphasis] society, and society exerts social constraints over our actions and sets limits to what we can do as individuals' (p. 30). However, as Widdicombe and Wooffitt point out, the danger of accepting the independent existence of society is that it suggests we are socially determined and therefore no longer controlling our individual experiences and lives. This apparent conflict becomes especially important when we are considering social change: what is it that brings about social change—society or individuals? This makes the division appear rather arbitrary and superficial. According to Widdicombe and Wooffitt (1995), it is important to challenge these assumptions.

There is increasing evidence to suggest that a gulf in meaning exists between ourselves as researchers and the young people we study when considering what it is to be a 'musician'. This is an area certainly worthy of further attention. The ideas presented in this chapter are far from exhaustive, but I hope they will provide a basis for future discussion and exploration. One of the features of Davies and Harré's (1990) account of self-identity is that once a young person has taken up a position within a discourse, such as 'I'm not really a musician', he or she inevitably will come to experience the world and his or her self from that perspective. This restricts the concepts, images, metaphors, ways of speaking, self-narratives and so on that are available and used in constructing a sense of self-identity in relation to music. It also entails an emotional commitment to the categories of musician and non-musician; young people are allocated to and see themselves as belonging to these categories. Young musicians' constructions of who they are and therefore what is possible or appropriate, and wrong or inappropriate forms of musical engagement, all derive from the ideology of lived experience. Only by raising our awareness of the possibilities and constraints afforded by particular ideologies can we hope to transcend the boundaries of what it means to be a musician.

References

Bempechat, J., London, P. and Dweck, C. (1991). Children's conceptions of ability in major domains: an interview and experimental study. *Child Study Journal*, 21, 11–36.

Burr, V. (1995). *An Introduction to Social Constructionism*. London: Routledge.

Cook, N. (1990). *Music, Imagination and Culture*. Oxford: Clarendon Press.

Cooley, C. (1902). *Human Nature and the Social Order*. New York: Scribner.

Cromby, J. and Nightingale, D.J. (1999). What's wrong with social constructionism? In D.J. Nightingale and J. Cromby (ed.), *Social Constructionist Psychology: A Critical Analysis of a Theory and Practice*, pp. 1–19. Buckingham, UK: Open University Press.

Crossley, M. L. (2000). *Introducing Narrative Psychology: Self, Trauma and the Construction of Meaning*. Buckingham, UK: Open University Press.

Csikszentmihalyi, M. and LeFevre, J. (1989). Optimal experience in work and leisure. *Journal of Personality and Social Psychology*, 56, 815–822.

Csikszentmihalyi, M., Rathunde, K. and Whalen, S. (1993). *Talented Teenagers: The Roots of Success and Failure*. Cambridge: Cambridge University Press.

Davies, B. and Harré, R. (1990). Positioning: the discursive production of selves. *Journal for the Theory of Social Behaviour*, 20, 43–63.

DeNora, T. (2000). *Music in Everyday Life*. Cambridge: Cambridge University Press.

Durkin, K. (1995). *Developmental Psychology: From Infancy to Old Age*. Oxford: Blackwell.

Dweck, C.S. (1986). Motivational processes affecting learning. *American Psychologist*, 41, 1040–1048.

Dweck, C.S. (1999). *Self-theories: Their Role in Motivation, Personality and Development*. Hove, UK: Psychology Press.

Dweck, C.S. and Leggett, E.L. (1988). A social–cognitive approach to motivation and personality. *Psychological Review*, 95, 256–273.

Eccles, J.S. (1987). Adolescence: gateway to gender role transcendence. In D.B. Carter (ed.), *Current Conceptions of Sex Roles and Sex Typing*, pp. 225–241. New York: Praeger.

Eccles, J.S. and Harold, R.D. (1992). Gender differences in educational and occupational patterns among the gifted. In N. Colangelo, S.G. Assouline and D.L. Ambroson (ed.), *Talent Develop-*

ment: *Proceedings from the 1991 Henry B. and Jocelyn Wallace National Research Symposium on Talent Development*, pp. 3–29. Unionville, NY: Trillium Press.

Eccles, J., Wigfield, A., Harold, R.D. and Blumenfeld, P. (1993). Age and gender differences in children's self- and task perceptions during elementary school. *Child Development*, **64**, 830–847.

Eccles, J.S., Wigfield, A. and Schiefele, U. (1998). Motivation to succeed. In N. Eisenberg (ed.), *Handbook of Child Development (5th edn., Vol. 3): Social, Emotional, and Personality Development*, pp. 1017–1095. New York: Wiley.

Elliott, E.S. and Dweck, C.S. (1988). Goals: an approach to motivation and achievement. *Journal of Personality and Social Psychology*, **54**, 5–12.

Geertz, C. (1979). From the native's point of view: on the nature of anthropological understanding. In P. Rabinow and W. Sullivan (ed.), *Interpretive Social Science: A Reader*, pp. 225–241. Berkeley, CA: University of California Press.

Gergen, K. (1991). *The Saturated Self: Dilemmas of Identity in Contemporary Life*. New York: Basic Books.

Gergen, K. J. and Davis, K.E. (1985). *The Social Construction of the Person*. New York: Springer-Verlag.

Giddens, A. (1991). *Modernity and Self Identity: Self and Society in the Late Modern Age*. Cambridge: Polity Press.

Green, L. (1997). *Music, Gender, Education*. Cambridge: Cambridge University Press.

Harré, R. (1983). *Personal Being: A Theory for Individual Psychology*. Oxford: Basil Blackwell.

Harré, R. (1998). *The Singular Self: An Introduction to the Psychology of Personhood*. London: Sage.

Harré, R. and Gillett, G. (1994). *The Discursive Mind*. London: Sage.

Heidegger, M. (1962). *Being and Time*. Oxford: Blackwell.

James, W. (1890). *The Principles of Psychology*, Vol. 1. New York: Holt.

Jaynes, J. (1979). *The Origin of Consciousness in the Breakdown of the Bicameral Mind*. London: Allen Lane.

Kemp, A.E. (1996). *The Musical Temperament: Psychology and Personality of Musicians*. Oxford: Oxford University Press.

Lovlie, L. (1992). Postmodernism and subjectivity. In S. Kvale (ed.), *Psychology and Postmoderism*, pp. 118–134. London: Sage.

Markus, H. and Nurius, P. (1987). Possible selves: the interface between motivation and the self-concept. In K. Yardley and T. Honess (ed.), *Self and Identity: Psychosocial Perspectives*, pp. 157–172. London: John Wiley and Sons Ltd.

Mead, G.H. (1934). *Mind, Self and Society*. Chicago: University of Chicago Press.

Merleau-Ponty, M. (1962). *Phenomenology of Perception* (translated by C. Smith). London: Cassel.

Michael, M. (1996). Constructing a constructive critique of social constructionism: finding a narrative space for the non-human. *New Ideas in Psychology*, **14**, 209–224.

Michael, M. (1999). A pardigm shift? Connections with other critiques of social constructionism. In D.J. Nightingale and J. Cromby (ed.), *Social Constructionist Psychology: A Critical Analysis of a Theory and Practice*. Buckingham, UK: Open University Press.

Mischel, W. (1968). *Personality and Assessment*. New York: Wiley.

Montemayor, R. and Eisen, M. (1977). The development of self-conceptions from childhood to adolescence. *Developmental Psychology*, **13**, 314–319.

Nightingale, D.J. and Cromby, J.E. (1999). *Social Constructionist Psychology: A Critical Analysis of Theory and Practice*. Buckingham, UK: Open University Press.

O'Neill, S.A. (1994). Children's conceptions of ability in three major domains. Poster presented at the *British Psychological Developmental Section Annual Conference*, University of Portsmouth, September 1994.

O'Neill, S.A. (1997a). Gender and music. In D.J. Hargreaves and A.C. North (ed.), *The Social Psychology of Music*, pp. 46–63. Oxford: Oxford University Press.

O'Neill, S.A. (1997b). The role of practice in children's early musical performance achievement. In H. Jorgensen and A.C. Lehmann (ed.), *Does Practice Make Perfect? Current Theory and Research on Instrumental Music Practice*, pp. 53–70. Oslo: NMH-publikasjoner.

O'Neill, S.A. (1999). Flow theory and the development of musical performance skills. *Bulletin of the Council for Research in Music Education*, **141**, 129–134.

O'Neill, S.A. and McPherson, G.E. (2001). Motivation. In R. Parncutt and G.E. McPherson (ed.), *The Science and Psychology of Musical Performance: Creative Strategies for Teaching and Learning*, pp. 31–46. Oxford: Oxford University Press.

O'Neill, S.A. and Sloboda, J.A. (1997). The effects of failure on children's ability to perform a musical test. *Psychology of Music*, **25**, 18–34.

O'Neill, S.A., Ivaldi, A. and Fox, C. (1999). Exposing gendered assumptions in young 'talented' women's construction of self. *Proceedings of the British Psychology Society Psychology of Women Section Conference*, University of Manchester, June 1999.

Parker, I. (1990). Discourse: definitions and contradictions. *Philosophical Psychology*, **3**, 189–204.

Piaget, J. (1936). *The Origin of Intelligence in the Child*. Harmondsworth: Penguin.

Pintrich, P. (1991). Current issues and new directions in motivational theory and research. *Educational Psychologist*, **26**, 199–205.

Potter, J. and Wetherall, M. (1987). *Discourse and Social Psychology: Beyond Attitudes and Behaviour*. London: Sage.

Potter, J., Wetherall, M., Gill, R. and Edwards, D. (1990). Discourse: noun, verb or social practice? *Philosophical Psychology*, **3**, 205–217.

Ruble, D.N. (1994). A phase model of transitions: cognitive and motivational consequences. *Advances in Experimental Social Psychology*, **26**, 163–214.

Schutz, A. (1962). On multiple realities. *Collected Papers*. The Hague: Martinus Nijhoff.

Senyshyn, Y. and O'Neill, S.A. (2001). Subjective experience of anxiety and musical performance: a relational perspective. *Philosophy of Music Education Review*, **9**(1), 42–53.

Stipek, D.J. and Mac Iver, D. (1989). Developmental change in children's assessment of intellectual competence. *Child Development*, **60**, 521–538.

Trevarthen, C. (1999). Musicality and the intrinsic motive pulse: evidence from human psychobiology and infant communication. *Musicae Scientiae, Special Issue (1999–2000)*, 155–215.

Widdicombe, S. and Wooffitt, R. (1995). *The Language of Youth Subcultures*. New York: Harvester Wheatsheaf.

Wigfield, A. (1994). Expectancy–value theory of achievement motivation: a developmental perspective. *Educational Psychology Review*, **6**, 49–78.

Wigfield, A., Eccles, J.S., Yoon, K.S., Harold, R.D., Arbreton, A., Freedman-Doan, K. and Blumenfeld, P.C. (1997). Changes in children's competence beliefs and subjective task values across the elementary school years: a three-year study. *Journal of Educational Psychology*, **89**, 451–469.

CHAPTER 6

THE SOLO PERFORMER'S IDENTITY

JANE W. DAVIDSON

Introduction

The previous chapter explored how self-identity is formed and how young people come to define themselves as musicians. The current chapter moves on from where the previous chapter concluded, accepting the definition of the musician's identity which emerged. The central topic for consideration here is the notion of 'being a performer', in particular the question: 'what makes a performer?' The chapter concentrates on the soloist, for it is well documented that soloists typically are more exposed to performance pressures—they do not have co-performers with whom to collaborate. Furthermore, in popular, folk and classical Western traditions, the soloist is often regarded as a person who needs to possess very high-level communicative abilities in order to engage the audience's attention and foster a sense of participation (see Davidson, 1997, for more discussion of solo versus co-performance). The discussion in this chapter reflects on the environmental circumstances, patterns of behaviour and personality traits that might influence the development of an individual's performance abilities. In particular, what makes a 'good' solo performance is considered.

Both media promotion and a compliance with the social tastes of a particular time can contribute toward specific individuals becoming notable or popular performers (see Frith, 1996, for more details). In this chapter, it is accepted that such social factors can strongly affect a performer's 'success'. Towards the end of the chapter, research is presented which demonstrates the degree to which some of these social influences shape the audience's assessment of performance quality. The chapter primarily focuses on individual differences within the socio-cultural environment of the Western solo performing tradition.

In this chapter, findings from research covering a wide range of relevant areas are explored. The results are discussed in the context of differences between myself (a solo performer) and Steve (an instrumental player but non-performer). Thus, I adopt a reflexive approach which not only seems particularly appropriate to issues connected with identity, but which is also useful in terms of drawing comparisons between the various areas of research explored and the personal examples given, thus linking theory and practice.

The chapter is written in two sections: Part A explores what factors might contribute to the performer's identity, and Part B focuses on which particular performer behaviours are perceived to be desirable and effective in the communication of a musical performance.

Part A: what makes a performer identity?

The Oxford Dictionary's definition of a performer is a person who is: 'an exhibitionist', engaged in 'carrying out notable feats' for the 'thrill of adulation' and 'sense of personal achievement'. In my personal experience as a solo classical singer, I can empathize with these definitions completely: I feel positive about going on stage and presenting myself to an audience. I do it for the challenge and thrill of the situation, coupled with a love of music. Steve, in contrast, plays classical guitar, an instrument with a vast solo repertoire. Steve is a fine guitarist who has practised the instrument regularly since childhood, so he has technical and expressive fluency equal to my own. However, Steve plays for himself, not public consumption. He is a musician, but not a public performer. What makes us so different? One way to begin to answer this question is to turn to the relevant research literature on the development of musical performance skills, to consider the external influences involved and to explore which of these might explain the differences between Steve and myself. The following subheadings have emerged from an examination of the research literature and are used as foci for discussion.

The influences of environmental factors on the development of the solo music performer

The provision of opportunities to experience 'peak emotions'

Sloboda (1991, 1998) has investigated the role of emotional experience in an individual's motivation to engage with music, and suggests that a 'peak emotional experience' with music in early childhood can help to develop life-long enthusiasm and the need to engage with it. At 7 years of age, I heard some older children rehearsing a musical at school. I was deeply affected by the music. I recall feeling tingles through my body when I first heard the music. My case seems typical of the experiences Sloboda describes, and so too were Steve's: he heard a guitar and was attracted to the musical sounds. The single key difference between us was that I immediately tried to re-create the performance I had heard. Indeed, my mother recalls that my enthusiasm to develop my version of the songs and stage action was overwhelming, and that I performed the music to my parents on a daily basis for several weeks. Thus, from my initial exposure to the medium of music, the concept of performance was central to my enjoyment and understanding of the music itself. Steve did not have a comparable experience, and from his earliest experiences with the instrument, the guitar was viewed as a solitary, escapist activity.

Casual but frequent exposure to music and performance contexts

Biographical accounts of famous solo music performers (see, for instance, Collier, 1983; Lehmann, 1997) show that frequent exposure to performing contexts figure strongly in their early lives, as do opportunities to explore the medium of music through experimentation in a non-threatening environment. For example, the jazz performer Louis Armstrong formed and sang in a street corner choir as a boy, and had opportunities to participate in communal jazz activities where mistakes were tolerated. He could choose the level of risk and difficulty of his performance, sometimes working as a chorister or bandsman, and gradually emerged as a soloist. Thus, he was able not only to learn the 'rules' of jazz harmony and improvisation, but also to experience performance, learning about different performing contexts.

In my own case, I attended a performance-oriented primary school where the staff encouraged all the students to create art products and present them in school assemblies. I invented puppet shows, classroom dramas, musicals and, gradually, as I gained in confidence and experience, I began to sing solos. Steve did not have these performance opportunities.

Role of key others

Davidson *et al.* (1997) studied over 250 young music learners, and discovered that they were highly externally motivated to participate in musical activities when they experienced the encouragement and support of key others such as peers, family and teachers. These types of influence are discussed in more detail in Chapter 3 by Lamont with regard to school friends and teachers, whilst, in Chapter 4, Borthwick and Davidson highlight the roles of parents and siblings in providing financial, practical and emotional circumstances for musical involvement. The critical finding of Davidson *et al.*'s research was that the encouragement need not come only from musicians, but rather from any highly supportive others. Typically, children who developed musical skills rapidly often had non-musician parents who sat through all of their practice and lessons. In addition to musical skills, the 'key others' supported the children in performances too. Indeed, Davidson *et al.* discovered that where the children possessed high levels of solo performance abilities, families typically had asked their children to play though pieces for them, and made efforts to give the children positively reinforcing performance experiences, such as getting them to play for visitors to the house. Most significantly, the children all reported that these performance experiences made them feel special, and so motivated them to seek out more performance opportunities. Throughout our schooling, Steve and I both had older children and teachers to provide musician role models, and our parents offered their full support. However, I enjoyed many family-initiated performance opportunities, whereas Steve did not. In fact, he was not encouraged to perform for anyone.

All of the influences described above seem to indicate that both musical and performance skills are developed optimally over time in unthreatening environments. The literature explored has focused on music learning, and so musical and performance abilities have tended to be examined as correlates: the better one is at music, the better one is at performance. Looking at personal anecdote, it becomes evident that Steve's case questions this idea for he has high-level musical skills, but no desire to perform. His biography has revealed that he had no opportunities to practise/acquire performance skills and interests in his early life.

I personally experienced many musical performance learning opportunities but, looking back and assessing my own life relative to the children in the study reported by Davidson *et al.*, I believe that it was my exposure to different types of performance that generally was a highly motivating and instructive experience for me. In particular, my parents had no musical skills and never listened to music at home, yet my father was a well-known competitive solo sportsman, and therefore a highly skilled solo performer in a different field. I believe that my exposure to his performances led me to crave the positive feelings my father reported to me about performance; and, most critically, by observing him and discussing his performances in detail throughout my childhood, I began to assimilate some skills required in order to produce a good performance. Looking back at the experience, I believe that I was able to transfer the skills observed in his sport and apply them to music (the specific skills required will be discussed later). Of course, my hypothesis about the important influence of my father in developing my performance skill is speculative but, given the very close bond between us, it seems likely that I would have been particularly influenced by him. (The power of the relationship between parent and child is pursued in detail in Borthwick and Davidson in Chapter 4.)

This is not an exhaustive list of the environmental factors contributing towards someone becoming a musician and a performer, and perhaps some factors are more significant than others. However, to date, no one has teased out the exact role of these important environmental factors. Research has demonstrated, however, that in order for a sustained interest in music to be achieved, motivation needs to be internalized and become self-generated (see Sloboda and Howe, 1991; Davidson *et al.*, 1997). Indeed, Davidson *et al.* discovered that intrinsic motivation kept children learning music at times when many of their peers were giving up, for example at the transition between primary and secondary school. Internal drives are believed to be related directly to personality (see Bayley, 1970), and so, in the section which follows, I shall explore the extent to which motivation and personality may influence one's ability to be a performing musician.

The motivation and personality to perform

Motivation

Maslow (1970) attempted to model individuals' motivations. He believed in a hierarchy of motives emerging from basic survival needs (food, water, rest, sex), and progressing to safety needs (security, protection, shelter). When these needs are attained, love and belongingness become important, then respect from others and self-esteem. Once self-esteem is in place, a search for meaning and knowledge can be undertaken, then aesthetic needs (beauty, order) can be explored and, eventually, one can focus on fulfilling one's full potential (self-actualization). To my knowledge, no one has applied Maslow's theory directly to musical contexts. It would appear that in both Steve's and my own case, musical participation engages us in all the upper hierarchical needs and provides an opportunity for personal growth and development, with respect, self-esteem and aesthetic pleasure being fulfilled. Our reasons for musical participation remain quite different, however.

Green and Gallwey (1986), Evans (1994) and Wilson (1997) all point out that self-esteem affects how one regards one's own capacities, and this in turn critically affects personal motivations to participate in certain contexts, to behave in particular ways and to display abilities in certain activities. Green and Gallwey argue that negative self-appraisal in a performance context can easily de-motivate a performer, as the ensuing self-doubt can distort perception, leading to further negative appraisal. Fortunately, Steve and I have never experienced these extreme negative reactions to the performance context, though I can recall feeling more or less motivated depending on my level of self-esteem, which was based on my confidence in my preparation and the perceived importance of the performance context and the audience. The critical point is that motivation is strongly affected by self-belief, vitally Dweck and Bempechat (1984) argue that belief about learning capacity is vitally important. They suggest that people believe themselves to possess either 'incremental' or 'entity' capacities. That is, those who could be described as 'entity theorists' would believe that their ability or role in a certain domain is fixed, whereas 'incrementalists' would believe that they will always improve next time. The researchers' practical investigations revealed that entity theorists feared that they might appear to lack ability in front of others. As a result of the desire to save face, entity theorists are much more likely to avoid tasks at which they are not likely to be successful, or might be seen to struggle. Entity theorists typically seek out situations where they have success with low effort and where they would be likely to outshine others (Dweck, 2000).

Considering Steve and myself, it could be that Steve is more of an entity theorist than I, since he does not seek out performance situations at all. There are, however, a number of ways to explain the motivational differences between Steve and myself. There have been periods of time in my life when I have behaved like an entity theorist with regard to beliefs I have held about my performing ability, and, contrarily, Steve has displayed incremental motivations in his desire to improve. Perhaps the best way to summarize the implications of these motivational theories is that individuals appear to behave in particular contexts according to broad principles, but individual motivations can change over time. A good example of change can be found in 'arousal theory' (see Geen *et al.*, 1984), which suggests that humans seek novelty and challenge in order to attain an optimal personal level of excitement from whatever is the task in hand, but that the optimal personal level varies depending on other concurrent life events.

Some theorists regard motivation primarily in terms of a general instinctual drive, whereas others, like those researching arousal and incremental/entity behaviours, acknowledge the role of individual differences as a result of varying social influences and personality (the inner predisposition to behave in certain ways; see Kemp, 1996, for further definitions of personality). Since social influences have already been discussed above (see section on the role of key others in the development of performance skills), an individual's personality and how this may shape the desire to engage in music performance should now be considered.

Personality

Research has shown that when musicians are compared with other people, they are found to display more introversion than the population in general (see Kemp, 1996). Examples of traits associated with introversion include being aloof, critical, introspective and individualistic. The requirements of musical skill acquisition would seem to match these characteristics: many numbers of hours need to be invested in lonely solo practice, which requires self-containment and an ability to be self-critical as well as the ability to take criticism in order to conquer the challenges of learning.

Solo performing musicians, such as pianists, conductors and singers, tend to be rather more extroverted than ensemble musicians such as string and woodwind players: they are more outgoing and adventurous (Kemp, 1996). Singers have been found to be the most independent of all. Kemp suggests that singers are the most 'exposed' of all musicians in that they have no instrument to 'protect' them from the audience's gaze, so that independence is a useful trait for them to possess. Research by Wubbenhorst (1994) reinforces this point in a study of American students, which revealed that students on performance courses scored much higher on extraversion dimensions in personality tests than those attending music teaching, or more theoretically oriented music courses.

A growing body of research (see, for example, O'Neill and Boulton, 1996; Maidlow and Bruce, 1999) demonstrates that not only are girls and boys attracted to different instruments, but that particular characteristics of instruments appeal to different individuals. Such findings raise interesting issues about whether or not it is the effect of a particular instrument that 'shapes' the individual who learns it, or whether it is the existing personality characteristics of individuals that attract them to the specific features of the instrument. Kemp discusses these issues in some depth and concludes that it is most probably an interactive consequence of environment and personal traits. Linking the studies of Kemp and Wubbenhorst, and the findings of the gender and instrumental choice studies, there does seem to be convincing evidence that a music performer may indeed display very particular personality characteristics.

Forrester (2000) suggests that personality is a projected representation of an individual's internal belief systems, emerging from genetic factors, life opportunity, social interaction and critical feedback. He believes that external factors such as a particular social context or task will trigger behaviours and responses which are deemed appropriate to individuals, emerging from and shaped by their internal belief systems. He suggests that this leads to a major dichotomy of self-defined perspectives on the personality. Namely, the version of the personality which is presented to the world—a self-defined 'public' image; and a version of the personality which tends to be of a more private nature, in which the more 'vulnerable' aspects of an individual such as self-doubts and extreme emotionality are revealed.

Forrester's view builds on Jung's psychodynamic view of personality. Psychodynamic approaches attempt to explain human characteristics and behaviour in terms of beliefs, fears and desires which typically operate at an unconscious level—see Berry (2000) for further details. Jung argued that each individual possesses a persona, or public mask, to protect their inner core or ego.

According to Goffman (1979), who modified Jung's ideas, the extent to which a projected self or mask is applied to a public situation will be determined by the information perceived in that situation. From studies in many different types of social context, Goffman believes that the process of learning how and when to use the appropriate 'projected self' or mask is the key to effective social interaction, public and intimate discourse.

Returning to Steve and I, and applying the performance 'mask' theory, I would argue that I learned to present a 'projection' early on, and that over the years I have learned to shift very easily between that state, which is for public performance, and other states more typical of other settings. Steve reports not being able to 'connect' with what he believes would be appropriate in the performance situation. It is as if he has not been able to construct a projected version of himself in music-making contexts.

An appropriate use of a projected mask would seem to be of critical importance in solo musical performance situations. On stage, my self-presentation is focused, confident and 'larger' than I would appear in, say, a one-on-one conversation in a cafe. Thus, assessing the theories and evidence available, and comparing these with my own reflections on Steve and myself, there is an emergent image of performers being individuals who possess self-concepts which permit them to enjoy public situations and to thrive in them. It seems that performance becomes a means through which part of the personality is expressed: from the evidence discussed, it is possible to argue that personality may be developed, to some extent, according to the performance task.

Motivation, personality and change: the emergence of a solo performing musician

In order to draw together the issues discussed so far, I turn now to research in which Karen Burland has followed the fortunes of 20 classical musicians from childhood performance success at a renowned specialist music school in England, through to adulthood (Burland and Davidson, 2002). These 20 participants had been part of a much larger study I carried out with Sloboda and Howe (see Davidson *et al.*, 1997 for an overview) in which we traced the biographical determinants of their childhood musical successes. We tracked down these 20 as a representative sample of the original 120 interviewees (see the design protocol in Burland and Davidson for details). All were between the ages of 10 and 18 years when we initially interviewed them, and all intended to become professional performers, claiming that music was central to their lives. However, 8 years later, when the sample were between 18 and 26 years of age, only half were in fact pursuing music performance as a profession, and the other half typically had kept music as a hobby, pursuing other careers. In one case, all involvement with music had ceased and, in another case, the young man did not perform music at all, but was involved in sound recording. Note that since the research I report is from a study Karen Burland and I undertook in 2000, I draw below on some unpublished raw data for illustrative examples, but other citations and more details of the study can be found in the published articles.

Detailed semi-structured follow-up interviews revealed that all the professional performers had received external support from teachers, parents and peers over the 8-year period. Four other key emergent factors linked all these participants: (1) over time, participation in music had become the key determinant of self-concept; (2) music-making had become perceived increasingly as having both positive physical and psychological benefits; (3) music performance had become a critical means of self-expression; and (4) a lifestyle had been developed in which a range of non-musical social and leisure activities were undertaken and used deliberately to promote a sense of general well-being.

These themes indicate that emotional and motivational aspects of these individuals' personalities had emerged, or been developed, which enabled them not only to sustain their love of music, but also to feel that music was a stabilizing factor in their lives. Being a performer was also an important issue. Looking at some of the data below, it could be argued that from childhood to adulthood these individuals went through the process of becoming self-identified as musical performers.

For these professional performers, music was an important determinant of self-concept. This was illustrated by sentiments such as:

I cannot imagine being me without music (21-year-old pianist).

Music and me, well, it's the same thing! (26-year-old harpsichordist).

To achieve psychological balance, one 24-year-old pianist commented that:

Music offers me stability, and I suppose a foundation in a way. It makes me feel as though I'm worth something... I can't really do anything else to the same standard and with the same passion and determination... I suppose it offers me some kind of self-satisfaction.

Music was a means of communicating this perception of self and of interacting with others. This is neatly encapsulated in the comments of a 25-year-old violinist:

Music is really quite a special thing. You can do it with people you don't really know very well, which you can't really do in any other way [with anything else].

It seems that for these individuals, performance allowed them to express themselves freely:

... Music performance is just so liberating—there's no kind of prejudice in it—it's just pure expression from one person to another... it's an all encompassing thing... When I'm playing I let people see me in a way that I won't when I'm talking (22-year-old oboist).

The 'desire' to perform featured very strongly with those who became professional performers. We felt that the data indicated the existence of a particular 'performer attitude'. As one highly successful 23-year-old pianist commented:

In performance it's good to have the 'attitude'... It's worth it for those small successes...

These musicians had a concept of themselves related to performance, and enhanced their self-esteem as a result of performance success. All accepted there would be hard times, but all believed that the good times would always compensate for the bad, which displays a truly 'incrementalist' attitude.

'Oh, there's always a good result, however bad things may seem at the time (24-year-old violinist).

Many of the performers wished they possessed more of a 'will' to succeed. The pianist quoted above added, for instance: 'Maybe if I had more of a "killer instinct", I'd be more successful.' The notion of 'killer instinct' emerged a number of times, and was interpreted not only as the determination required to 'keep going', but also as the drive to push others out of the way should it be necessary, and to assist in putting oneself in the limelight, for all recognized that to become a performer meant getting noticed:

When you practise you need to be cool in order to learn all the notes and control what they mean for yourself, but when you perform you need to be more like a circus act, going out there and showing off, showing the audience that you are good (25-year-old violinist).

This point links back to the idea of having different personae, or masks, and that it is necessary to develop a projected persona if you are to become a performer. None of the interviewees who kept music only as a hobby discussed the notion of a performing personality. However, this could be because they did not consider it to be part of their own musical experience. Perhaps the maintenance of other hobbies such as reading and swimming alongside music helped these performers to place music within a broader context of life and/or provided ways to maintain or even intensify interests and skills in music.

None of those who did not become professional performers expressed sentiments about seeing music as being highly integrated with the self, and none regarded performance as a positive part of music-making. In childhood, as with the current professional performers, music-making had been the most important part of their lives. Indeed, all had practised more than those who became professional performers. However, comparing the two sets of early data, it became apparent that those who gave up performing in adulthood were less self-motivated in childhood *and* had no hobbies outside of music. In our judgement, this pattern of results could be interpreted to indicate that these children had put too much effort into music—effort which sometimes was forced upon them by others or which they 'inflicted' upon themselves in the struggle to succeed. Indeed, many of them looked back on childhood practice as 'boring' and 'heavy'. Indeed, one 24-year-old pianist said:

I cannot understand why I did so much practice. Well, I suppose I used to think I was getting better, but I got to really hate it ... Maybe it was because others expected me to it ... Anyway, I seemed to do nothing but practice!

We could tentatively suggest that some of these children initially were externally motivated, but that the effort involved in making music became a burden rather than a pleasure. The professional performers, in contrast, showed an incremental theory of music-making throughout their childhood and current adult experiences. This is revealed in the following statement by a 25-year-old violinist:

I always wanted to get better ... The challenge ... I am still like that. Music is about becoming better.

Burland and Davidson's data have demonstrated that even out of very similar circumstances which led to the acquisition of high-level musical skills, individuals develop in different ways and that in order for a performer to emerge, several key factors are required. Given that it was only the performers who emphasized their desire to project a stage persona, I would suggest that learning how to present the self on stage is a critical variable for performers.

Observing and assessing performance behaviours (arguably the expressions of the performing persona) are ways in which we can begin to understand what makes a performance 'good' from the audience's point of view. Thus, in the second half of this chapter, I turn to a discussion of performance behaviour. Of course, as was stated earlier, socio-cultural factors such as taste and fashion have significant roles to play, and so an individual who is perceived positively in one music performance context may be perceived less favourably in another. For this reason, the discussion is limited to solo Western vocal performance, though some contrasts between classical and pop ballad singing are drawn. Thus, there is a shift from the performer's experience to what the audience perceives, thus enabling a discussion of what a good performer offers the audience.

Part B: the perceived characteristics of the good solo music performer

Judging singers

Daniela Coimbra and I (Davidson and Coimbra, 2001) recently worked with the assessors of classical singers in a music conservatory to explore which characteristics were identified as being critically important for a 'good' solo performer. The assessors were all highly experienced judges and voice teachers. We discovered that alongside the possession of musical skills (control and flexibility of timbre, range and intonation), characteristics defined by the assessors as 'the performing personality' were perceived to be highly important. (Note that 'performing personality' was the assessors' term. We believe it is analogous to the Jungian concept of 'persona' mentioned earlier in the chapter.) We did not ask specifically about personal or musical characteristics, but rather asked the assessors of second and third year vocal studies students (with a mean age of 22 years) taking examinations to offer grades and detailed comments on the strengths and weaknesses of what they observed in the performances. Working from video footage of the performances, transcripts of the discussions between the assessors and written documentation of the assessment procedure, we subjected these data to a 'grounded' qualitative analysis (in line with Smith, 1995). From the analysis, we were able to extract the criteria the assessors used. For the sake of this discussion, I now focus on the judgements that were made about the singers.

The single most striking 'performance personality' theme to emerge from the data was the emphasis placed on physical appearance. Criticisms of what the young singers actually did on stage were often highly personal in nature:

Odd make-up and ill-fitting cardigan

A rather puppet like physical appearance

Bow ankles and sweater covered hands . . . a bit motherly matronly in this outfit.

Without an appropriate level of physical appeal, a key element of 'performance' was missing. Allied to this, non-verbal communication was also identified as being of crucial importance. These included the use of facial expression and eye contact, as shown in comments such as:

A self-possessed beam

A visual 'performing' element missing. A problem of self-image: does he need/want to develop as a performer?

There is an incredible energy flowing out of the entire surface of her body [to the audience].

Very appealing visual/facial expression

or, on the contrary,

Eyes dead. Blank face

The next most strongly emergent theme was 'artistry', i.e. the communication not only of the music, but the personal interpretation of that music to the audience. This had two components. The first was emotional intention: comments such as the performance should be 'heartfelt', 'from the centre of the person' and, therefore, with 'self-possession' were used time and again to describe what the performer needed to attain. We interpreted these terms to mean that an expressive performance should be created, emerging out of the individual's personality and its presentation on stage. The second component was the significance of the singer showing that he/she was committed to interacting with the audience. The singers did this to various degrees and in different styles, ranging from physically approaching the audience to simply smiling, or introducing the performance pieces to explain their performance intentions.

The assessors' perception of the singer's attitude at the start of their performances had a significant effect on the establishment of the initial mood in the room, as can be observed in the following examples:

Positive statements:

Your introductions and choice of repertoire fill me with instant joy

This was a charming presentation, revealing a charming personality

Negative statements:

Introductions—Boring

Rather too jolly and josh in the introductions

The more focused the singer was on transmitting the musical intention, the more the assessors seemed to be captivated and, therefore, considered the singer to be 'appealing'. The full relevance of 'appeal' was encapsulated in one of the assessor's statements:

The singer is so focused that nothing interferes with our relationship, and so, not only the composer's message is important, but the singer also acknowledges that I am here and I am important too.

If the singer was not sufficiently 'present', there was a perception that the singer was 'hiding'. Lack of energy or interest in portraying the song was considered as a lack in part of the performance itself:

A lovely sound, but rather disappointing as she doesn't get involved as an artist

On the other hand, some singers distracted the audience from the contents of the song, drawing the focusing of attention more on his/her 'self', hence lacking the desirable involvement in the music:

. . . Ultimately tiring to listen to because of the over giving

The assessors even felt patronized by some of the singers:

Perhaps too much of the persona comes through . . . and the result is slightly disrespectful of the seriousness of the situation.

As the analysis progressed, it became apparent that the assessors were aiming for the singers to possess a 'performing personality' in which stage presence was the means through which part of the personality, that connected with an outward focus, was presented. All the assessors talked about the most successful performers sharing a particular kind of personality, one that was large scale and projected. Their descriptions were combined with concepts of acting, in that the performers empathized with a mood in their musical material or showed the audience ideas, but did not present the intimacies of their own personalities. Linking back to the theories developed by Jung and Goffman discussed in Part A of the chapter, it seems that a 'persona' with 'a public mask' is what the assessors were looking for in a good performer.

These data indicate, of course, that performer states are evident to the audience, and that appropriate public behaviour is a prerequisite to the perception of a good solo vocal performance.

On several occasions, however, a process of identification between the 'performing' and the 'inner' personality was made:

Charming girl—charming voice

A sweet and sunny personality. A sweet and sunny voice

This is an engaging performing personality showing great intensity. It is all engaged and heartfelt with the self

These data suggest that to be a good performer, one has to be 'public' in presentational style, but also to show something of one's individuality and inner state. A slightly ironic and complex presentation is required—sufficiently external to be public, yet intimate:

Beautiful multi-layered poised sincerity

Deeply felt performance—partly real and partly excellent role-playing

When looking at the best-rated performers' profile, 'good performance' was also related to expressions such as 'engagement', 'appeal', 'charm', 'commitment' and 'depth of feeling':

... It is great to see someone feeling all that emotional stuff when singing. He got involved and cared about what he was doing. Lots of promise ...

This extract suggests that solo classical singers are culturally expected to display their emotions, but how much of this is genuinely heartfelt or 'acted' is clearly a complex issue, given the emphasis on the public 'persona'. The origins of 'acting' based on empathy and previous experience are discussed at length in method books such as those by Boal (1992) and Stanislavsky (1967). Some training establishments for opera singers do deal with these techniques, and it seems that the demands of 'acting' will affect singers' conceptions of themselves and their 'performer identities'. Indeed, Kemp's (1996) discussion of whether it is the instrument, and/or the cultural role of that type of musician which most affects the individual, needs careful consideration. The key question becomes whether training develops the role, or whether a certain type of personality is drawn to solo performance on a particular musical instrument. The stereotype of the 'luvvy', the 'loud' and 'extravagant' personality of the operatic Diva, could indeed have its roots in cultural expectations, but it may be that 'loud' personalities are drawn to becoming opera singers. These issues require much more research but, as a first stage, critical reflection of the type presented so far begins to formulate the key questions.

I have written elsewhere about the different kinds of social groups and the roles individuals play within them in musical contexts (Davidson, 1997), and the chapters by Tarrant *et al.* (Chapter 8) and MacDonald and Miell (Chapter 10) in the current volume emphasize the critical role played by social groups in the construction of an individual's musical identity. I shall now deepen the discussion of the solo vocal performer's identity by exploring how the soloist works on stage, communicating the 'performer identity'. Although my data come from Western culture, and are based on singing, two different genres of solo singing performance are explored: classical and pop.

The performing personality in action

Having established that assessors look for particular performance behaviours, I felt that it was critically important to know what specific and observable behaviours contributed to the 'performing personality' on stage. My previous empirical studies of music performers (Davidson, 1993, 1995, 2002) had demonstrated that different types of expressive information are communicated to observers through body movement, and Gellrich (1991) has shown that a set of specifically learned mimetic movements and gestures furnish a performance with expressive intention. A fairly extensive literature on physical gesture in spoken language (cf. Ekman and Friesen, 1969; Ellis and Beattie, 1986) indicates that gestural repertoires emerge which are associated with specific meanings. I therefore devised a preliminary study to explore what solo singers do on stage with their music and their bodies to communicate with the audience (Davidson, 2000, 2001a). All the data used in these studies came from video recordings of live performances. The performances were given by myself, as a classical singer, and Annie Lennox, as a pop singer. Different musical styles were chosen deliberately to provide contrast within the Western solo performance tradition. These performances were subjected to repeated observations to explore the nature of the behaviours used in communication. My own performances provided the grounding for the subsequent analyses as I could reflect critically on my own actions and attempt to understand my motives—again, the approach was reflexive. Interpretations of all the analyses were obtained by asking two expert musician evaluators for their independent feedback and commentaries on the raw material, and the interpretations of it.

The analyses (derived from emergent themes from the observations, in line with Interpretative Phenomenological Analysis; see Smith, 1995) revealed that during the course of a full 1 hour programme, I used a small number of communicative gestures of seemingly very different types. Observations suggested that they were expressive of the following.

1. Movements directly related to material in the texts of the poems: for instance, a priest giving a sermon was portrayed with outstretched preacher-like gestures.

2. Movements linking together sections of the music or ideas between musical passages: for example, both hands in a slow moving 'begging dog' position to connect one phase end to the opening of the next song.

3. Gestures with clear technical orientation: for example, lifting and turning hand and forearm 'illustrating' the action of the soft palette lifting.

4. Movements of direct instructional nature about musical entrances and exits to the accompanist—such as head nods to indicate 'now'.

These movements were interpreted as being:

1. performance process-oriented—to assist the moment-by-moment issues of co-ordination—making the performance start, remain fairly co-ordinated and finish;

2. expressive of my emotional intention; and

3. rhetorical in terms of both the narrative of the poem and the music.

Additionally, they revealed a 'story' about how I had been trained to move to produce the performance. The palette-lifting gesture, for example, presumably had been learned in singing lessons and then integrated into my behaviour in performance. I also preserved a fairly intense forward body posture, with my eye contact being maintained with the audience. It was evident that my whole focus was towards communicating these different elements of myself to the audience.

When observing the film footage, I was struck by the 'larger-than-life' presentation, and my seemingly spontaneous adoption of stereotypical behaviours such as the use of rather exaggerated frowns and poses. I realized that I was indeed producing what the assessors in the conservatory study I had undertaken with Coimbra had specified as being prerequisites to good, publically projected communication. There was information of an intimate and personal nature (themes of love, mothering, etc. were all present and communicated in the movements and sounds I produced), but all were formalized and clearly codified in a stereotypical manner of presentation. In other words, it was a mildly abstracted representation of 'real' behaviour, but presented in a symbolic form. The video observations led me and the independent observers to note that throughout the performance I seemed fully engaged in the performance task, and that my behaviours seemed to engage the audience—the behaviours were certainly easy to decode in the analysis process. The value of the symbolic and representational nature of the behaviours seemed to be that the audience had the potential to perceive me in the role of 'performer', but I also believed that they saw some of the 'real' me too, i.e. the private, personal me behind the abstracted behaviours.

To pursue these matters further, I undertook two very detailed analyses of Annie Lennox singing 'Who's that girl?' from the videos of concerts in Central Park, New York in 1995, and at London Docklands in 1999 (video references BMG 74321 333213 and BMG 74321 743473) (see Davidson, 2001a for full details). I codified all behaviours that accompanied the singing in terms of Ekman and Friesen's (1969) classification, looking specifically for the following: *adaptors* (movements of self-stimulation such as touching the face or scratching the head); *regulators* (typically, movements punctuating turn-taking and entrances and exits in conversation); *illustrators* (gestures that clearly demonstrate what is being said such as miming the holding and rocking of a baby whilst talking about one); and *emblems* (gestures with learned cultural meanings such as a 'thumb's up' to indicate 'good' in some cultures).

These analyses provided extremely useful data, demonstrating a similar array of gestures to those I had used—marking musical entrances and exits, movements illustrating texts, etc.—but one notable exception was an overt display solely for the audience's benefit which was given the label 'show', and which was not connected to the musical or textual content of the songs. 'Show' may be a critical feature of live pop performance where there is arguably a more overt social requirement to entertain the audience—pop audiences typically participate more directly in the performance by singing and dancing along to the songs. Also, the audience typically is very large and often far away so that such demonstrations may be more appropriate to the performance space as well as the performance culture. Indeed, perhaps I did not engage in 'show' because it is not part of the classical tradition to make such overt gestures. Also, my audience was in a small concert room and so I did not need to make such extravagant gestures in order to draw the audience into my interpretation of the songs. Of course, I am aware that classical singers such as Luciano Pavarotti do 'show off' to their audiences—for instance, mopping the brow with a handkerchief to indicate the hard work involved in singing all those top Cs. However, his performances most typically occur in large concert venues where he does not have any sense of personal contact with the audience. Additionally, and perhaps critically, Annie Lennox and Luciano Pavarotti both occupy positions of 'star status' where promotion of themselves is just as important as the communication of the musical message.

Frith (1996) gives support to the suggestions above, noting that singers in the popular tradition deal with three roles on stage: the 'character' of the person singing the song; their role as 'stars' with all the accompanying stage etiquette; and the more stable personal traits and characteristics normally associated with their personality. Analysis of my own performance focuses more on the moment-by-moment issues of the performance context, but it does illustrate the different elements of self being presented to the audience; however, I do not have to deal with the 'star' status and so do not engage my audience in the same way. The audience does not have such an expectation of me.

Obviously, further studies are necessary before firm conclusions can be drawn. For example, it would be interesting to examine performers on different instruments to investigate whether the labelling of emblem, illustrator, 'show', etc. are robust categories; it would also be useful to study performers giving performances of the same repertoire in different contexts. Such studies could deal with questions about how the performer emerges, and how a 'performance personality' is more or less successfully developed.

To summarize the findings presented in this section, it seems that a key part of a good performance is for the soloist to 'show off' to the audience. Indeed, it seems that to have a performance personality is to be able to 'show off' in a number of different ways. The main point to emerge from the video data is that the singer needs to 'show off' in a culturally appropriate manner.

Final word

It is evident that many factors contribute to a person developing an identity as a 'solo performer'. The reflexive approach I have adopted certainly reveals that recognizable characteristics exist which give performers the confidence and zeal to thrive in the performing context. Apparently I possess these characteristics, and Steve does not. Whilst some aspects of the performer's identity, such as extraversion, may be less susceptible to training than others, many aspects are plastic and can be both learned and trained. It would seem, therefore, that it is possible for some individuals who make music to develop a sense of themselves as being 'performers'. Of course, as is the case for Steve, performer characteristics may not be desirable for all musicians.

References

Bayley, N. (1970). Development of mental ability. In P. Mussen (ed.), *Carmichael's Manual of Child Psychology*, Vol. 1, pp. 231–254. New York: Wiley.

Berry, R. (2000). *Jung*. London: Hodder and Stoughton.

Boal, A. (1992). *Games for Non-actors*. London: Routledge.

Burland, K. and Davidson, J.W. (2002). Training the talented. *Music Education Research*. **4**(1), 123–142.

Collier, J.L. (1983). *Louis Armstrong: An American Genius*. Oxford: Oxford University Press.

Davidson, J.W.(1993). Visual perception of performance manner in the movements of solo musicians. *Psychology of Music*, **21**, 103–113.

Davidson, J.W. (1995). What does the visual information contained in music performances offer the observer? Some preliminary thoughts. In R. Steinberg (ed.), *The Music Machine: Psychophysiology and Psychopathology of the Sense of Music*, pp. 103–115. Heidelberg: Springer.

Davidson, J.W. (1997). The social in musical performance. In D.J. Hargreaves and A.C. North (ed.), *The Social Psychology of Music*, pp. 209–228. Oxford: Oxford University Press.

Davidson, J.W. (2000). Exploring the body in the production and perception of performance. In Woods, C., Luck, G.B., Brochard, R., O'Neill, S.A. and Sloboda, J.A. (ed.), *Proceedings of the Sixth International Conference on Music Perception and Cognition*. Keele, Staffordshire, UK: Department of Psychology. CD-ROM.

Davidson, J.W. (2002). Understanding the expressive movements of a solo pianist. *Musikpsychologie*. V, 235–256.

Davidson, J.W. (2001a). The role of the body in the production and perception of solo vocal performance: a case study of Annie Lennox. *Musicae Scientiae*. V, 235–256.

Davidson, J.W. and Coimbra, D.C.C. (2001). Investigating performance evaluation by assessors of singers in a music college setting. *Musicae Scientiae*, **5**, 33–54.

Davidson, J.W., Howe, M.J.A. and Sloboda, J.A. (1997). Environmental factors in the development of musical performance skill in the first twenty years of life. In D.J. Hargreaves and A.C. North (ed.), *The Social Psychology of Music*, pp. 188–203. Oxford: Oxford University Press,

Dweck, C.S. (2000). *Self Theories: Their Role in Motivation, Personality and Development*. New York: Psychology Press.

Dweck, C.S. and Bempechat, J. (1983). Children's theories of intelligence. In S. Paris, G. Olsen and H. Stevenson (ed.), *Learning and Motivation in the Classroom*, pp. 56–71. Hillsdale, NJ: Erlbaum.

Ekman, P. and Friesen, W.V. (1969). The repertory of nonverbal behaviour: categories, origins, usage, and coding. *Semiotica*, **1**, 49–98.

Ellis, A. and Beattie, G. (1986). *The Psychology of Language and Communication*. London: Weidenfield and Nicolson.

Evans, A. (1994). *The Secrets of Musical Confidence*. London: Thorsons.

Frith, S. (1996). *Performance Rites*. Oxford: Oxford University Press.

Forrester, M. (2000). *Psychology of the Image*. London: Psychology Press.

Geen, R.G., Beatty, W.W. and Arkin, R.M. (1984). *Human Motivation: Physiological, Behavioural and Social Approaches*. Boston: Allyn & Bacon.

Gellrich, M. (1991). Concentration and tension. *British Journal of Music Education*, 8, 167–79.

Goffman, E. (1979). *Gender Advertisement*. London: Macmillan.

Green, B. and Gallwey, W.T. (1987). *The Inner Game of Music*. New York: Pan.

Kemp. A.E. (1996). *The Musical Temperament*. Oxford: Oxford University Press.

Lehmann, A.C. (1997). The acquisition of expertise in music: efficiency of deliberate practice as a moderating variable in accounting for sub-expert performance. In I. Deliege and J.A. Sloboda (ed.), *Perception and Cognition of Music*, pp. 161–190. Hove, UK: Psychology Press.

Maidlow, S. and Bruce, R. (1999). The role of psychology research in understanding the sex/gender paradox in music. *Psychology of Music*, 27, 147–158.

Maslow, A.H. (1970). *Motivation and Personality*, 2nd edn. New York: Harper Collins.

O'Neill, S.A. and Boulton, M. (1996). Boys' and girls' preferences for musical instruments: a function of gender? *Psychology of Music*, 24, 171–183.

Sloboda, J.A. (1991). Music structure and emotional response: some empirical findings. *Psychology of Music*, 19, 110–120.

Sloboda, J.A. (1998). Does music mean anything? *Musicae Scientiae*, 2, 21–32.

Sloboda, J.A. and Howe, M.J.A. (1991). Biographical precursors of musical excellence: an interview study. *Psychology of Music*, 19, 3–21.

Smith, J.A. (1995). Semi-structured interviewing. In J.A. Smith, R. Harre and L. van Langenhove (ed.), *Rethinking Methods in Psychology*, pp. 1–26. London: Sage.

Stanislavsky, K. (1967). *An Actor Prepares*. London: Routledge.

Wilson, G. (1997). Performance anxiety. In D.J. Hargreaves and A.C. North (ed.), *The Social Psychology of Music*, pp. 229–245. Oxford: Oxford University Press.

Wubbenhorst, T. (1994). Personality characteristics of music educators and performers. *Psychology of Music*, 22, 63–74.

PART II

DEVELOPING IDENTITIES THROUGH MUSIC

CHAPTER 7

GENDER IDENTITY AND MUSIC

NICOLA DIBBEN

Introduction

All human societies make social distinctions based on gender: for example, many societies label some work as 'women's work' and some as 'men's work', and in the domain of music some kinds of musical activities are deemed 'female' or 'male'. Why should musical activities be gendered in this way? And what role does music have in the psychological sense of oneself as male or female? In this chapter, I present evidence for the role of music in the construction of gender identity. The approach adopted here which provides the explanatory framework for the research reported is a social constructionist perspective (although biological and cognitive approaches are also discussed briefly). Issues addressed in this chapter are the gendering of music as an activity, the gendering of musical practices and tastes, and the way in which musical texts may position the (gendered) subject.

Theories of gender identity and development

Accounts of gender have tended to draw a distinction between (biological) sex, on the one hand (a distinction between male and female, based on differences in chromosomes and the genitals), and socially constructed gender on the other (masculine and feminine, i.e. the characteristics and behaviour ascribed to each of the sexes). For many people, these categories (particularly sex and gender identity) map onto each other: for example, a biological male is likely to think of himself as a boy or a man (although not necessarily) but he may not have a masculine role (i.e. the norm of acceptable behaviour for males in a particular society). This distinction between sex and gender provides the basis for two main views of gender identity which are often framed in terms of the dual influences of biology and of socialization. A commonly accepted view is that biology and the environment interact and that it is this complex interaction which produces the phenomenon we experience; however, many different theoretical positions have been adopted to explain gender identity and development (for a review, see Turner, 1995) and I review some of these briefly here before discussing gender identity from the perspective of the social constructionist position.

The biological perspective maintains that gender characteristics are pre-given, and determined by biological sex; the idea, for example, that women's biological role as mothers makes them inherently more caring. One view of gender development is that biological factors predispose boys and girls to behave in certain ways and to have certain predispositions for learning. A number of hormonal explanations have been proposed: the action of sex hormones on the fetal brain producing brain specialization and later differences; the influence of sex hormones on our thinking and behaviour during adult life; and differences in brain maturation between boys and girls in later life. In addition, socio-biological accounts suggest that genetic and evolutionary factors give rise to gender differences and social organization. In broad terms, this is the idea that genes control human attributes (e.g. aggressiveness) and that the operation of natural and sexual selection has resulted in genetic predispositions of men towards aggression and of women towards nurturing. By basing gender identity on nature, specifically the physical body as the site which sets the boundary of who we are, identity is treated as fixed and transhistorical.

With the emergence of feminist theory in the 1970s, and anthropological and psychological data on the variability of gender roles and behaviour, the role of social factors became increasingly recognized. Feminist writers have been particularly resistant to biological accounts due to the determinism which seems to underlie them, and because they can be read as legitimizing male aggression and sexual exploitation of women as natural and desirable. The evidence for biological influences is equivocal: biological differences between the sexes are less than might be assumed (Kaplan and Rodgers, 1990), and where differences do exist society attaches far greater importance to them than is perhaps warranted (Birke, 1992). In addition, cross-cultural comparisons suggest that gender differences and divisions of labour are not the same in all societies, suggesting that socialization (the acquisition of culturally appropriate values and beliefs) may have a greater influence than biology (see Burr, 1998).

In broad terms, socialization theories suggest that most people develop a stable sense of gender identity in the first few years of life as a consequence of enculturation. Internalizing gender as part of one's personality goes beyond knowing one is male or female—one argument is that as children grow up within a particular society, they undergo 'gender typing', i.e. they integrate culturally defined norms of what is gender-appropriate into their self-concept. Social learning theory applies behaviourist principles of learning to the acquisition of gender, and argues that children learn gendered behaviour from their environment by virtue of reinforcement, punishment and extinction of sex-inappropriate behaviour, and by exposure of boys and girls to different kinds of activities and role models (Mischel, 1970). This theory relies on the concept of 'identification': this is the idea that children spontaneously imitate behaviour without direct training or reward based on an intimate relationship with the person being imitated, although there is also evidence that children imitate adult models even when not directly reinforced for doing so—imitating models who are themselves reinforced (Bandura, 1977).

While the influence of these processes is generally accepted, psychologists question whether this alone is enough to account for gender typing. A second perspective on socialization emphasizes the role of the child's awareness of their own gender identity. Cognitive–developmental theory (Kohlberg, 1966, 1969) argues that children's attitudes and beliefs about gender roles guide their interaction with the environment, i.e. they watch and imitate same-sex models because they are aware that that is what someone of the same sex as themselves does, and they come to value gender-appropriate aspects of themselves positively. From an early age, children categorize other people on the basis of social dimensions, of which gender is one of the first distinctions children make; however, there is evidence that children understand some things about sex and gender before others: by the age of 2 years, children can perform gender labelling (giving the correct gender label to a picture of a person) and are aware of their own gender identity (they can assign a picture of themselves to the correct gender category although they may believe that someone can change genders by changing their clothes or hair); by the age of about 3 years, children are aware of sex stereotypes concerning activities, thus children become aware of sex stereotypes of musical behaviours—both of real differences (such as the fact that the majority of drummers in pop groups are men) and of widely held beliefs (such as whether boys or girls should play which kinds of musical instrument). However, according to cognitive–developmental theory, it is not until the age of 6 or 7 years, with the understanding of gender constancy, that it is possible for motivations to emerge to adopt particular behaviours: once they know what they are, children turn to the cultural expectations for people of their own sex and come to value sex-appropriate behaviour. According to this perspective, identification is an outcome of gender typing, not a cause of it. (This theory is not universally accepted, however, because research does not support the idea that children become gender typed only after acquiring a sense of gender constancy.) Although it does not deny social learning theory, cognitive–developmental theory adds to it by suggesting that children socialize themselves to be masculine or feminine. The child models those who are like him or her self and who are high in prestige and competence, and external rewards and punishments are far less important from this perspective.

Underlying many of these socialization theories of gender development is the idea that although gender is not determined by biological sex, it is the social expression of the facts of biological sex difference. However, some critics increasingly doubt there are any core premises from which gender derives: recent research casts doubt on the idea of male/female as a biological absolute opposite and argues that it is a convenient social construct (Kaplan and Rodgers, 1990; Birke, 1992). Categories of sexual difference commonly thought of as immutable turn out to be changeable, and by social influences, not just medical 'discoveries' (Lacqueur, 1990). From classical antiquity to the end of the 17th century, Western popular belief and medical texts depicted a one-sex model of sexual characteristics in which female genitals were seen as an inverted, interior version of male genitals. By the 19th century, however, this view had been discarded in favour of the idea of unbridgeable sexual difference, driven not by new scientific discoveries, but by a need to counter women's demands for full citizenship. From this perspective, the marking of sexual difference through dress, behaviour and a whole range of other domains, including music, is part of a continuing effort to sustain the social definition of gender—an effort that is necessary precisely because the biological differences cannot sustain the gender categories (Connell, 1987).

Instead, some theories draw attention to gender as a learnt phenomenon, and claim that gendered identities are produced by means of repetitions of 'performative' (Butler, 1990) or 'representational' (de Lauretis, 1987) practices. This strand of gender theory has been influenced by Foucault's argument that sex is an effect, a product of discursive practices, rather than an origin. The idea of identity categories as effects of institutions, practices and discourses has been an important influence on gender theory over the last decade. In the words of Simone de Beauvoir (1988) 'one is not born a woman but becomes one', moreover, one is under a cultural compulsion to become a man or a woman (what she refers to as the 'imaginable domain of gender'). Judith Butler goes even further in her critique arguing that not only is sex as culturally constructed as gender, but that there may be no distinction between sex and gender at all (Butler, 1990, p. 7). According to Butler, what produces the phenomenon of 'natural sex'—the apparently natural correlation of bodies with sexes—is the 'sedimentation' of gender norms. In addition, because, according to this view, there is no essence that gender expresses, nor an objective ideal to which it aspires, the acts of gender create the idea of gender:

... gender is always a doing, though not a doing by a subject who might be said to pre-exist the deed ... There is no gender identity behind the expressions of gender; that identity is performatively constituted by the very 'expressions' that are said to be its results. (Butler, 1990, p. 25)

The 'performative' view of gender is congruent with social-constructionist views of identity in which identity is something we *do* rather than something we are (see O'Neill, Chapter 5, this volume). According to this account, language and all symbolic systems provide the concepts with which we think, and our understanding of the world is socially constructed through our interactions. For example, Widdicombe and Woofitt ' ... view identities as *achieved*; not fixed but negotiated products of the ongoing flow of interaction' (Widdicombe and Woofitt, 1995, p. 131).

Through the existence of differences in the kinds of musical behaviours men and women engage in, it is possible to see how music might feasibly play a role in gender development and maintenance. From a biological perspective, differences in male and female aptitudes for music and musical behaviours are a result of biological differences. From the perspective of socialization, music may offer models of culturally appropriate male and female behaviour which act as the basis for imitation and modelling. From the perspective of 'performative' theories of gender, engagement in musical practices may construct and sustain individual or collective identity. It is this last perspective which is explored in the rest of the chapter. I first consider the way in which gender identity is developed and 'performed' through music in these ways, including participation in musical performance and composition, musical tastes and preferences, and collecting, before considering the kinds of gendered representations which music offers.

Musical practices and the construction of gender identity

An observable feature of gender identity is that men and women engage in different kinds of behaviours and activities and are represented in very different ways: for example, in Western culture, women are often portrayed as passive in relation to active male characters, they are shown engaging in a far narrower range of activities than men, and are situated in the domestic rather than the public sphere. These gender roles are also observable in musical behaviour, beliefs and preferences. There is a huge literature on the gender typing of musical practices; therefore, the following gives some illustrative examples rather than a comprehensive overview.

The gendering of music

Within a Western culture structured in terms of a mind–body split, music's appeal to the body predisposes it to be assigned to the feminine. Indeed, feminist scholars have argued that male musicians have compensated for this by emphasizing the rational in music, claiming objectivity and transcendence for it, and prohibiting female participation (McClary, 1991). However, as Richards has argued, one should not essentialize music as feminine or physical, but should consider music as a phenomenon 'which is remade with divergent meanings in its inscription within particular discourses' (Richards, 1998, p. 165). In other words, generalized cultural polarities are useless in understanding taste choices, or the gendering of musical participation; specification is needed of the social relations of particular contexts. It is therefore necessary to look at the way in which gender is enacted in particular musical, historical and cultural contexts.

The gender typing of musical performance and composition

Historically, musical participation has been differentiated by gender: for example, women are largely absent from historical accounts of Western European art music (although not from others; see Koskoff, 1987). Although part of this is a bias in the way in which history has been written (over the past two decades one branch of musicological research has sought to rectify this through compensatory music history; e.g. Neuls-Bates, 1982; Pendle, 1991; Marshall, 1993; Fuller, 1994), it is true that women have been largely absent from many of the more professionalized aspects of European art music composition and performance, having been denied musical training in all but the most domesticated forms of music-making and facilitated in those most affirmative of a patriarchal construction of femininity (Citron, 1993; Green, 1997; Bayton, 1998). For example, women's involvement in domestic music-making in the 18th century (such as playing keyboards as an accompaniment to singing) is congruent with women's association with the private rather than public spheres; and the association of women with nature and the body has made singing a more acceptable activity than some other instruments more associated with technology. Although participation in music in Western cultures is now apparently equally available to men and women, large discrepancies still exist in the extent to which different kinds of musical activities are engaged in. Distinctions between the kinds of musical practices men and women engage in also exist in many other cultures (Koskoff, 1987). In this section, I review some of the evidence for gender roles in music and the way in which they participate in the construction of gender identity.

One area of study of the operation of gendered musical practices and meanings has been in the school music classroom. In her book *Music, Gender, Education*, Lucy Green uses the school music classroom to illuminate processes involved in the construction of gender identity through musical participation, beliefs and preferences. Using questionnaires, interviews and observation, Green found a number of widely held beliefs about the gender-appropriateness of musical practices: according to teachers, girls were more successful at singing (a belief which agreed with pupil's perceptions), girls were more active as instrumentalists and more involved in classical music, and girls' attitudes were understood by teachers as linked to 'expressivity', 'decoration' and 'delicacy' (Green, 1997, pp. 151–152). Girls were also seen by both pupils and teachers to lack the necessary abilities for composition—a lack which constitutes their femininity. Green argues that boys and girls 'experience their own music as a reflection and legitimation of their own gender identities' (Green, 1997, p. 229), thus boys presented themselves as more positive about their own composition, and positioned their own work positively in relation to others.

As Green notes, girls are not just learning music but negotiating a gender identity, and classical music in school provides an affirmation of gender for girls in the form of a safe and private form of display. For example, studies of preference of music and musical activities among school children have found that while positive attitudes towards music increase with age, girls report more positive attitudes and competence beliefs towards music than boys (Crowther and Durkin, 1982; Eccles *et al.*, 1993), a finding which agrees with Green's study of attitudes to music in school (Green, 1997). Research suggests that music in school generally is regarded as a 'feminine' subject (Boldizar, 1991), although this appears to be changing due to the introduction of music technology into classroom music-making: the performance of popular music involves drums, electronic instruments, and interrupts femininity, which provides a space for masculinity (Comber *et al.*, 1993).

One of the domains in which gender beliefs can be seen to operate most powerfully is in the gender stereotyping of musical instruments (for a review, see O'Neill, 1997). Research has found that children and adolescents stereotype musical instruments as either 'masculine' or 'feminine', and that children display sex differences in their instrumental choices (Crowther and Durkin, 1982) and preferences (Abeles and Porter, 1978). Studies of the kinds of instruments boys and girls (age 9–10 years) would like to play found gender differences, with boys preferring drums, guitar and trumpet, and girls preferring flute, piano and violin (O'Neill and Boulton, 1996). Preferences for musical instruments show age-related differences in gender stereotyping: younger children (age 5 years) showed no differences in the extent to which they preferred instruments viewed by adults as masculine or feminine, whereas older children (age 10 years) showed a marked gender difference (Abeles and Porter, 1978). Research also suggests that boys have a narrower range of 'appropriate' instruments from which to select than girls (Delzell and Leppla, 1992; O'Neill and Boulton, 1996). There is also evidence that parents may encourage their children to choose instruments on the basis of gender stereotypes (Abeles and Porter, 1978).

Children's gender-stereotyped beliefs about musical instruments (and behaviour) have been interpreted within the framework of gender typing, i.e. that these stereotypes form part of gender role development. This kind of behaviour shows that boys are engaging in an avoidance of femininity (O'Neill, 1997)—the equivalent of which (avoidance of masculinity) girls engage in at a later age (Hill and Lynch, 1982). Indeed, Green reports that secondary school teachers interviewed about children's involvement in musical activities in school observed both boys and girls engaging in a restriction of musical activities to gender-stereotyped behaviour (Green, 1993). A consequence of gender boundary violation is that children are far less popular with their peers (O'Neill and Boulton, 1995), thus there is reason to think that social forces are at work affirming this stereotyping. There is some evidence that gender models can be used to overcome gender stereotyping in music but, although these stereotypes seem amenable to change, interventions do not seem to have a lasting effect (O'Neill, 1997).

Evidence from other cultures shows other processes at work in determining children's involvement in music. In his study of Bulgarian music of the 1930s, Rice (1994) points out that gender was one of the most important factors in determining the acquisition of musical skills. While most boys had the opportunity to learn simple instruments such as the shepherd's flute while herding animals, girls were learning domestic skills in the home such as cooking, sewing and weaving, which meant they did not have free hands. Instead, girls sang while they worked, learning songs from the other female family members as they learnt 'female' skills. Rice observes that performance style and the issues dealt with in songs also differed by gender: in particular, the cultural expectation for women to behave with modesty and deference towards men discouraged women from singing in public, and from the explicit displays of improvisation and creativity, which men engaged in more frequently.

Another example is Sugarman's study of Prespa Albanian wedding celebrations (1977). Sugarman argues that Prespa Albanians believe women and men to have different 'natures' and therefore their singing styles are expected to be different. In addition, because they have different roles within the family and community, they are also expected to have different roles as singers and to address different themes within the songs. The activities around these weddings are segregated by gender, as are the song repertoires and performance styles. The polyphonic songs are structured around three vocal lines which move around the same pitch collection, and which therefore require voices with roughly similar tessituras. Women's singing is nasal and muted, as appropriate to an intimate, indoor setting, and is described as 'thin' by the Prespa Albanians. Men, on the other hand, are said to sing with a 'thick' voice (not nasal), a quality associated with the voices of young men, and understood as indicative of strength and virility suitable to the heroic themes of some of the song texts. Whereas there are only two main categories of women's songs, men's songs deal with a much wider range of themes. These examples illustrate the way in which gender can determine the acquisition and display of musical skills, and also the way in which music articulates gender differences which are part of the larger social organization of a community.

Musical taste and gender identity

Taste in music (musical consumption) is viewed within Western culture as personal and as an important way in which we define ourselves and others, because music is culturally positioned as an expressive and affective medium. However, taste is not 'natural' or 'innocent', but central to the way in which people define themselves. Essentially, this view involves a shift from thinking of consumption as the utilitarian fulfillment of needs to consumption as identity construction. Following Bourdieu (1984), the role of taste has been theorized not as 'natural' or 'personal' but as a means by which social distinctions are made (e.g. Frith, 1983; Shepherd, 1991; Richards, 1998).

Studies of musical consumption show clear patterns of gender- and age-based genre preferences (for reviews, see Russell, 1997; Zillman and Gan, 1997). For example, studies of American and British music consumption reveal the importance of dancing (discos and clubs) for women as opposed to men. Dancing is the only out-of-home leisure activity that women engage in more than men (who are more likely to attend a sporting event, attend live concerts and visit the cinema; Central Statistical Office General Household Surveys 1972–1986, cited in Thornton, 1995, p. 103). A preference for 'love songs', romantic popular music and dancing exhibited by young girls has been attributed to an emphasis within female culture on finding a husband and establishing a home (Frith, 1983; McRobbie, 2000).

Distinctions between male and female musical tastes can be interpreted in terms of the maintenance of a positive social identity. Drawing on social identity theory, Tarrant *et al.* (Chapter 8, this volume) argue that the social context in which affiliation with music takes place for adolescents is of central importance: musical preference is an important factor in in-group and out-group membership, for self-esteem and for the maintenance of a positive social identity. According to this perspective, affiliation of groups with particular genres means adolescents associate those groups with the 'meta-information' which that affiliation activates. The music provides extra-musical information on which social judgements are made, and this information is used to form a positive evaluation of an adolescent's own group in order to maintain a positive social identity. Although at a local level, musical tastes may provide a means for males and females to maintain positive social identities, one implication of this perspective is that it may be difficult for females to maintain a positive social identity through music viewed from a larger social perspective. For example, the musical tastes of females are often decried by the media: in the UK, young girls' fandom of boy and girl bands is ridiculed and the bands are criticized for 'artificiality' and 'banality' and juxtaposed to the 'authenticity' of rock (perceived as a male domain). Within this larger social context, it may be difficult for female tastes to affirm a positive social identity since the access to power and resources to define value in the public realm is held primarily by males.

Like Green (1997), Richards' study of adolescents' musical tastes found that boys and girls differentiate themselves in terms of musical preferences. Significantly, however, Richards argues that the difference between boys and girls was in how they spoke about their engagement in music rather than the type of music they listened to. Richards argues for the 'need to consider tastes in music as features of discourse rather than in terms of a more abstracted relationship between the formal characteristics of music and particular subjectivities' (Richards, 1998, p. 172). Both girls and boys were unwilling to invest in fixed taste positions (a strategy commensurate with the need in adolescence to keep tastes and identities mobile) and were only willing to engage in fixing when it was to avoid being attributed with musical tastes which interrupted traditional gender roles.

There is further evidence from ethnographic studies that music's role in identity construction is influenced by social context. For example, Koizumi found that the way in which the gendered meanings of popular music were used by Japanese high school students differed over different contexts (Koizumi, 1999). In formal sites (i.e. a school context), both female and male pupils attempted to conceal their own favourite music, but used different strategies to do so: whereas male pupils subordinated their favourite music to perceived peer tastes, female pupils either mentioned 'safe' artists in the classroom only, or spoke ambiguously to conceal their favourite music. In a semi-formal site (a High School band event), males were much more willing to talk about their own music, even though the music actually performed in the event included conventional and conformant messages. Koizumi argues that in the informal site, pupils no longer needed to worry about the judgements of others and so in this setting engaged in different musical behaviours: for example, the girls participated in music in a way which emphasized physicality (an aspect which is less evident in school settings due to the exclusion of dance from the school curriculum). Empirical research has shown that the preferences expressed by young people change according to the particular social context they are in at any time, highlighting the inappropriateness of attributing any sort of fixity to notions of identity and highlighting the role of musical preference in self-presentation (Finnäs, 1989; Richards, 1998; Koizumi, 1999). These studies highlight the way in which a sense of self arises from social interaction through music, differs according to social context and depends on language—evidence congruent with the social constructionist position (Burr, 1995).

Music, remembering and collecting

One of the primary uses of music which people engage in is that for memory retrieval: remembering key people in their lives, using an associated piece of music to relive an event or emotionally critical moment from the past—often a relationship—and more generally using music as a means of self-recording (as with photographs, diaries, souvenirs and collecting). An ethnographic study by DeNora on the use of music in the lives of British and American women found that music was a significant resource in women's remembering and emotional life (DeNora, 2000, pp. 66–74). Given the masculine stereotype of men's lesser emotional expressivity, one might expect men to report fewer uses of music in this way. Indeed, a study by Christenson and Peterson found that their women participants more frequently described their use of music in terms of 'secondary' (sic) uses (e.g. in order to improve mood, as a background activity, etc.) and they conclude by drawing a distinction between men's use of music as 'central and personal' and women's as 'instrumental and social' (Christenson and Peterson, 1988, p. 299). Using music to achieve what you 'need' is a common way in which people speak about their uses of music for relaxation, for example 'needing' to hear one particular piece of music at a particular moment rather than another. It is not only the use of music in this way which is 'identity work' but the way in which people talk about their 'needs': it is a 'discourse of the self'—a way of creating the self as something we have knowledge into and about (DeNora, 2000).

There is a small amount of evidence that music collecting behaviours are gendered. For example, adolescent boys report spending more money on recordings and hi-fi equipment than do girls (Richards, 1998), and there is some evidence that boys enjoy opportunities to display the quantity and sometimes the range of their collections to a greater extent (Thornton, 1995; Richards, 1998). As with other forms of collecting, record collecting may function as a way of marking out an individual identity in the context of family and friends, as well as acting as a practical form of remembering. Richards also suggests that by acting as a display of earning power, this kind of activity is affirmative of a masculine work ethic and so affirms a particular kind of masculine identity. Richards describes the way in which one boy (David) talks about his collection, describing it in terms of an avoidance of 'emotional' records, and choosing instead on the basis of 'sound' and 'quality' (Richards, 1998, p. 155). The emphasis here is on rational discrimination, choice and control—qualities affirmative of 'macho' masculinity. Interestingly, it is not only the music one likes that turns out to be significant in the construction of identity, but the music one has stopped listening to, and that one must eradicate from the record collection: most people try and deny or laugh at past tastes, although they might hold on to music with personal resonance (Richards, 1998, p. 105; DeNora, 2000, pp. 72–73).

Thus, the kind of music collected, the way collections are used and the act of collecting itself appear to have a gendered basis as part of the way in which a range of musical beliefs, acts and preferences mark gender difference. However, just as in other forms of cultural representation, music not only provides a way of marking and enacting gender, it also presents models of gender. How music 'represents' gender, and how these representations are engaged with, are considered in the next section.

Representations of gender in music

Theories of gender identity suggest that learning of gender-appropriate behaviour is due partly to gender role models offered in the media. A count of the number of representations of men and women in musical activities reveals many inequalities: for example, a study of representations of men and women in popular music television, radio and magazines in the UK during the 1980s and 1990s revealed that more men than women were represented overall, and that when women were featured it was as vocalists rather than as instrumentalists (Bayton, 1998). A second approach to the study of representations is through content analysis, which is used to reveal the messages in those representations. Analysis of music videos shows gender role stereotyping of occupational roles and behaviours in which male characters are more adventurous, assertive and aggressive than females, and in which females are more affectionate, dependent and nurturing (Seidman, 1992; Sommersflanagan *et al.*, 1993). Analysis of 19th century opera has highlighted the way in which these operas require the female heroines' death in order to achieve narrative and tonal resolution (Clément, 1988). However, representations do not simply produce meanings through which we make sense of the world; the social constructionist perspective adopted here argues that representations create the possibilities of what we are, constructing places from which individuals position themselves. This section considers both the signifying practices and symbolic forms through which gendered meanings are produced in music, and the subject positions it offers.

An important strand of 'new musicological' research has been the way in which musical 'works' contribute to constructions of gender. Gender ideologies in music have been investigated through critical readings of (often idealized) performances and works (e.g. McClary, 1991; Walser, 1993; Pfeil, 1995). Most critical enquiry has focused on vocal music (i.e. music with words) due to the grounding this provides for interpretation. In the case of instrumental music, commentaries have often based their gendered readings on the gendered language used by contemporary critics, or on contemporary beliefs about genres and gender appropriateness. Although there is not scope in this chapter to do more than consider the issue briefly, it is worth considering how music comes to be heard in terms of gendered meanings. There are a number of possible sources of gendered meanings in music: for example, the influence of role models engaging in particular kinds of musical activity, the discourse surrounding music and music's accompanying texts, lyrics and images. It has been argued that the texts and other visual images accompanying musical practices (e.g. programme notes, music criticism, musicological discourse) bind together musical structures and gendered meanings, and through these means (through the sedimentation of such meanings in musical material) the music acquires apparently 'inherent' gendered meanings (Green, 1997).

Evidence that listeners hear musical materials in terms of gendered meanings derives from a variety of sources. For example, Tagg (1989) found high levels of agreement between participants regarding the gendered meanings associated with television theme tunes: tunes associated with female characters had a slower average tempo than those for male characters, were legato and tended to change in dynamic level, whereas tunes associated with male characters tended to have more rhythmically and intervallically active bass lines, and greater rhythmic irregularity. Listeners' descriptions also indicated sex stereotyping of instruments (tunes associated with female characters featured the piano, strings, flute and mandolin whereas those associated with male characters were played by electric guitar, trumpet and xylophone) and of genres (female characters were associated with tunes that were classical–romantic or classically modal in tonal language, whereas the male tunes used rock or fusion harmonies).

The associations of particular kinds of musical materials in Western art and popular music with masculinity and femininity can be traced through music history. McClary has argued that, beginning with the rise of opera in the 17th century, composers developed a 'semiotics' of gender—conventions for constructing masculinity and femininity in music (McClary, 1991). Because these codes change over time, studying music can reveal gender organization available at a particular time. McClary's comparison of the delineation of Orfeo and Euridice in Monteverdi's opera L'Orfeo illustrates how the contrast between Orfeo's rhetorical power and Euridice's simplicity and innocence is constructed through tonal–harmonic means (McClary, 1991, pp. 38–48). In Orfeo's aria 'Rosa del ciel', he commands the sun be still and listen to him and his rhetorical power derives from the ability of his song to arouse the expectations and channel the desires of listeners. So, for example, in the opening section, Orfeo's embellished recitation over sustained bass notes not only defies musical conventions of the day, but arouses and controls listener's expectations for tonal and melodic progression (Figure 7.1). Euridice's reply, in contrast, is far less goal-directed than Orfeo's and therefore affirmative of her gender role as a young and innocent female character.

Orfeo presents a paradox for Western conceptions of masculinity: on the one hand he must sing to demonstrate his rhetorical skill and mastery, yet this elaborate display is precisely what threatens to undermine his masculinity. These same contradictions are apparent in contemporary music-making. For example, Walser has argued that Heavy Metal stages fantasies of masculine power and control, signified by technical mastery of the electric guitar, use of vocal extremes, power chords, distortion and sheer volume

Figure 7.1 Monteverdi's 'Rosa del ciel' *L'Orfeo*. Extract showing delaying of tonal expectations. (Cited in McClary, 1991, p. 40.) Reproduced with permission from Cambridge University Press.

(Walser, 1993). Walser points out that the enactment of virtuosity as a signifier of transcendent freedom and controlling power draws upon classical models: see, for example, the references to classical virtuosic style in Van Halen's 'Eruption' (Figure 7.2). Walser argues that the overwhelmingly male teenage audience for Heavy Metal generally lacks social, physical and economic power but is besieged with messages that promote power as an obligatory component of masculinity. The fantasies of masculinity provided by Heavy Metal (and other forms of popular culture) therefore serve as a means by which such power can be enacted and as a way in which fans can confirm and alter their gender identities through involvement with it (Walser, 1993, p. 109).

Figure 7.2 Van Halen's (1978) 'Eruption'. Extract showing reference to classical figuration. (Cited in Walser, 1993, p. 74.) Reproduced with permission from Wesleyan University Press.

The implication of some of these analyses is that music not only provides representations of masculinity and femininity, but that it can encourage listeners to adopt a
particular subject position. This approach derives from film theory. For example,
Mulvey has argued that Hollywood cinema constructs a masculinized gaze which
controls events on screen along with the female image (Mulvey, 1989). Contrast this
with Modleski's reading of soap operas in which the subject position created in this case
is a 'decentreing' which confirms women's domestic position (Modleski, 1982): the
implication of this reading is that the text is able to position the female spectator such
that feminine-stereotyped characteristics such as passivity and self-sacrifice are affirmed
(although subsequent research has criticized these kinds of approaches for producing
generalized readings; e.g. Ang, 1985). Within musicology, critical analyses of particular
works have investigated the way in which musical texts address a particular (gendered)
audience and encourage the listener to take up a particular subject position (e.g. Bradby,
1990; Clarke, 1999; Dibben, 1999, 2000, 2001; Clarke and Dibben, 2000). One issue
highlighted by these commentaries is that music which apparently affirms stereotyped
gender roles can also afford resistant or subversive uses. For example, the Spice Girls
can be viewed as empowering young girls by offering a more independent stance than is
sometimes found in pop music (Dibben, 1999), and flamboyant male performers may
offer a means for men to experience or imagine behaviours which are not normally
available to them. Furthermore, camp performance and the emergence of gay and
bisexual imagery (e.g. Bowie, Madonna) suggest that pop music is one area in which
gender roles and relationships can be explored and assumptions challenged.

As well as positioning listeners in terms of a particular (gendered) subjectivity, music
can have a disciplinary function on the experiencing subject in terms of the kind of physical
involvement it affords. For example, DeNora reports one informant for whom musical
structures provided a way to live out ideal social relationships: one female informant
stated that being an alto in a choir allows her to participate in a group activity without
being in the spotlight (DeNora, 2000, p. 69)—a kind of participation which is affirmative
of a patriarchal construction of femininity as associated with the body (singing), and
with a supportive rather than a leading and, therefore, a displaying role. Matthew Head's
analysis of 18th century German keyboard music for women reveals its disciplining
function in terms of the kinds of physical states and displays it allows, as well as revealing
a rather more ambivalent discourse of bourgeois femininity (Head, 1999).

There are a number of criticisms of the approaches to representation outlined above.
First, although the models offered in such representations have been thought to be an
important source of sex-role information, there has been a failure to theorize how this
influence operates at a psychological level. Identifying the existence of images does not
prove that they cause gender differences and inequalities, and there is debate about the
extent to which messages are taken in. Secondly, much recent research is explicitly
critical of the emphasis on the musical 'work' implicit in the gendered readings offered
by musicologists such as McClary. Indeed, the implication of both DeNora and Richards' research is that the musical 'work' is by and large irrelevant. DeNora argues that

Music takes it meaning from many things apart from its intertextual relationship with other
musical works (and with the history of those works)... equally important to the matter of

music's social 'effects' is the question of how musical materials relate to extra-musical matters such as occasions and circumstances of use, and personal associations... (DeNora, 2000, p. 61).

Much more research is needed into the way in which music is used by people in their everyday lives. This is not to dismiss the analyses provided by musicologists as irrelevant to gender, but to recognize that they are readings made from a particular subject position, with particular political purposes in mind. One role of the kind of critical readings which McClary and others engage in is to circulate meanings of music. Seen in this way, musicological writings are another instance of the way in which gendered meanings are produced, reproduced and (sometimes) laid bare.

Conclusions: the 'gendering' of identity through music

This discussion has presented unequivocal evidence for the marking of gender by musical preferences, beliefs and practices. I have argued that this is part of a wider and continuing effort to sustain the social definition of gender, and a sense of the gendered self. As already mentioned, music constitutes one of the most popular leisure pursuits of young people, it is integrated into people's lives in a way which is particularly unique (music is heard in a wide variety of locations, while on the move and while engaged in other activities) and it affords the repetition necessary to the constant reachievement of identity highlighted by so many theorists (e.g. Walser, 1993). Music, then, is particularly well situated to afford opportunities for the construction of (gender) identity.

One of the issues highlighted by the research presented here is the problematic character of attempting to draw conclusions regarding the way music is used in relation to gender identity alone, since it intersects with other aspects of identity such as generation, socio-economic status, ethnicity, and so on. In addition, there is strong indication that performances of gender are contingent on the context of construction, highlighting the need for research into identity to situate any findings within a particular socio-historical context. Nonetheless, it is possible to identify general processes by which music is involved in the construction of gender identity: identity is constructed through the musical activities people participate in, through their musical preferences and through their beliefs about what constitutes gender-appropriate musical behaviour. The effect of this gender typing, however, is that it constrains the opportunities and engagement with music which are possible for an individual at any particular time.

Analysis of music from the past reveals the differing ways in which gender is encoded in music, and the organization of gender relations in different historical periods. Musical representations of gender may act as models for gender-appropriate behaviour, as a means by which gender beliefs are circulated and as a way of enabling the listener to experience particular gendered subject positions. The ideological power of music to position listeners in this way is easily overlooked when music is viewed simply as 'entertainment'. Music's power to enact and perpetuate gender beliefs should not be underestimated, but neither should music's capacity to afford the exploration of gender identities, which offers individuals the chance to imagine, and perhaps experience, gender positions in a way which might not otherwise be possible.

References

Abeles, H.F. and Porter, S.Y. (1978). The sex-stereotyping of musical instruments. *Journal of Research in Music Education*, **26**, 65–75.

Ang, I. (1985). *Watching Dallas: Soap Opera and the Melodramatic Imagination*. Methuen, New York.

Bandura, A. (1977). *Social Learning Theory*. London: Prentice-Hall.

Bayton, M. (1998). *Frock Rock: Women Performing Popular Music*. Oxford: Oxford University Press.

Birke, L. (1992). In pursuit of difference: scientific studies of women and men. In G. Kirkup and L.S. Keller (ed.), *Inventing Women: Science, Technology and Gender*, pp. 81–102. Cambridge: Polity Press/The Open University.

Boldizar, J.P. (1991). Assessing sex typing and androgyny in children: The Children's Sex Role Inventory. *Developmental Psychology*, **27**, 505–515.

Bourdieu, P. (1984). *Distinction: A Social Critique of the Judgement of Taste*. London: RKP.

Bradby, B. (1990). Do-talk and don't talk: the division of the gendered subject in Girl-Group music. In S. Frith and A. Goodwin (ed.), *On Record: Rock, Pop and the Written Word*, pp. 341–368. New York: Pantheon.

Burr, V. (1995). *An Introduction to Social Constructionism*. Routledge, London.

Burr, V. (1998). *Gender and Social Psychology*. London: Routledge.

Butler, J. (1990). *Gender Trouble: Feminism and the Subversion of Identity*. London: Routledge.

Christenson, P. and Peterson, J.B. (1988). Genre and gender in the structure of musical preferences. *Communication Research*, XV/3, June.

Citron, M. (1993). *Gender and the Musical Canon*. Cambridge: Cambridge University Press.

Clarke, E.F. (1999). Subject-position and the specification of invariants in music by Frank Zappa and P.J. Harvey. *Music Analysis*, **18**, 347–374.

Clarke, E.F. and Dibben, N. (2000). Sex, Pulp and critique. *Popular Music*, **19**, 231–241.

Clément, C. (1988). *Opera or the Undoing of Women*. Minnesota: University of Minnesota Press.

Comber, C., Hargreaves, D.J. and Colley, A. (1993). Girls, boys and technology in music education. *British Journal of Music Education*, **10**, 123–34.

Connell, R. (1987). *Gender and Power*. Cambridge: Polity Press.

Crowther, R. and Durkin, K. (1982). Sex- and age-related differences in the musical behaviour, interests and attitudes towards music of 232 secondary school students. *Educational Studies*, **20**, 13–18.

de Beauvoir, S. (1988). *The Second Sex* (translated and edited by H.M. Parshley). London: Pan Books.

de Lauretis, T. (1989). *Technologies of Gender*. Basingstoke, UK: Macmillan.

Delzell, J.K. and Leppla, D.A. (1992). Gender associations of musical instruments and preferences of fourth grade students for selected instruments. *Journal of Research in Music Education*, **40**, 93–103.

DeNora, T. (2000). *Music in Everyday Life*. Cambridge: Cambridge University Press.

Dibben, N. (1999). Representations of femininity in popular music. *Popular Music*, **18**, 331–355.

Dibben, N. (2000). The sound of 'Synthetic Fury': dance music, machines and masculinity. *Review of Popular Culture*, **11**, 75–84.

Dibben, N. (2001). Pulp, pornography and spectatorship. *Journal of the Royal Musical Association*, **126**, 83–106.

Eccles, J., Wigfield, A. Harold, R.D. and Blumenfeld, P. (1993). Age and gender differences in children's self- and task perceptions during elementary school. *Child Development,* **64**, 830–847.

Finnäs, L. (1989). A comparison between young people's privately and publicly expressed musical preferences. *Psychology of Music,* **17**, 132–145.

Foucault, M. (1984). *The History of Sexuality,* Vol. 1. Harmondsworth, UK: Penguin.

Frith, S. (1983). *Sound Effects: Youth, Leisure and the Politics of Rock 'n' roll.* London: Constable.

Fuller, S. (1994). *The Pandora Guide to Women Composers: Britain and the United States 1629–present.* London: Harper Collins.

Green, L. (1997). *Music, Gender, Education.* Cambridge: Cambridge University Press.

Head, M. (1999). 'If the pretty little hand won't stretch': music for the fair sex in eighteenth-century Germany. *Journal of the American Musicological Society,* **52**, 203–254.

Hill, J.P. and Lynch, M.E. (1982). The intensification of gender-related expectations during early adolescence. In J. Brooks-Gunn and A.C. Petersen (ed.), *Girls at Puberty: Biological and Psychological Perspective,* pp. 201–229. New York: Plenum.

Kaplan, G.T. and Rodgers, L.J. (1990). The definition of male and female: biological reductionism and the sanctions of normality. In S. Gunew (ed.), *Feminist Knowledge: Critique and Construct,* pp. 205–228. London: Routledge.

Kohlberg, L. (1966). A cognitive–developmental analysis of children's sex-role concepts and attitudes. In E.E. Maccoby (ed.), *The Development of Sex Differences,* pp. 82–173. Stanford: Stanford University Press.

Kohlberg, L. (1969). Stages and sequences: the cognitive–developmental approach to socialization. In D.A. Goslin (ed.), *Handbook of Socialization Theory and Research,* pp. 347–380. Chicago: Rand McNall.

Koskoff, E. (ed.) (1987). *Women and Music in Cross-Cultural Perspective.* Westport, CT: Greenwood Press.

Koizumi, K. (1999). Koukousei to popular ongaku [High school students and popular music: an ethnography of the process of 'being gendered' in educational sites] In J. Kitagawa (ed.), *Narihibiku sei: Popular Music and Gender in Japan.* Tokyo: Keiso Shobo.

Lacqueur, T. (1990). *Making Sex: Body and Gender from the Greeks to Freud.* Cambridge, MA: Harvard University Press.

Marshall, K. (ed.) (1993). *Rediscovering the Muses: Women's Musical Traditions.* Boston: Northeastern University Press.

McClary, S. (1991). *Feminine Endings: Music, Gender and Sexuality.* Minneapolis: University of Minnesota Press.

McRobbie, A. (2000). *Feminism and Youth Culture,* 2nd edn. Basingstoke, UK: Macmillan.

Mischel, W. (1970). Sex typing and socialization. In P.H. Mussen (ed.), *Carmichael's Manual of Child Psychology,* Vol. 2, 3rd edn, pp. 3–72. New York: Wiley.

Modleski, T. (1982). The search for tomorrow in today's soap operas. *Loving With a Vengeance: Mass Produced Fantasies for Women.* New York: Routledge.

Mulvey, L. (1989). Visual pleasure and narrative cinema. In *Visual and Other Pleasures.* Basingstoke, UK: Macmillan.

Neuls-Bates, C. (ed.) (1982). *Women in Music: An Anthology of Source Readings from the Middle Ages to the Present.* New York: Harper & Row.

O'Neill, S.A. (1997). Gender and music. In D.J. Hargreaves and A.C. North (ed.), *The Social Psychology of Music,* pp. 46–60. Oxford: Oxford University Press.

O'Neill, S.A. and Boulton, M.J. (1995). Is there a gender bias towards musical instruments? *Music Journal*, **60**, 358–359.

O'Neill, S.A. and Boulton, M.J. (1996). Boys' and girls' preferences for musical instruments: a function of gender? *Psychology of Music*, **24**, 171–183.

Pendle, K. (ed.) (1991). *Women and Music: A History*. Bloomington and Indianapolis: Indiana University Press.

Pfeil, F. (1995). *White Guys: Studies in Postmodern Domination and Difference*. London: Verso.

Rice, T. (1994). *May it Fill Your Soul. Experiencing Bulgarian Music*. Chicago: University of Chicago Press.

Richards, C. (1998). *Teen Spirits: Music and Identity in Media Education*. London: UCL Press.

Russell, P.A. (1997). Musical tastes and society. In D.J. Hargreaves and A.C. North (ed.), *The Social Psychology of Music*, pp. 141–158. Oxford: Oxford University Press.

Seidman, S.A. (1992). An investigation of sex-role stereotyping in music videos. *Journal of Broadcasting and Electronic Media*, **36**, 209–216.

Shepherd, J. (1991). *Music as Social Text*, pp. 174–185. Cambridge: Polity Press.

Sommersflanagan, R., Sommersflanagan, J. and Davis, B. (1993). What's happening on music television: a gender-role content analysis. *Sex Roles*, **28**, 745–753.

Sugarman, J.C. (1997). *Engendering Song: Singing and Subjectivity at Prespa Albanian Weddings*. Chicago: University of Chicago Press.

Tagg, P. (1989). An anthropology of stereotypes in TV music. *Swedish Musicological Journal*, 19–42.

Thornton, S. (1995). *Club Cultures: Music, Media and Subcultural Capital*. Cambridge: Polity Press.

Turner, P.J. (1995). *Sex, Gender and Identity*. Leicester, UK: British Psychological Society.

Walser, R. (1993). *Running With the Devil: Power, Gender and Madness in Heavy Metal Music*. Hanover: Weslyan University Press.

Widdicombe, S. and Wooffitt, R. (1995). *The Language of Youth Subcultures*. Sussex, UK: Harvester Wheatsheaf.

Zillman, D. and Gan, S.-L. (1997). Musical taste in adolescence. In D.J. Hargreaves and A.C. North (ed.), *The Social Psychology of Music*, pp. 161–187. Oxford: Oxford University Press.

CHAPTER 8

YOUTH IDENTITY AND MUSIC

MARK TARRANT, ADRIAN C. NORTH AND
DAVID J. HARGREAVES

Several recent publications have focused on the role of music in young people's lives (e.g. Larson, 1995; Zillmann and Gan, 1997; North and Hargreaves, 1999; North *et al.*, 2000; Welch, 2001). A prevalent theme throughout this research is the distinction between musical behaviour which takes place in formal (in school) and informal (out of school) contexts. Whilst this distinction is unproblematic at primary level (see Mills, 1997; Lamont, Chapter 3, this volume), at secondary level it becomes especially prominent as adolescents begin to devalue school-organized music, and instead begin to favour musical activities that they can organize themselves (Boal-Palheiros and Hargreaves, 2001).

This chapter explores how the needs of the adolescent and adolescent development more generally contribute to this shift in the nature of musical activity. We consider the relationship between identity and music from two theoretical perspectives. First, we consider research which focuses on the identity 'status' of the individual at any given time (see Marcia, 1966), and then contrast this with research from a 'social identity perspective' (Tajfel, 1978a; Tajfel and Turner, 1979) which emphasizes the contribution of the social (peer) group in structuring musical behaviour. The latter has not been investigated extensively in the music literature, and we believe that it can promote a more comprehensive understanding of musical behaviour in adolescence, and across the lifespan as a whole.

Identity in adolescence

Although there is often disagreement about many of the processes of adolescence, it is undoubtedly a period associated with an increasing self-awareness and confidence in one's identity (Waterman, 1982; Arnett, 1995a). A prominent approach to the study of identity remains that espoused by Marcia (1966, 1980; see Erikson, 1968). Research in this tradition portrays the adolescent as experiencing an 'identity crisis' which involves the exploration of various possible identities. This crisis subsequently is resolved through a commitment to a particular identity (Marcia, 1966; see Newman and Newman, 1988).

Marcia identified four identity 'states' which characterize this process, namely diffusion, foreclosure, moratorium and achievement. Identity 'diffusion' refers to an absence of commitment to a particular identity (which may or may not be accompanied by identity exploration). This is a state typically experienced in early adolescence. Identity 'foreclosure' represents a commitment to an identity without the prior experience of an identity crisis (e.g. when an adolescent pursues a particular occupation because his or her parents are already employed in that field). Identity 'moratorium' refers to a state of identity crisis in which the individual may have engaged in some exploration of altern-ative identities, but has yet to make a firm commitment to one particular identity. Finally, an adolescent in a state of identity 'achievement' has explored alternative iden-tities, has experienced a crisis and has made a commitment to a particular identity which currently is being pursued.

Music and identity development

The media (including television and magazines) provide important sources of informa-tion and advice upon which decisions about identity can be made (Swidler, 1986; Arnett, 1995a,b; see Kleiber *et al.*, 1986; Shaw *et al.*, 1995). Adolescents' involvement with music in particular has attracted considerable attention in this regard. Patterns of this involve-ment have been reviewed extensively only recently (Zillmann and Gan, 1997), and it is not necessary to repeat these here. Suffice it to say that a consistent observation of research has been that involvement with (mainly popular) music is especially prominent during adolescence, and that this appears to be greater than involvement with other forms of media (Lyle and Hoffman, 1972; Davis, 1985; Larson *et al.*, 1989; Geter and Streisand, 1995). Indeed, for many adolescents, listening to music is *the* most preferred leisure activity (Fitzgerald *et al.*, 1995), and many regard music as one of their most special, important or treasured possessions (Kamptner, 1995).

Drawing on some of the processes which characterize identity formation, researchers have suggested that the appeal of music during adolescence stems from its ability to address salient developmental issues (Larson and Kubey, 1983; see also Bleich *et al.*, 1991). These issues, or 'developmental tasks' (Roscoe and Peterson, 1984), include acquiring a set of values and beliefs, performing socially responsible behaviour, devel-oping emotional independence from parents and achieving mature relations with peers (Coleman, 1979; Palmonari *et al.*, 1990; Kirchler *et al.*, 1993). Although empirical research is lacking, it seems that one of the appeals of music to adolescents lies in its ability to help them cope with the fluctuations in mood to which these tasks naturally give rise (e.g. Wooten, 1992; Arnett, 1995a; Larson, 1995; see also Lyle and Hoffman, 1972; Kurdek, 1987).

This potential of music was demonstrated recently in a study by North *et al.* (2000) who questioned British adolescents directly about their motivations for listening to music. Participants ($n = 2465$) aged 13–14 years were presented with a list of 12 potential reasons why people might listen to music, and were asked to indicate the degree to which each reason explained their own listening behaviour. Three factors accounted for the participants' responses, the first of which was listening to music in order to 'fulfil emotional needs' (p. 263). Items which loaded highest on this factor included 'listening to relieve tension and stress' and 'listening to express emotions'.

However, adolescents' use of music seems to extend beyond that of mood regula-tion. The second factor identified in North *et al.*'s study suggested that music listening might be guided by impression management needs. Indeed, this factor actually explained *more* of the variance in responses than did the previous factor, and comprised items such as 'listening in order to create a particular self-image', 'listening to be trendy/cool' and 'listening in order to please others' (e.g. peers). A near-identical factor resolution was reported by Tarrant *et al.* (2000) in their study of British and American adolescents (see also Roe, 1985; Sun and Lull, 1986; Behne, 1997; Sloboda *et al.*, 2000).

It is not yet clear whether overt displays of one's musical allegiance are guided specifically by identity needs, although there is good reason to believe that they might be. Adolescence research has long acknowledged the role of the social context in identity formation, and has shown how adolescents rely increasingly on others in their peer network when forming self-evaluations (Coleman, 1979; Larson and Richards, 1991; Robinson, 1995). The importance of this peer network is reflected by evidence that most adolescents report belonging to a peer group and are motivated to maintain good relations with their groups (Palmonari *et al.*, 1990; Kirchler *et al.*, 1993; Heaven, 1994). By demonstrating appropriate musical behaviour, therefore, adolescents may maintain the positive relations with their peer groups necessary for successful identity development (cf. Buhrmester, 1992; Parkhurst and Asher, 1992).

Early support for this idea was provided by Brown and O'Leary (1971). These authors identified a positive relationship between adolescents' perceived knowledge about Top 10 music and the number of times they were nominated as popular by class mates: the more informed they were about popular music, the more popular they were with peers (see also Johnstone and Katz, 1957; Adoni, 1978). Yet, peer relations are not maintained solely through the expression of musical *likes*: adolescents are equally aware of the importance of showing others the kinds of music that they *dislike*. For example, adolescents in Finnäs' (1989) study reported different degrees of liking for 'unpopular' music depending on whether ratings were made in private or in the company of peers. Specifically, ratings were least favourable when they had to be stated publicly.

Brown and O'Leary (1971) and Finnäs (1989) highlight the importance placed by adolescents on their peer network when making decisions about musical preference. Their findings reiterate the argument that the social context is a crucial factor in the musical behaviour of adolescents (as for other age groups; see, for example, Konecni, 1982; Hargreaves and North, 1997; North *et al.*, 2002). Whilst the 'ego-psychological' approach to identity espoused by Marcia (1966, 1980) and others acknowledges the role of the social (peer) context in identity formation, its primary focus is on the identity 'status' of the *individual* (see Jackson and Bosma, 1992; Waterman, 1982). Whilst this approach is useful in so far as it can help identify individual factors in musical behaviour (e.g. adolescents' uses of music to regulate mood), it might be limited in its ability to explain the wider impact of the peer group on that behaviour.

An alternative approach to identity which focuses more on the social group context is research in the tradition of 'social identity theory' (or SIT; see Tajfel, 1978a; Tajfel and Turner, 1979). Although not developed specifically to explain adolescent development, we believe that this approach offers a model of identity which will give more insights into adolescents' musical behaviour than those which emerge from the ego-psychological approach alone (cf. Jackson and Bosma 1992).

Social identity theory

Social identity theory (SIT) starts from the assumption that we are all members of social groups, whether these be large-scale social categories such as gender or race to which individuals are ascribed automatically, or smaller scale categories such as peer groups, for which membership usually is earned (Tajfel, 1981). The categorization of the self as a member of a particular group (the 'in-group') necessarily excludes certain other individuals (who are categorized as members of an 'out-group'). According to the theory, this categorization instigates a sense of self—a social identity—which guides behaviour. This identity can be contrasted with that which is salient in the absence of any obvious social categorization. In such instances, the self is defined in terms of personal, idiosyncratic attributes such as personality and/or physical and intellectual traits, and is referred to accordingly as personal identity.

In SIT, interactions between two or more people can be distinguished according to whether they are guided predominantly by personal identity or by social identity. When personal identity is salient, behaviour is based on individual characteristics only. This is referred to as *interpersonal* behaviour. When social identity is salient, behaviour is based upon an acknowledgement of one's own and others' group membership. When the subjects of the interaction come from different groups, behaviour is referred to as *intergroup* behaviour (Tajfel and Turner, 1979).

For Tajfel (1978a), the distinction between interpersonal behaviour and intergroup behaviour is largely theoretical. He argues that it would not be possible to engage in an encounter that is not somehow influenced by a social category membership (e.g. such as gender). However, behaviour of a purely intergroup nature is possible: an individual could act entirely in terms of his or her group membership, particularly when there is no face-to-face contact (e.g. such as when an air force bombs an enemy country—see Tajfel, 1978a). What is important, though, is the degree to which individuals perceive the interaction as being predominantly interpersonal or intergroup in nature. The more the situation is perceived as an intergroup one, the more uniform individuals' attitudes and behaviour will be towards the out-group (cf. Linville and Jones, 1980).

According to SIT, the presence of a social categorization motivates individuals to behave in ways which secure a positive evaluation of the in-group. This is achieved through a process of social comparison (cf. Festinger, 1954). By comparing the in-group and an out-group, in-group members should be able to portray their group more positively, or as somehow 'better off' than the out-group. In doing so, they are able to fulfil the need for positive social identity and self-esteem (Tajfel, 1978a; see also Abrams and Hogg, 1988).

Numerous studies have tested this hypothesis. In a series of experiments, Tajfel and his colleagues demonstrated the basic effects of social categorization through experiments involving what has become known as the 'minimal group paradigm'(e.g. Tajfel *et al.*, 1971; Billig and Tajfel, 1973). In a typical experiment, participants were allocated to one of two groups on the basis of some arbitrary task (e.g. such as an aesthetic preference task). Following this, participants were introduced to the experimental task which required them to distribute resources (e.g. money) among different members of the in-group and the out-group.

Participants in these studies have shown remarkable consistency in their behaviour. Rather than operating on a principle of fairness, or on one which ensures the maximum reward possible for the in-group, participants typically choose the option of 'maximum difference': they assign the most resources possible to the in-group and the least possible to the out-group. These studies have provided the clearest demonstration that the act of merely categorizing people into groups is sufficient to promote behaviour which ensures positive outcomes for the in-group (see also Turner *et al.*, 1979; Howard and Rothbart, 1980; Hunter *et al.*, 1996).

Social identity in adolescence

The potential benefits of a social identity approach to the study of adolescent identity have been outlined in the research literature (e.g. Gavin and Furman, 1989; Palmonari *et al.*, 1990; Jackson and Bosma, 1992; Cotterell, 1996; see also Widdicombe and Wooffitt, 1995). This work suggests that adolescents make group-based social comparisons in order to secure a positive evaluation of their peer groups, and hence maintain a positive self-concept (cf. Sherif *et al.*, 1961). In short, the benefits derived from peer group membership in adolescence are seen as being realized through intergroup processes (see Cotterell, 1996).

The few studies that have addressed these predictions generally support the theory. Following Palmonari *et al.*'s (1990) study of American adolescents, Tarrant (2002) investigated the peer group behaviour of male and female adolescents in the UK. Participants made a series of comparisons between the characteristics of their own peer group and those of a self-nominated out-group. As expected, participants evaluated their own group consistently more favourably than the out-group. Specifically, the in-group was described as being, amongst other things, more 'fun', more 'honest' and more 'intelligent' than the out-group, and as less 'boring', less 'ignorant' and less 'unfriendly' than the out-group.

Tarrant *et al.* (2001b) extended this research by investigating how adolescents used social and passive pursuits (rather than trait adjectives) in forming an appropriate social identity. Again, participants demonstrated the intergroup bias so often observed in traditional tests of SIT. The in-group was perceived to be more interested in, and better at, pursuits which were valued positively (e.g. enjoyment and knowledge of media), and the out-group was perceived to be more interested in, and better at, pursuits which were valued negatively (e.g. enjoyment of academic pursuits). These two studies also offered support for the hypothesized relationship between discrimination and social identity: in both studies, those participants who reported the highest levels of discrimination also reported the highest levels of group identification (cf. Hinkle *et al.*, 1989).

Musical behaviour and the maintenance of social identity

The application of SIT to the study of adolescence is a relatively new line of enquiry which might also make a valuable contribution to the social psychology of music. Since peer groups are such a central feature of adolescence (Coleman, 1974; Palmonari *et al.*, 1990) and since adolescents are motivated to form positive evaluations of these groups, then statements about music might contribute to identity formation by facilitating intergroup differentiation. In other words, we propose that a major appeal of music to adolescents lies in its ability to help them form positive social identities.

Of course, this proposal is not entirely novel. Sociological research has already acknowledged the potential identity-serving function of affiliation with music. In this literature, statements about music are seen to act as a label, or 'badge' of identification (e.g. Frith, 1981), upon which judgements about someone's likely group membership can be made (see Denholm *et al.*, 1992). Ultimately, it is suggested that such judgements can form a basis for discriminatory behaviour. For example, Dolfsma (1999) suggested that the 'badge' function of music helps adolescents express a particular identity which serves to differentiate their peer groups from others (cf. Russell 1997), and in his ethnographic study of Bruce Springsteen fans, Cavicchi (1998) showed how fans go to considerable lengths to reinforce this differentiation by emphasizing the qualities of 'real' versus 'ordinary' listeners. Cavicchi argued that such behaviour helped fans strengthen their social identity and feelings of community (see also Larson, 1995; Bryson, 1996; Bennett, 1999).

Whilst this research undoubtedly identifies some practical applications of the social identity approach, it nevertheless fails to consider precisely *how* music fulfils the function of differentiation. One possible explanation can be drawn from Kelley's (1950) seminal work on person perception. Extending the earlier research of Asch (1946), Kelley showed how people rely on trait information in forming judgements of others. A sample of college students was told that their usual tutor would be replaced by a guest lecturer, and that they were to evaluate this lecturer following his talk. Prior to the talk, participants were given some background information about the lecturer. This was the same for all participants in all but one respect: some of them were told that the lecturer had, amongst other things, a 'warm' personality, and others were told that he had a 'cold' personality. Participants who received the 'warm' description subsequently evaluated the lecturer more favourably than those who had received the 'cold' description; they were also more willing to interact with the lecturer during the session. Kelley concluded that the traits 'warm' and 'cold' are 'central' qualities which offer additional information (or *meta-information*: see Yzerbyt *et al.*, 1994) about the likely characteristics of a person.

Statements about music might also act as 'central' qualities by conveying meta-information about the listener, which in turn can be used to make a social judgement. North and Hargreaves (1999) examined this possibility directly. Adolescents were presented with a short vignette which described a male or female target individual the same age as themselves. The target's interest in music was manipulated such that in each condition he or she was presented as being a fan of one of four musical styles. The participants were required to state their degree of agreement with 12 statements about the target, six of which were positive and six of which were negative. Participants held normative expectations about the characteristics of fans of different musical styles, and their evaluations of the targets varied according to these expectations. Specifically, targets who expressed a preference for styles of music perceived to be prestigious (e.g. popular music) were perceived more positively than targets who expressed a preference for less prestigious styles (e.g. country and western, and ballet music; see also Zillmann and Bhatia, 1989).

North and Hargreaves' (1999) study exposed a process by which music can facilitate impression formation. If adolescents can identify the differential social connotations of different styles of music, then it follows that they might also use this knowledge to construct a particular self-image by aligning themselves to greater or lesser extents with that music. A similar process might also take place at a group level: by aligning their peer groups with certain styles of music, adolescents might be able to present those groups in such a way as to secure a positive social identity. Understood as such, the relationship between music and identity can be stated more precisely as follows:

1. through the affiliation of their peer groups with certain styles of music, adolescents associate those groups with the meta-information which such affiliation activates;

2. through intergroup comparison, this affiliation can be exaggerated or diminished according to the value connotation of that meta-information, and in response to social identity needs.

We describe below three of our own studies which have tested these assumptions. The first two studies examined how adolescents use music to form identity-appropriate *evaluations* of their peer groups (evaluation effects). The third study, in the tradition of intergroup attribution research, considered how principles of SIT can further our understanding of the *attributions* that adolescents make for their own and others' musical behaviour (attribution effects).

Study 1: social categorization and musical affiliation

Our first study (Tarrant *et al.*, 2001a) involved 124 British adolescents aged 14–15 years. A subsample of 27 participants took part in a pilot study designed to identify styles of music that were positively and negatively stereotyped. They were asked to nominate as many styles of music as they could that they liked and disliked, and then rate fans of 'liked' and 'disliked' music on 10 personality-type characteristics.

Analysis of the 'fan' ratings showed that fans of liked music were seen as more 'popular', more 'in touch with youth issues', easier 'to get along with', more 'fashionable' and more 'fun' than were fans of disliked music. Conversely, fans of disliked music were seen as more likely to 'not have many friends', and to be more 'boring' and more 'snobbish' than were fans of liked music.

Participants in the main study first completed a self-esteem scale (namely the evaluative self-description questionnaire of Julian *et al.*, 1966). Following this, they were required to make a series of comparisons between pupils at their own school (i.e. the in-group) and pupils at a different school (i.e. the out-group) (the present discussion deals only with the specifically *musical* effects: see Tarrant *et al.*, 2001a for a full discussion). Six musical style labels (selected from the pilot study) were presented to the participants. These styles had been described in the pilot study as ones which were either liked (and the fans of which had been described positively) or disliked (and the fans of which had been described negatively). They were presented together with the names of two bands or artists which play in that style. The styles (and bands) in the *liked* category were 'dance' (The Prodigy and Sash); 'pop' (Hanson and All Saints); and 'indie' (The Verve and Oasis), and the styles in the *disliked* category were 'classical' (Beethoven and Mozart); 'jazz' (Count Basie and Duke Ellington); and 'heavy metal' (Iron Maiden and Metallica). Participants were asked to estimate the in-group and out-group's liking for

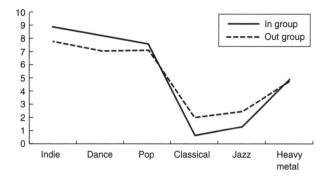

Figure 8.1 Participants' preference ratings assigned to the in-group and out-group.

each style. We predicted that the in-group would be associated to a greater extent than the out-group with positively stereotyped music, and that the in-group would be associated to a lesser extent than the out-group with negatively stereotyped music.

With the exception of ratings assigned to Heavy Metal music, which did not differ between the groups, the participants responded consistently in ways which favoured their in-group. As expected, the in-group was estimated as liking positively stereotyped music *more* than the out-group, and was estimated as liking negatively stereotyped music *less* than the out-group (see Figure 8.1).

According to SIT, intergroup discrimination is motivated by a need for positive social identity and self-esteem (Tajfel, 1978a; Abrams and Hogg, 1988). Specifically, lowered or threatened self-esteem should lead to increased discrimination (which in turn should restore self-esteem; see Abrams and Hogg, 1988). To test this hypothesis, the participants' levels of self-esteem were correlated with their ratings of the in-group and out-group, and the result offered some support for the predicted effects. First, self-esteem was related to the out-group ratings for negatively stereotyped music such that at lower levels of self-esteem, the out-group was assumed to like the music more. Secondly, for ratings of negatively valued music, self-esteem was related to in-group favouritism (calculated as the difference score between the in-group and out-group ratings). This suggested that at lower levels of self-esteem, the in-group distanced itself more from the out-group in terms of its stated degree of liking for that music (i.e. they said that the out-group liked it *more* and the in-group liked it *less*).

Study 2: context effects in musical preference statements

Study 1 used a methodology derived directly from the social identity literature, and identified a role for music in adolescents' group behaviour which had not been demonstrated previously. Our second study (Tarrant *et al.*, 2001b) extended these findings by targeting the *context* in which judgements about musical preference take place. We investigated the role of music in relation to the other interests and activities that young people have, and sought in doing so to establish more precisely the value of music in adolescents' social identity maintenance.

Using essentially the same methodology as the previous study, 149 British adolescents were asked to make comparisons between their own peer group and a peer group of which they were not a member. A list of 26 items reflecting the activities and interests that adolescents might or might not be involved with, or concerned with, was presented to the participants. The following six styles of music were included in the list: 'dance', 'pop', 'indie', 'classical', 'jazz' and 'country and western'. Participants were asked to rate how well each item could be used to describe the in-group and the out-group, and also to state how desirable their own group thought it was to be associated with each one.

The 26 items were first organized according to whether they were positively or negatively valued by the participants (by comparing each item's rating with the scale midpoint). The ratings assigned to the in-group and out-group in each of these two categories were then compared, as before. As expected, the in-group was associated to a greater extent than the out-group with positively valued items, and was associated to a lesser extent than the out-group with negatively valued items (see Tables 8.1 and 8.2).

Although participants' responses to the music were clearly biased in favour of their own group, their responses to negatively valued music were particularly strong. The low rankings for 'desirability of association' assigned to country and western and classical music could be interpreted as reflecting the participants' strong motivation to avoid being associated with these styles, and with the negative connotations which accompany them (cf. Finnäs, 1989; North and Hargreaves, 1999). However, on their own, these rankings did not indicate that music was *more* important to social identity *maintenance* than the other items. To test this, we correlated the participants' 'desirability of association' ratings with their levels of intergroup differentiation (see Study 1). If the music items featured most prominently in the participants' discriminatory behaviour, then this would be evidence for the assertion that music is central to adolescents' identity.

The analysis supported this assertion. For positively valued items, there was a positive relationship between item desirability and intergroup differentiation in that the *more* desirable the item, the greater the perceived difference between the two groups. For

Table 8.1 Mean ratings assigned to the in-group and out-group for positively valued items

Item	Mean desirability rating	Mean for in-group	Mean for out-group
Fun	8.81	8.61	5.07*
Wear fashionable clothes	8.57	6.14	5.50
Enjoy watching comedy programmes/films	7.89	8.17	6.53*
Popular with others	7.87	7.72	5.75*
Enjoy listening to 'pop' music	7.54	7.69	6.58*
Good at computer/video games	7.52	8.27	6.37*
Enjoy watching action films	7.46	6.79	6.38
Enjoy listening to 'dance' music	7.44	6.95	5.86*
Intelligent	7.18	7.34	5.08*
Good at football	7.05	6.98	6.56
Knowledgeable about current music fashions	6.89	7.14	5.63*
Enjoy watching music TV programmes	6.77	6.36	5.82
Enjoy watching sports programmes	6.43	5.88	5.60

* Indicates significant difference between in-group and out-group rating ($P < 0.05$).

Table 8.2 Mean ratings assigned to the in-group and out-group for negatively valued items

Item	Mean desirability rating	Mean for in-group	Mean for out-group
Enjoy listening to 'country and western' music	0.83	0.52	1.82*
Enjoy listening to 'classical' music	0.83	0.73	1.65*
Boring	0.97	2.85	5.36*
Enjoy listening to 'jazz' music	1.40	1.07	1.90*
Enjoy reading school books	2.13	4.38	5.05*
Enjoy watching current affairs programmes	2.66	1.82	2.67*
Enjoy watching romantic comedies	3.26	3.37	3.71
Enjoy listening to 'indie' music	3.69	5.34	4.88
Often go on family outings	4.26	3.88	3.77
Good at hockey	4.40	5.46	5.03
Always follow teachers' instructions	4.55	4.98	4.67

* Indicates significant difference between in-group and out-group rating ($P < 0.05$).

negatively valued items, the effect was the opposite: here the *less* desirable the item, the greater the degree of differentiation between the in-group and out-group. Stated simply, this analysis indicated that in order to protect their social identity, participants relied primarily on those items that they valued most positively (e.g. be fun; wear fashionable clothes; enjoy *popular music*) and also most negatively (e.g. enjoy *country and western music*; enjoy *classical music*).

Study 3: attributions for others' musical behaviour

Studies 1 and 2 confirmed the utility of the social identity perspective in explaining adolescent behaviour, and established that adolescents use statements about music to form favourable evaluations of their peer groups. Our final study (Tarrant and North, 2000) developed this research further by considering how these statements might be used to make social judgements about the actual behaviour exhibited by different groups. To do this, we drew upon intergroup attribution research, which has shown how individuals attribute the behaviour of in-groups and out-groups to different causes in response to social identity needs.

Previous research has focused mainly on three kinds of intergroup attributions. First, the 'locus of causality' dimension considers the extent to which the cause of a behaviour is attributed to internal (e.g. disposition) or external (e.g. situation) characteristics of the group. Secondly, the 'stability' dimension refers to whether the cause is perceived to be constant or variable over time. Finally, the 'globality' dimension considers perceptions of whether the cause of a behaviour is likely to affect a variety of outcomes, or whether it is more specific to a given behaviour (see Islam and Hewstone, 1993). Research conducted in a variety of contexts has broadly supported the prediction that compared with an out-group, the in-group's positive behaviour is attributed more to internal, stable and global causes, whilst negative behaviour is attributed less to those causes (see Hewstone, 1990 for a review).

Our interest was in whether such a bias would be evident in young people's attributions for others' musical behaviour. Fifty-five British participants were given information about a member of the in-group and out-group who supposedly had performed a positive and a negative behaviour (attending a rock/pop concert and attending a classical music concert, respectively). They were asked to explain the target's behaviour using a series of scales. These scales addressed the locus of causality dimension (e.g. 'the person's decision to go to the event was likely to have been an entirely individual one'), the stability dimension (e.g. 'the person is likely to go to similar events often') and the globality dimension (e.g. 'the person is likely to perform related behaviours in the future').

The results were in line with our expectations. For the locus of causality dimension, participants made a higher internal attribution for the in-group's positive behaviour, and a lower internal attribution for the in-group's negative behaviour, than they did for the corresponding behaviour of the out-group. For the stability dimension, participants made a higher stability attribution for the in-group's positive behaviour, and a lower stability attribution for the in-group's negative behaviour, than they did for the same behaviour of the out-group. Finally, for the globality dimension, they made a higher global attribution for the in-group's positive behaviour, and a lower global attribution for the in-group's negative behaviour, than they did for the corresponding behaviour of the out-group.

Discussion

We introduced this chapter by highlighting the distinction between the musical behaviour which takes place in formal and informal contexts in adolescence. It now seems clear that this distinction is in part reflected by the demands of normal identity development. The adult-organized, supervisory nature of the formal education system provides a context within which adolescents can explore important identity issues (e.g. concerning vocational choices): however, the decreased identification with school (and music) that occurs during adolescence (see Lamont, Chapter 3, this volume) suggests that other needs cannot be resolved entirely in a school environment. Instead, it is the unsupervised, informal activities which increasingly are typified by music (Fitzgerald et al., 1995), which enable a more complete exploration of identity issues (including issues of, for example, role experimentation and self-evaluation: Roscoe and Peterson, 1984; Muus, 1988; see Coleman, 1974).

As our studies have shown, the benefits to identity and self-esteem that are derived from interactions with peers seem in part to be realized through intergroup behaviour. Working within the framework of SIT, we have shown how by engaging in social comparisons, adolescents are able to portray their own peer groups more positively than other groups in their network, and are thus able to sustain positive self-evaluations. Whilst we are not suggesting that engagement with music is the only means by which adolescents achieve this, it does seem that music can play a prominent role in this respect.

By considering the wider social context in which musical behaviour takes place, we have sought to redress the balance between more traditional individualistic approaches to the study of identity, and those which acknowledge fully the impact of the social group. However, this distinction raises the interesting issue of whether adolescents' musical behaviour is determined primarily by its individual social function (e.g. its ability to address the emotional needs of the individual) or by music's potential to serve a group differentiation function (through its use as a 'badge').

It is possible though that this argument is not as polarized as it first appears. For example, Finnäs' (1989) finding that adolescents' ratings of music differed according to whether they were made privately or in the company of peers might indicate that adolescents' music listening fulfils both individual *and* group concerns. A similar conclusion can be drawn from North *et al.*'s (2000) and Tarrant *et al.*'s (2000) studies of listening behaviour. Nevertheless, Finnäs' study does serve as a powerful reminder of the ability of the peer group to dictate adolescents' behaviour. Perhaps the most rounded identity will be the one which accommodates both the demands of the peer group *and* the personal needs of the individual.

Future research

Although our primary emphasis here has been on the application of social psychological theory to the study of adolescent musical identity, the implications of our research go beyond the study of adolescence. Indeed, SIT was developed originally to explain intergroup relations in general, i.e. it was not age-specific. Therefore, it is entirely appropriate to use the theory to predict the musical behaviour of groups organized along other defining criteria, and also forms of musical behaviour other than musical affiliation. Below, we outline briefly two distinct fields where a social identity perspective might prove informative.

National and cultural identity

SIT could be employed to further our understanding of the music embraced by groups on a broader cultural level than those considered here. Research has already identified clear differences in the musical preferences of majority and minority groups in multicultural societies such as the UK (Gregory, 1997; Russell, 1997), and several studies imply that the expression of such preferences mediates social identity by helping group members distinguish themselves from other groups (Denisoff and Levine, 1972; Peterson and DiMaggio, 1975; see also Zillmann *et al.*, 1995; Russell, 1997; Deyhle, 1998; cf. Tajfel, 1978b). SIT could be used to test this possibility directly. SIT might also be able to make a contribution to research on national identity, some of which has already shown how the use of symbolic music (e.g. national anthems) by a nation can vary according to that nation's political status (Ruud, 1997; see Folkestad, Chapter 9, this volume). Given the current increase in interest in issues concerning national and cultural identity (e.g. Hopkins *et al.*, 1997; Rutland and Cinnirella, 2000), the SIT perspective on the role of music in the construction and maintenance of these identities seems particularly timely.

Social identity and musical performance

The social identity perspective might also help develop a better understanding of the psychology of musical performance: empirical research could build upon that which has already addressed influences on performance in non-musical contexts. Of particular relevance here are findings from the field of occupational psychology, which indicate that a positive relationship exists between social identity and task performance. It has been found, for example, that employees who identify strongly with their employer produce more high-quality work than those with lower levels of employer identification (Pilegge and Holtz, 1997; Scott, 1997; Van Knippenberg, 2000). It seems reasonable to propose that such a relationship will also exist in musical contexts. The social identity perspective might explain how musical groups contribute to the development of self-concept, for example, and how the evaluation of those groups by the members contributes to the work ethic and performance quality of the group (cf. Murningham and Conlon, 1991).

Conclusion

Although the suggestion that affiliation with music helps adolescents to negotiate an appropriate 'identity' is not a new one, our understanding of this process has proved somewhat limited. In this chapter, we have attempted to show how young people's musical behaviour is guided not only by individual identity needs, but also by group identity needs. Regardless of the level of analysis adopted, it is clear that the relationship between identity and music develops within a social context, and that future studies must continue to acknowledge this. A comprehensive explanation of musical behaviour will only develop when these influences are identified.

References

Abrams, D. and Hogg, M.A. (1988). Comments on the motivational status of self-esteem in social identity and intergroup discrimination. *European Journal of Social Psychology*, **18**, 317–334.

Adoni, H. (1978). The functions of mass media in the political socialization of adolescents. *Communication Research*, **6**, 84–106.

Arnett, J.J. (1995a). Adolescents' uses of media for self-socialization. *Journal of Youth and Adolescence*, **24**, 519–533.

Arnett, J.J. (1995b). Broad and narrow socialization: the family in the context of a multidimensional theory. *Journal of Marriage and the Family*, **57**, 617–628.

Asch, S.E. (1946). Forming impressions of personality. *Journal of Abnormal and Social Psychology*, **41**, 258–290.

Behne, K.E. (1997). The development of 'musikerleben' in adolescence: how and why young people listen to music. In I. Deliège and J. Sloboda (ed.), *Perception and Cognition of Music*. Hove, UK: Psychology Press.

Bennett, A. (1999). Subcultures or neo-tribes? Rethinking the relationship between youth, style and musical taste. *Sociology*, **33**, 599–617.

Billig, M. and Tajfel, H. (1973). Social categorization and similarity of intergroup behaviour. *European Journal of Social Psychology*, **3**, 27–52.

Bleich, S., Zillmann, D. and Weaver, J. (1991). Enjoyment and consumption of defiant rock music as a function of adolescent rebelliousness. *Journal of Broadcasting and Electronic Media*, **35**, 351–366.

Boal-Palheiros, G.M. and Hargreaves, D.J. (2001). Listening to music at home and at school. *British Journal of Music Education*, **18**, 101–116.

Brown, R.L. and O'Leary, M. (1971). Pop music in an English secondary school system. *American Behavioral Scientist*, **14**, 400–413.

Bryson, B. (1996). 'Anything but heavy metal': symbolic exclusion and musical dislikes. *American Sociological Review*, **61**, 884–899.

Buhrmester, D. (1992). The developmental courses of sibling and peer relationships. In F. Boer and J. Dunn (ed.), *Children's Sibling Relationships: Developmental and Clinical Issues*. Hillsdale, NJ: Erlbaum.

Cavicchi, D. (1998). *Tramps Like Us: Music and Meaning Among Springsteen Fans*. New York: Oxford University Press.

Coleman, J.C. (1974). *Relationships in Adolescence*. London: Routledge.

Coleman, J.C. (1979). *The School Years*. London: Methuen.

Cotterell, J. (1996). *Social Networks and Social Influences in Adolescence*. New York: Routledge.

Davis, S. (1985). Pop lyrics: a mirror and molder of society. *Et Cetera*, 167–169.

Dehyle, D. (1998). From break dancing to heavy metal: Navajo youth, resistance, and identity. *Youth and Society*, **30**, 3–31.

Denholm, C., Horniblow, T., and Smalley, R. (1992). The times they're still a'changing: characteristics of Tasmanian adolescent peer groups. *Youth Studies Australia*, **11**, 18–25.

Denisoff, R.S. and Levine, M. (1972). Youth and popular music: a test of the taste culture hypothesis. *Youth and Society*, **4**, 237–255.

Dolfsma, W. (1999). The consumption of music and the expression of values: a social economic explanation for the advent of pop music. *American Journal of Economics and Sociology*, **58**, 1019–1046.

Erikson, E.H. (1968). *Identity: Youth and Crisis*. New York: Norton.

Festinger, L. (1954). A theory of social comparison processes. *Human Relations*, 7, 117–140.

Finnäs, L. (1989). A comparison between young people's privately and publicly expressed musical preferences. *Psychology of Music*, **17**, 132–145.

Fitzgerald, M., Joseph, A.P., Hayes, M. and O'Regan, M. (1995). Leisure activities of adolescent schoolchildren. *Journal of Adolescence*, **18**, 349–358.

Frith, S. (1981). *Sound Effects: Youth, Leisure, and the Politics of Rock 'n' roll*. New York: Pantheon.

Gavin, L.A. and Furman, W. (1989). Age differences in adolescents' perceptions of their peer groups. *Developmental Psychology*, **25**, 827–834.

Geter, T. and Streisand, B. (1995). Recording sound sales: the music industry rocks and rolls to the newest financial rhythms. *US News and World Report*, 67–72.

Gregory, A. (1997). The roles of music in society: the ethnomusicological perspective. In D.J. Hargreaves and A.C. North (ed.), *The Social Psychology of Music*. Oxford: Oxford University Press.

Hargreaves, D.J. and North, A.C. (ed.) (1997). *The Social Psychology of Music*. Oxford: Oxford University Press.

Heaven, P.C.L. (1994). *Contemporary Adolescence: A Social Psychological Approach*. Melbourne: Macmillan.

Hewstone, M. (1990). The 'ultimate attribution error'? A review of the literature on intergroup causal attribution. *European Journal of Social Psychology*, **20**, 311–335.

Hinkle, S., Taylor, L.A., Fox-Cardamone, L. and Crook, K.F. (1989). Intragroup identification and intergroup differentiation: a multicomponent approach. *British Journal of Social Psychology*, **28**, 305–317.

Hopkins, N., Regan, M. and Abell, J. (1997). On the context dependence of national stereotypes: some Scottish data. *British Journal of Social Psychology*, **39**, 553–563.

Howard, J.W. and Rothbart, M. (1980). Social categorization and memory for in-group and out-group behaviour. *Journal of Personality and Social Psychology*, **38**, 301–310.

Hunter, J.A., Platow, M.J., Howard, M.L. and Stringer, M. (1996). Social identity and intergroup evaluative bias: realistic categories and domain specific self-esteem in a conflict setting. *European Journal of Social Psychology*, **26**, 631–647.

Islam, M.R. and Hewstone, M. (1993). Intergroup attributions and affective consequences in majority and minority groups. *Journal of Personality and Social Psychology*, **64**, 936–950.

Jackson, S. and Bosma, H.A. (1992). Developmental research on adolescence: European perspectives for the 1990s and beyond. *British Journal of Developmental Psychology*, **10**, 319–337.

Johnstone, J. and Katz, E. (1957). Youth and popular music: a study in the sociology of taste. *American Journal of Sociology*, **62**, 563–568.

Julian, J.W., Bishop, D.W. and Fiedler, F.E. (1966). Quasi-therapeutic effects of intergroup competition. *Journal of Personality and Social Psychology*, **3**, 321–327.

Kamptner, N.L. (1995). Treasured possessions and their meanings in adolescent males and females. *Adolescence*, **30**, 301–318.

Kelley, H.H. (1950). The warm–cold variable in first impressions of persons. *Journal of Personality*, **18**, 431–439.

Kirchler, E., Palmonari, A. and Pombeni, M.L. (1993). Developmental tasks and adolescents' relationships with their family. In S. Jackson and H. Rodriguez-Tomé (ed.), *Adolescence and its Social Worlds*. Hove, UK: Lawrence Erlbaum.

Kleiber, D.A., Larson, R. and Csikszentmihayli, M. (1986). The experience of leisure in adolescence. *Journal of Leisure Research*, **18**, 169–176.

Konecni, V.J. (1982). Social interaction and musical preference. In D. Deutsch (ed.), *The Psychology of Music*. Florida: Academic Press.

Kurdek, L.A. (1987). Gender differences in the psychological symptomatology and coping strategies of young adolescents. *Journal of Early Adolescence*, **7**, 395–410.

Larson, R.W. (1995). Secrets in the bedroom: adolescents' private use of media. *Journal of Youth and Adolescence*, **24**, 535–550.

Larson, R. and Kubey, R.K. (1983). Television and music: contrasting media in adolescent life. *Youth and Society*, **15**, 13–31.

Larson, R. and Richards, M.H. (1991). Daily companionship in late childhood and early adolescence: changing developmental contexts. *Child Development*, **62**, 284–300.

Larson, R., Kubey, R. and Colletti, J. (1989). Changing channels: early adolescent media choices and shifting investments in family and friends. *Journal of Youth and Adolescence*, **18**, 583–599.

Linville, P.W. and Jones, E.E. (1980). Polarized appraisals of outgroup members. *Journal of Personality and Social Psychology*, **38**, 689–703.

Lyle, J. and Hoffman, H.R. (1972). Children's use of television and other media. In E.A. Rubinstein, G.A. Comstock and J.P. Murray (ed.), *Television and Social Behavior. Reports and Papers: Vol. IV. Television in Day-to-day Life: Patterns of Use*. US National Institute of Mental Health, Washington DC: US Government Printing Office.

Marcia, J. (1966). Development and validation of ego-identity status. *Journal of Personality and Social Psychology*, **3**, 551–558.

Marcia, J. (1980). Identity in adolescence. In J. Adelson (ed.), *Handbook of Adolescent Psychology*. New York: Wiley.

Mills, J. (1997). A comparison of the quality of class music teaching in primary and secondary schools in England. *Bulletin of the Council for Research in Music Education*, **133**, 72–76.

Murningham, J.K. and Conlon, D.E. (1991). The dynamics of intense work groups: a study of British string quartets. *Administrative Science Quarterly, June*, 165–186.

Muus, R. (1988). *Theories of Adolescence*, 5th edn. New York: Random House.

Newman, B. and Newman, P. (1988). Differences between childhood and adulthood: the identity watershed. *Adolescence*, 23, 551–557.

North, A.C. and Hargreaves, D.J. (1999). Music and adolescent identity. *Music Education Research*, 1, 75–92.

North, A.C., Hargreaves, D.J. and O'Neill, S.A. (2000). The importance of music to adolescents. *British Journal of Educational Psychology*, 70, 255–272.

North, A.C., Hargreaves, D.J. and Tarrant, M. (in press 2002). Social psychology and music education. In R.J. Colwell and C.P. Richardson (ed.), *Second Handbook of Research on Music Teaching and Learning*. Oxford: Oxford University Press.

Palmonari, A., Pombeni, M.L. and Kirchler, E. (1990). Adolescents and their peer groups: a study on the significance of peers, social categorization processes and coping with developmental tasks. *Social Behaviour*, 5, 33–48.

Parkhurst, J.T. and Asher, S.R. (1992). Peer rejection in middle school: subgroup differences in behavior, loneliness, and interpersonal concerns. *Developmental Psychology*, 28, 231–241.

Peterson, R.A. and DiMaggio, P. (1975). From region to class, the changing locus of country music: a test of the massification hypothesis. *Social Forces*, 53, 495–506.

Pilegge, A.J. and Holtz, R. (1997). The effects of social identity on the self-set goals and task performance of high and low self-esteem individuals. *Organizational Behavior and Human Decision Processes*, 70, 17–26.

Robinson, N.S. (1995). Evaluating the nature of perceived support and its relation to perceived self-worth in adolescents. *Journal of Research on Adolescence*, 5, 253–280.

Roe, K. (1985). Swedish youth and music: listening patterns and motivations. *Communication Research*, 12, 353–362.

Roscoe, B. and Peterson, K. (1984). Older adolescents: a self-report of engagement in developmental tasks. *Adolescence*, 19, 391–396.

Russell, P.A. (1997). Musical tastes and society. In D.J Hargreaves and A.C. North (ed.), *The Social Psychology of Music*. Oxford: Oxford University Press.

Rutland, A. and Cinnirella, M. (2000). Context effects on Scottish national and European self-categorization: the importance of category accessibility, fragility and relations. *British Journal of Social Psychology*, 39, 495–519.

Ruud, E. (1997). *Musikk og identitet* [Music and Identity]. Oslo: Universitetsforlaget.

Scott, S.G. (1997). Social identification effects in product and process development teams. *Journal of Engineering and Technology Management*, 14, 97–127.

Shaw, S.M., Kleiber, D.A. and Caldwell, L.L. (1995). Leisure and identity formation in male and female adolescents: a preliminary examination. *Journal of Leisure Research*, 27, 245–263.

Sherif, M., Harvey, O.J., White, B.J., Hood, W.R. and Sherif, C.W. (1961). *Intergroup Conflict and Cooperation: The Robbers Cave Experiment*. Norman: University of Oklahoma Book Exchange.

Sloboda, J.A., O'Neill, S.A. and Ivaldi, A. (2000). Everyday experiences of music: an experience-sampling study. Paper presented at *The 6th International Conference. Music Perception and Cognition*, University of Keele, Keele, UK.

Sun, S.-W. and Lull, J. (1986). The adolescent audience for music videos and why they watch. *Journal of Communication*, 36, 115–125.

Swidler, A. (1986). Culture in action: symbols and strategies. *American Sociological Review*, **51**, 273–286.

Tajfel, H. (1978a). *Differentiation Between Social Groups: Studies in the Social Psychology of Intergroup Relations*. London: Academic Press.

Tajfel, H. (1978b). *The Social Psychology of Minorities*. London: Minority Rights Group.

Tajfel, H. (1981). *Human Groups and Social Categories*. Cambridge: Cambridge University Press.

Tajfel, H. and Turner, J.C. (1979). An integrative theory of intergroup conflict. In W.G. Austin and S. Worschel (ed.), *The Social Psychology of Intergroup Relations*. Monterey, CA: Brooks/Cole.

Tajfel, H., Flament, C., Billig, M.G. and Bundy, R.P. (1971). Social categorization and intergroup behaviour. *European Journal of Social Psychology*, **1**, 149–178.

Tarrant, M. (2002). Adolescent peer groups and social identity. *Social Development*, **11**, 110–123.

Tarrant, M. and North, A.C. (in press 2002). Explanations for positive and negative behaviour: the intergroup attribution bias in achieved groups. *Current Psychology*.

Tarrant, M., North, A.C. and Hargreaves, D.J. (2000). English and American adolescents' reasons for listening to music. *Psychology of Music*, **28**, 166–173.

Tarrant, M., Hargreaves, D.J., and North, A.C. (2001a). Social categorization, self-esteem, and the estimated musical preferences of male adolescents. *The Journal of Social Psychology*, **141**, 565–581.

Tarrant, M., North, A.C., Edridge, M.D., Kirk, L.E., Smith, E.A. and Turner, R.E. (2001b). Social identity in adolescence. *Journal of Adolescence*, **24**, 597–609.

Turner, J.C., Brown, R.J. and Tajfel, H. (1979). Social comparison and group interest in ingroup favouritism. *European Journal of Social Psychology*, **9**, 187–204.

Van Knippenberg, D. (2000). Work motivation and performance: a social identity perspective. *Applied Psychology—An International Review*, **49**, 357–371.

Waterman, A.S. (1982). Identity development from adolescence to adulthood: an extension of theory and a review of research. *Developmental Psychology*, **18**, 341–358.

Welch, G.F (2001). UK. In D.J. Hargreaves and A.C. North (ed.), *Musical Development and Learning: The International Perspective*. London: Continuum.

Widdicombe, S. and Wooffitt, R. (1995). *The Language of Youth Subcultures: Social Identity in Action*. London: Harvester Wheatsheaf.

Wooten, M.A. (1992). The effects of heavy metal music on affects shifts of adolescents in an inpatient psychiatric setting. *Music Therapy Perspectives*, **10**, 93–98.

Yzerbyt, V.Y., Schadron, G., Leyens, J.-P. and Rocher, S. (1994). Social judgeability: the impact of meta-informational cues on the use of stereotypes. *Journal of Personality and Social Psychology*, **66**, 48–55.

Zillmann, D. and Bhatia, A. (1989). Effects of associating with musical genres on heterosexual attraction. *Communication Research*, **16**, 263–288.

Zillmann, D. and Gan, S. (1997). Musical taste in adolescence. In D.J. Hargreaves and A.C. North (ed.), *The Social Psychology of Music*, pp. 161–187. Oxford: Oxford University Press.

Zillmann, D., Aust, C.F., Hoffman, K.D., Love, C.C., Ordman, V.L., Pope, J.T., Seigler, P.D. and Gibson, R.J. (1995). Radical rap: does it further ethnic division? *Basic and Applied Social Psychology*, **16**, 1–25.

CHAPTER 9

NATIONAL IDENTITY AND MUSIC

GÖRAN FOLKESTAD

Introduction

Arriving at the hotel abroad, my children notice with delight that 'they're playing Swedish music in the elevator'. This music was cover versions of hit songs by Abba. At the opening of the Olympics 2000 in Sydney, the Swedish team marched in to the tune of *The Winner Takes It All*, once again by Abba. Another feature of the Sydney Olympics was that the official music that accompanied every broadcast from the games included the didjeridoo and other Aboriginal cultural markers. What questions regarding the relationship between national identity and music do these examples raise?

Throughout time, people have used music as a means of expression and identification. Although the purposes and functions of music can vary within as well as between cultures, they have many common features; from the Stone Age to modern times, and from the jungles of Africa and Borneo to the suburbs of the big cities (Malinowski, 1922; Malm, 1967; Nettl, 1983). Music is, and has always been, an important part of human life. It can enable people to make daily work easier and to celebrate and dance; to protest against oppression and to establish contact with the Gods; to tell the history of the past and to dream about the future; to encourage the fighter and to calm the worried; to shout out pain and bring messages of love; to keep weariness away and to make babies fall asleep.

Music has always played an important part in forming the identities of individuals and of groups of people. It provides a means of defining oneself as an individual belonging to and allied with a certain group, and of defining others as belonging to other groups which are separate from ones own. The development of a musical identity is not only a matter of age, gender, musical taste and other preferences, but is also a result of the cultural, ethnic, religious and national contexts in which people live. Individuals forming their musical identities are part of, influenced by and a product of several such collective musical identities, and these exist in parallel and on several levels—including the local, the regional, the national and the global.

Ruud (1997) writes in his book *Music and Identity* about the relationship between the global and the local, and concludes that 'the debate on the global and the local affects every presentation of music and belonging, music and identity' (p. 159). The book is based on a longitudinal research project carried out in Norway with 60 music therapy students. On the basis of the collected interviews and autobiographies, Ruud states that 'it is in this point of tension between our national and local belongings, and the international media world, that our identification with music finds its place' (p. 159).

Hebert and Campbell (2000) also suggested that 'among all of the activities humans possess as means by which to create such a powerful sense of identity and community, music may be among the most personal and the most meaningful' (p. 16).

In their book *Music, Media, Multiculture*, Lundberg *et al.* (2000) present a 5-year research project including 11 field studies carried out in Sweden, West India, Eastern Africa and Syria. They comment that 'never before have so many styles, genres, forms and ways of expression been accessible simultaneously' (p. 15). They conclude that 'the sources of this increasing diversity are many, among which are migration, tourism, a global trade market and new technology' (p. 15). This *diversity* and *multiculture* is based upon cultural identities: *culture* and *identity* are 'together, and separately, the most important organising concepts in today's society' (p. 16).

Given this context, the present chapter will try to bring together what might be seen as two contradictory perspectives: the formation of a global youth culture on the one hand, and the development of distinct national identities on the other. The chapter focuses on the issue of national identity and music from the perspective of music education. However, as research in music education is interdisciplinary in character, the literature and research referred to arise from different theoretical points of view and from fields of research including psychology, ethnology, anthropology, sociology, education and ethnomusicology.

A preliminary review of existing research seems to indicate that very little empirical research has its main focus on national identity and music, or uses national identity as a central explanatory concept for issues in music education. The fact that this area has not been explored before is a positive challenge rather than a disadvantage: one main aim of the chapter will be to establish what might be the dimensions of this potentially exciting area of study. Formulating definitions and key problems is in itself an important task. This is potentially a very fruitful and important area for empirical research, and the chapter will strive to indicate what some of the important directions might be.

The concept of national identity needs to be carefully considered and redefined at a time when the musical preferences of young people seem to be based more upon global chart music than upon any specific 'national' music. Thus, in the first section, a preliminary distinction between the concepts of *national identity*, *cultural identity* and *ethnic identity* and their relationships with each other will be made. In the following sections, the idea of national identity *in* music will be presented: how this manifested itself in the development of the national romanticism in the 19th century, and what were its implications for music education. In conclusion, some projects and studies on contemporary music education in multicultural settings are presented. These raise the issue of the relationships between national, cultural and ethnic identities in music education, and the consequences of teaching world musics in formal educational settings.

National, ethnic and cultural identities

Yeh (2001) points out that China incorporates 56 nationalities with numerous different languages, and Farrell (2001) suggests that 'it is unrealistic, and hopelessly reductive, to speak of one Indian music—there are many' (p. 56). Whilst the Zulu people are one of the ethnic groups forming the new multicultural South African nation, *Zulu Nation* appears as one of the substyles of the rap culture of New York City. These examples typify the difficulty and complexity of the concepts of 'nation' and of 'national identity', and we need to distinguish between the concepts of national, ethnic and cultural identity.

Defining national identity might be described as a 'top-down' project, in which the 'official' definition of national identity is based on the different cultural and ethnic identities within the regions that are defined as a nation. Nationality becomes the cement which makes different regions stay together despite their reciprocal cultural and ethnic differences. Ruud (1996) argues that 'nationalism is a doctrine which states that the legitimate political unit is identical with the ethnical. In other words, what it is all about is the marriage between state and culture' (p. 100).

This becomes a central issue in the process of creating a common national school education system and when a national curriculum is formulated on the basis of a common foundation of values, all of which are important if not essential in a nationalistic project. As an example, McPherson and Dunbar-Hall (2001) point out that today, as a result of a political strife manifested in the development of national curricula during the past four decades, 'Australian school systems consider all music worthy of study, and former boundaries governing content and topic choice have been removed' (p. 20). They continue by stating that:

The strong multicultural nature of Australian music education . . . is a means of implementing the concept-based approach to music education, in that the diverse cultures which make up Australia provide a rich source of illustrations of the materials and processes of music. It also provides a means of tailoring education to reflect students' backgrounds, needs and interests, and is indicative of the general political and educational situation in Australia. (pp. 21–22)

Today, this political aspect of forming a national identity is especially evident in the creation of 'new' nations such as South Africa, in which people of many cultures and ethnic heritage are put together. Thorsén (1997) points out that South Africa now finds itself in a state of dramatic change, and argues that 'the formation of a music education system on a national level today often necessitates decisions on multiculturalism' (p. 91). A fundamental issue in the development of a national curriculum is how to form a national identity with which all citizens, despite their individual backgrounds, can affiliate. Primos (2001) suggests that 'it is impossible to consider music learning and development in Africa without being drawn into historical, cultural and political issues (p. 1).

China, India, Australia and South Africa are all examples of large-scale geographic areas combined to form one nation or state. There are also examples of smaller countries in which 'the national' as a unit of identity is gradually being replaced either by an overarching structure, as for example in the European Union, or by the regional or the local, such as the Welsh, the Basque or the Catalonian. One of the fundamental ambitions of the European Union project might be seen as the dissolution of the distinctive national characters typical for the nation states into a common Europe. One effect of this has been the re-establishment of the regional, based on ethic and cultural identities developed long before nationalistic ambitions created today's nations.

In contrast to national identity, cultural identity might be described as a 'bottom-up' concept. Most cultural utterances, such as music, typically originate from popular forms developed either long before today's national boundaries were drawn, or among groups of people sharing the same musical preferences, for example, despite their national and/or ethnic affiliations. This means that cultural identity has a direct bearing on the music itself, and the musical context in which it exists. This also means that an individual can have more than one cultural identity, and it might be that the global multicultural person of today is characterized by having the possibility of and ability to choose and change between several cultural identities. To illustrate: I have one national identity (I'm a Swede), and an ethnic identity (I'm a white Christian), but my cultural identity is the result of my lifelong encounters with a multitude of cultural utterances from various nations and ethnic groups. Accordingly, my musical roots and belongings are thus to be found in Western classical music, Afro-American rock and pop music, and Swedish as well as Indian folk music, amongst others.

Ethnic identity and ethnicity are more porous concepts, combining both 'top-down' and 'bottom-up' perspectives. In some contexts, 'ethnic' is synonymous with the national and with nationality, whereas in others it refers to folklore, describing the close links with popular culture. In that sense, 'ethnic' and 'ethno-' are used very broadly; in *ethnomusicology*, for example, 'ethno-' indicates that the object of study is folkloric or is popular music, analysed in a local context. This contrasts with traditional musicology, in which Western classical music is the main focus, and is mainly analysed from an intramusical perspective (Nettl, 1983).

Ruud (1997) points out that 'ethnicity is of course about cultural and personal intrinsic value, about identity and dignity. The music becomes an area on which one can present oneself and one's distinctive character in a positive way, and by doing that reach respect for ones difference' (p. 165). Quite often, 'ethnic diversity' is used inaccurately as a synonym for 'cultural diversity', and vice versa, not the least in official documents and official reports (Lundberg *et al.*, 2000), which further contribute to the confusion and complexity in defining these concepts. We must conclude that these concepts need to be defined explicitly in relation to the context in which they are used.

National identity in music

The most significant period of Western art music, with respect to explicit formulations of national identity in music, was the so-called 'national romantic period' of the 19th century. The 'national romantic' composers, such as Sibelius, Smetana and Kodaly, brought in elements from folklore music into their art music compositions, thereby achieving a national character in their music (Grout, 1960).

However, folklore music rarely was transferred into the compositions by direct transcription, but rather was used as inspiration. In this sense, the folklore music was filtered through the screen of the established forms and tonal languages of art music. One exception to this was Grieg, who actually transcribed Norwegian folk music as played by folk musicians on the Hardanger fiddle, for example, and used the transcriptions verbatim in his compositions. This may be one of the reasons why Grieg's music still has a central position in what Norwegians regard as their national identity in music, which makes Grieg 'a core example of how a rich and distinctive folklore culture was assimilated into a national romantic project' (Ruud, 1996, p. 100).

The impact of national musics, including national anthems, as a symbol for national identity seems to be especially strong in countries in which people were not allowed to express their nationality in public for certain periods of time. Ruud (1997) suggests that in the case of Norway, memories of the German occupation during the Second World War are still prevalent, and this may be an explanation as to why singing the national anthem and marching in the streets on May 17, the national day of Norway, has a very special meaning which is deeply impressed on the soul of every Norwegian.

In Sweden, on the other hand, which throughout history has acted as a great power rather than being subordinated, and whose sovereignty has never been seriously threatened, national symbols such as music expressing national identity have a much less prominent role in everyday life. Similar differences in attitudes towards the role of national musics might be found, for example, in Wales, Scotland and England, and in the Basque country, Catalonia and Spain, respectively, as a consequence of their relationship to each other throughout history.

Accordingly, national identity varies from country to country and from region to region. As Ruud suggests, it may be that the awareness of a common national musical identity independent of social, religious or ethnic background is more prevalent and stronger in countries that have fought for freedom throughout history than in countries which have lived in peace for a long time.

The need to express and preserve cultural expressions of national identity in music and dance, and to educate the growing generation in order to encourage its members to become part of a national and ethnic heritage, becomes even more important when the cultural context cannot be taken for granted. The visibility, accentuation and preservation of national identity seems to be particularly important for people who have for different reasons been uprooted from their origin by having moved to another country, such as immigrants or refugees.

In his doctoral dissertation *Giving form to an origin*, Ronström (1992) describes an ethnomusicological study among Yugoslavians in Stockholm, Sweden. The aim of the study was to investigate the significance of dancing and music-making in their attempts to create and maintain a world of their own. The empirical material stems from field-work conducted at Yugoslavian dance and music events in Stockholm during 1984–1988, and in Yugoslavia in 1986. One conclusion of the study is that 'dancing and music-making play an important role in maintaining the Yugoslav institutions, for the socialisation of new group members, and for the feeling of being a Yugoslav' (p. 2). Dancing is also 'of great importance for the learning of ethnically specific gender roles' (p. 266). The specific ways of performing music and dance serve to maintain a Yugoslavian frame of reference in a non-Yugoslavian surrounding, and 'the important question about the group's prospects for survival becomes closely linked to the opportunity and ability for these persons to continue to perform their art' (p. 266).

Yugoslavia is a good example of a geographical area containing several regions, and a multitude of cultural and ethnic heritages, which was politically constructed and defined as a nation. This nation subsequently has dissolved into its ethnic and cultural constituents as a result of political power struggles.

Music has two main functions in expressing and communicating national identity, which might be called '*inside-looking-in*', an in-group perspective, and '*outside-looking-in*', an out-of-group perspective. In the first of these, music is used in order to strengthen the bonds within the group, and to make the members of the group feel that they belong to one another. In the second, the aim of the music is to be recognized by others as being a typical member of one nation or particular group, and to make people outside the group identify the members of the group as such.

In the anthropological literature, the insider/outsider perspectives are referred to as the *emic* and *etic* perspectives respectively, and this forms the basis of some basic concepts of research methodology in ethnomusicology (Baumann, 1993). In brief, the emic and etic perspectives represent two contrasting descriptions of a phenomenon: the insider description given by the members of the culture, using their own concepts and discourse, and that given by the outsider, which assumes the adoption of concepts, categories and discourses from the research culture (Saether, 2002). However, as Herndon (1993) points out, these perspectives should not be regarded as mutually exclusive, but rather as a continuum, such that 'the outsider can learn to *act* like an insider' (p. 65), and 'the insider can learn to *analyse* like an outsider' (p. 66).

In his study of the music among Syrians in Sweden, Hammarlund (1990) defines these functions and kinds of music as *emblematic* and *catalytic*. Emblematic music is directed outwards and has national symbolic meanings. In situations in which the main purpose is to play for other people, or to impress national ideas upon the home group, 'traditionalistic' music is used. 'It is lifted up as an emblem in front of the group, as a cultural flag around which associations to cultural heritage, past greatness etc. flock' (p. 92). The other function is the catalytic: in this case, music works as 'a catalyst in the social chemistry which produces the feeling of belonging to a group' (p. 94).

This means that the emblematic function is to present a simplified and conventionalized version of the music which is geared towards the perceived experiences of the audience. All forms of music and dance can be used as symbols for groups of people, although some seem to function better than others (Ronström, 1992). In Europe, 'the "ethnic specific" music is often folk lore music which is ascribed especially old progenitors' (p. 217).

However, in North America, where the commercial- and media-based popular culture functions 'as an umbrella over the whole society ... modern forms of music are used as "ethnic trademarks"' (Ronström, 1992, p. 217). Slobin (1984), writing about Jews in the USA and Ukrainians in Canada, describes how these groups use country and western music to mediate 'the transition from being Europeans to being Americans' (p. 34).

What might be seen as typically national music 'from the inside' does not necessarily have to be regarded as such by others 'from the outside'. In an article describing how the use of popular music might improve music education in American schools, Hebert and Campbell (2000) argue that many Americans regard Afro-American musics such as jazz and rock music, for example, as part of their national musical heritage and as a critical signifier of themselves. They put forward the view that 'whether psychedelic or soul, metal, grunge, or hip hop, an American spirit is embodied in the roots of rock, maintained even as it is appropriated and rejuvenated within the musical creations of other nations' (p. 16).

Others around the world, however, do not regard rock music as a typical and exclusive symbol of American identity, but rather as a significant representative of global music genres, and as an important ingredient in global youth culture. According to this, Bruce Springsteen singing *Born in the USA* probably has a different and deeper meaning for American listeners than it has for non-Americans, for whom it might be just another chorus in just another rock song.

National identity in music education

One result of the 'national romantic' period described in the previous section was that artists and their works were used for educational purposes, in which the aim of using art music, literature and paintings in school teaching was to bring about education in nationality, and to accomplish the formation of national identities.

An example of this is Kodaly's use of elements of Hungarian folk music in his compositions to strengthen Hungarian nationalism and the Hungarian identity (Kodaly, 1974; Ruud, 1996). Few have so clearly and explicitly formulated their belief in the importance of grounding children's education in national and cultural elements. Today, Kodaly's music teaching method is still practised, and his ideas are taken as one possible point of departure for the promotion of the national elements of music in music education. There is some similarity between Kodaly's ideas, developed in the context of his cultural and political struggle for a strong Hungarian national identity, and those which are put forward in parts of Europe today when, for example, regions want to emphasize their independence vis-à-vis the national supremacy.

We can see the difference if we see on spring days in public parts how a foreign-born governess hammers into Hungarian children's heads the subconscious elements of her own language and music. Such children will have changed souls and will be unable all through their lives to speak and feel Hungarian. When they have grown up and are appointed, thanks to their family, to some leading position, they will not understand either the language or the soul of the Hungarians. There is nobody to enlighten such parents as to what they are doing to their children: they are excluding them from the national community. The basic layer of the soul can not be made from two different substances. A person can have only one mother tongue—musically, too. (Kodaly, 1974, p. 131)

This detailed (and provocative) quotation, if taken literally, could almost be interpreted as an utterance of racism. However, it does demonstrate the complexity and difficulty of promoting national identity in music education in order to include some people, but simultaneously trying to avoid excluding or oppressing others.

The period of national romanticism in Western music history reached its end by the Second World War. One of the reasons for the war, with all its horrors, might have been the emphasis on national and ethnic differences for political purposes: these were accentuated in the national romantic era. As Jørgensen (1983) puts it, 'the years of war had shown that an emphasis on national interests could result in catastrophes' (p. 118). Accordingly, the utopian idea of modernist composers after the war was to remove national characteristics from their music, and to create a new common, internationally united tonal language.

In music education, however, the idea of a national identity in music remained. Even today, some national music curricula strive to maintain repertoires which express national characteristics in one way or another, and which serve to stress the importance of national heritage to the rising generation. Ruud (1996) refers to this repertoire of well-known traditional songs as having had a stabilizing function on the relationship between national and local affiliations. When points of view are expressed today about the amount of singing in schools, or about the reintroduction of well-known traditional national songs in order to achieve a common value system, nationalism seems to re-emerge as a central value. 'With an increased internationalisation, not the least the mass media's promotion of rock music as the new transcultural language, the table might be laid for a reaction involving the flourishing of the heritage of the national romantics' (p. 99). Ruud suggests that this was obvious in the implementation of the new national music curriculum in Norway, in which the importance of putting the folk song back in place in music education was emphasized. The result, however, was a curriculum with 'a balance between the local, the national and the international' (Jørgensen, 2001, p. 18).

In this section, I have given some examples of how national musics have been high-lighted in formal music education with the purpose of improving the national identity of children. What we can learn from history, however, might be that too much focus on the national does not necessarily have positive effects: music education should have its main emphasis on music as a cultural rather than as a national phenomenon.

Music education in multicultural settings

Music is a significant part of the cultural heritage of every nation and race . . . For this reason alone, its place is justified in the school curriculum. (New South Wales Department of Education, 1963, quoted in Dunbar-Hall and Wemyss, 2000, pp. 25–26)

As stated earlier, *nationality* and, accordingly, *national identity* are basically political concepts. As music has such an immense impact on, and plays such an essential part in, the formation of the self-identity, every idea emphasizing national identity in music education becomes not only an educational but also a political statement. The same seems to be true of *ethnicity* and *ethnic identity* to some extent. It might of course be argued that this applies to every other subject in school, and to every other aspect of music education, but the issue becomes extremely sensitive in the integration of the national and ethnic dimensions of music into school teaching.

Thorsén (1997), writing about music education in South Africa, points out that 'as in many debates on multicultural music education, an underlying pattern of striving for *unity* and *diversity* is apparent' (p. 105). He describes how education based on segrega-tion is to be replaced by the implementation of the policy of the Rainbow Nation, and suggests that 'to merge traditions from Africa, Europe, North America and Asia into a multicultural music education in a short space of time is indeed a vast and complicated mission' (p. 91). He continues by arguing that diversity is 'a sensitive issue in a nation that has been stigmatised by the myths of "natural differences"' (p. 105).

Björck's (2001) study of the influence of gender and music on the identity process of young, black South African music students found that the students are in a state of transition in the 'new' South Africa in a number of ways. First, they are pioneers because they chose to study subjects and to have careers in fields previously inaccessible to people of their skin colour. Secondly, they are redefining existing gender positions as they search for new ways to become men and women in the field of music. In doing this, the students manoeuvre in the spaces between individualism and the collective, and between the local and the global.

The term *cultural* identity seems to be more neutral in the sense that it has a more direct bearing on the music itself and on musical expression, rather than on the values it represents. It might be easier for people to meet and play music together as representatives of different musical traditions than as representatives of different nationalities or ethnic groups. This is probably why the terms 'national' and 'ethnic' are avoided in educational contexts (other than in political statements such as curricula), and terms such as *multicultural* and *cultural diversity* are preferred. One result of the increasing interest in national, cultural and ethnic issues in music education is the establishment of a global network named Cultural Diversity in Music Education (CDIME), which has arranged five international symposia on teaching world music since 1992. During these conferences, the challenges of integrating world music with mainstream music teaching and research in music and music education are explored.

At the 1999 conference, held at Malmö Academy of Music, Lund University, Sweden, the theme was 'World Music and National Folk Music' and the main proposal under discussion was that the emergence of world music as a global phenomenon is increasingly reflected at the national level by the revival and enhancement of folk music and fusion of pop and indigenous traditions. This gave rise to essential questions such as: what are the dynamics of the interplay between different traditions, and how can the local and the global interact? How can world music and folk music be taught in institutions, and how can they influence and contribute to music education and training?

Two other key issues are how this development affects higher music education, such as in music teacher training programmes, and the relationship between world music and the classical canon. Traditionally, Western classical music is perceived to be of greater prestige than world music. Differences in status and prestige are also reflected in the distinctions between historical versus contemporary forms, between 'high arts' versus local culture, between scores and notation versus oral tradition, and between imitation versus creativity and improvisation.

The inclusion of world musics in music education has a lot in common with the way in which other forms of popular music, such as rock and jazz, have found their way into the classrooms. Like world music, 'popular music' is a broad concept which is constantly undergoing change, and which needs to be defined whenever it is used. For example, today's rock music can no longer be described unambiguously as youth music, but rather as one musical genre among others which is liked by some members of all generations. Whilst some young people still use rock music as an expression of rebellion, the genre is also represented by 'grandparents' such as Tina Turner and Mick Jagger, and rock artists appear as guests and friends of presidents and other prominent people. In the eyes of some of today's young people, rock represents the establishment against which they wish to revolt (Folkestad, 2000).

Similarly, using ethnically related music is a way of expressing support for one's own personal identity and cultural heritage for some musicians, whilst for others it is simply one of many stylistically interesting means of musical expression. Many forms of world musics and popular music are (1) based on playing by ear rather than by notation; (2) created and performed to a large extent as collective processes; and (3) learned by employing traditions that mostly include informal learning situations outside formal educational school settings.

What consequences and implications does this have for the place of these musics in contemporary formalized music education, and for the development of teaching methods which harmonize with their origin? Increasing cultural diversity and implementing world musics in music education should develop and change some aspects of formal music education (Gruvstedt *et al.*, 2000; Tingbäck, 2000). However, the experiences of previous multicultural projects in music education show that schools containing children representing many different cultures, in the sense that they have different cultural backgrounds, cannot necessarily be described as multicultural: the different cultures' views of learning and musical content do not necessarily penetrate everyday life in those schools.

It is therefore a delicate matter to create a situation, in and out of school, which can promote and stimulate a cultural plurality in which a variety of national, cultural and ethnic identities can be recognized, accepted and developed side by side. Individuals should be given the chance to form their own identities, but this should not happening at somebody else's expense, such as by being used as a means of demonstrating political power or oppression, or creating boundaries between groups of people.

Conclusions

I have argued that the issues of national, cultural and ethnic identity in and through music are not only of general interest, but indeed represent one of the key challenges for tomorrow's music education. It is important not only to learn about and develop one's own distinctive character, but also to learn about the distinctive characters of others, and both of these processes should take place in parallel. By the mutual acknowledgement of others' cultural means of expression, and by letting children make music together, mutually respecting each others' differences and uniqueness, the breeding ground for hostility towards foreigners might be removed. By obtaining security in one's own identity whilst simultaneously achieving knowledge and understanding of others, the possibilities of and prerequisites for a genuinely multicultural society might be created. As Ruud (1996) states, 'it is thus reasonable to argue that the music life might be an especially important arena for cultural meetings and for the learning of reciprocity and communication' (p. 107).

In this perspective, global youth culture and its music, because it is the same regardless of the national, ethnic or cultural heritage of the context in which it operates, might have a non-segregating and uniting function. In a globalized world, particularly in the market for pop music, music is less of a force for national identification than perhaps it used to be. Music might help develop identities and allegiances that are not national, but instead are more cultural: some pop music appeals to identifiable groups of people across national and ethnic boundaries, for example.

In this chapter, I have tried to bring together what might be seen as two contradictory perspectives: the formation of a global youth cultural identity on the one hand, and the development of distinct national musical identities on the other. The paradox might be that the unique character and identity of national musics and national music identities will not only remain, but may even be strengthened as an effect of globalization, and the power of the Internet and international chart music.

In conclusion: what does the fact that one can hear a didjeridoo at a Swedish wedding in a Middle Age stone church tell us about today's and tomorrow's society? What does it tell us about the future that Assyria, a country that has not existed in 2600 years, is rising again as a nation—on the Internet? And what does it tell us about the tension between globalization and localization that rap music has found its way back to Africa, after being developed in American exile (Lundberg *et al.*, 2000)?

Issues regarding national, cultural and ethnic identities in music are likely to be increasingly important in music education at all levels. Further research in this field will become increasingly important, as it has the potential to contribute valuable knowledge for educators who implement and develop multicultural musical activities in and out of school.

References

Baumann, M.P. (ed.) (1993). Emics and etic in ethnomusicology. *Journal of the International Institute for Traditional Music*, **35** (1).

Björck, C. (2001). *Identities in Transition. Young Black South Africans Heading for a Career in Music*. Göteborg: Göteborg University.

Dunbar-Hall, P. and Wemyss, K. (2000). The effects of the study of popular music on music education. *International Journal of Music Education*, **36**, 23–34.

Farrell, G. (2001). India. In D.J. Hargreaves and A.C. North (eds.), *Musical Development and Learning: The International Perspective*, pp. 56–72. London: Continuum.

Folkestad, G. (2000). Editorial. *International Journal of Music Education*, **36**, 1–3.

Grout, D.J. (1960). *A History of Western Music*. London: J.M. Dent and Sons, Ltd.

Gruvstedt, M.B., Olsson, B.I. and Saether, E. (2000). *World music school. Music undervisning i en mångkulturell skola*. [World music school. Music education in a multicultural school]. Malmö: Malmö Academy of Music.

Hammarlund, A. (1990). Från Gudstjänarnas Berg till Folkets Hus. In O. Ronström (ed.), *Musik och kultur* [Music and Culture], pp. 65–98. Lund: Studentlitteratur.

Hebert, G.H. and Campbell, P.S. (2000). Rock music in American schools: positions and practices since the 1960s. *International Journal of Music Education*, **36**, 14–22.

Herndon, M. (1993). Insiders, outsiders: knowing our limits, limiting our knowing. *Journal of the International Institute for Traditional Music*, **35**, 63–80.

Jørgensen, H. (1983). Nasjonale toner i sang og musikkundervisning [National music in song and music education]. In E.S.H. Jørgensen (ed.), *En levende tradisjon* [A Living Tradition], pp. 117–121. Oslo: Norsk Musikforlag A/S.

Jørgensen, H. (2001). Sang og musikk i grunnskole og lærerutdanning 1945–2000 [Song and music in the basic school system and in teacher training in Norway 1945–2000]. *Studia Musicologica Norvegica*, **27**, 1–23.

Kodaly, Z. (1974). Children's choirs (1929). *The Selected Writings of Zoltan Kodaly*, pp. 119–126. London: Boosey and Hawkes.

Lundberg, D., Malm, K. and Ronström, O. (2000). *Musik, medier, mångkultur. Förändringar i svenska musiklandskap.* [Music, Media, Multiculture. Changes in Swedish Music Landscape]. Hedemora: Gidlunds Förlag.

Malinowski, B. (1922). *Argonauts of the Western Pacific.* London: Routledge and Kegan Paul.

Malm, W. P. (1967). *Music Cultures of the Pacific, the Near East, and Asia.* Englewood Cliffs, NJ: Prentice-Hall, Inc.

McPherson, G. and Dunbar-Hall, P. (2001). Australia. In D.J. Hargreaves and A.C. North (eds.), *Musical Development and Learning: The International Perspective*, pp. 14–26. London: Continuum.

Nettl, B. (1983). *The Study of Ethnomusicology. Twenty-nine Issues and Concepts.* Chicago: University of Illinois Press.

Primos, K. (2001). Africa. In D.J. Hargreaves and A.C. North (eds.), *Musical Development and Learning: The International Perspective*, pp. 1–13. London: Continuum.

Ronström, O. (1992). Att gestalta ett ursprung. En musiketnologisk studie av dansande och musicerande bland jugoslaver i Stockholm. [Giving form to an origin. An Ethnomusicological study of dancing and music-making among Yugoslavs in Stockholm]. Doctoral thesis, Institutet för folklivsforskning, Stockholm.

Ruud, E. (1996). *Musikk og verdier* [Music and Values]. Oslo: Universitetsforlaget.

Ruud, E. (1997). *Musikk og identitet* [Music and Identity]. Oslo: Universitetsforlaget.

Saether, E. (2002). *The Oral University. On Mandinka Jalis and their Possible Impact on Western Music Teacher Training.* Malmö: Malmö Academy of Music.

Slobin, M. (1984). Klezmer music: an American ethnic genre. *Yearbook for Traditional Music*, XVI, 34–41.

Tingbäck, B. (2000). *Euriadne.* Göteborg: Musik i Väst.

Thorsén, S.-M. (1997). Music education in South Africa—striving for unity and diversity. *Svensk Tidskrift för Musikforskning*, 1, 91–109.

Yeh, C.-s. (2001). China. In D.J. Hargreaves and A.C. North (eds.), *Musical Development and Learning: The International Perspective*, pp. 27–39. London: Continuum.

CHAPTER 10

MUSIC FOR INDIVIDUALS WITH SPECIAL NEEDS: A CATALYST FOR DEVELOPMENTS IN IDENTITY,COMMUNICATION, AND MUSICAL ABILITY

RAYMOND A.R. MACDONALD AND DOROTHY MIELL

Introduction

In the following chapter, Wendy Magee discusses the impacts on an individual's personal identity of both acquiring a serious illness and subsequently of taking part in music therapy. She highlights the manner in which physical illness can change self-perceptions to produce what is termed a 'damaged self', and goes on to highlight how music therapy can be used to help change some of these negative self-perceptions using clinical improvisation. In this chapter, we take a related yet distinctive approach to the therapeutic potential of music. Here we focus on a range of music interventions (of which music therapy is one), used by a particular organization with individuals who have special needs. We present a brief overview of the type of musical activities, including teaching musical skills, performing music and music therapy interventions, organized by the Sounds of Progress (SOP) company in Glasgow, Scotland. Findings from experimental research demonstrate both musical and psychological developments as a result of taking part in SOP music teaching workshops, and a possible theoretical model for explaining these developments is presented. The chapter then turns to a discussion of the findings from in-depth interviews with three individuals who have participated in a range of SOP music activities. They reflect on the range of developments in their identity resulting from their involvement with music. Throughout, the implications of these findings for broader issues concerning musical identities are drawn out and explored.

We take a broad view of personal identity throughout the chapter. Individual aspects of musical and communicative ability are viewed as being important contributors not only to an individual's sense of self-esteem and efficacy in particular skill areas, but also to their more general personal identity. Underpinning this broad-based view of personal identity and music is an assumption about the intrinsically social nature of engagement in any musical activities. While there is a long history of research in music psychology which has looked at the effects of music listening and participation upon specific variables such as cognitive functioning, there is also increasing recognition by researchers that music is primarily a social activity, and that issues surrounding the social context must be taken into consideration when attempting to understand the effects of music participation, including those on the development of personal identity (Hargreaves and North, 1997; Miell and MacDonald, 2000).

Sounds of Progress

The musical activities discussed in this chapter are focused on the work of Sounds of Progress (SOP), an integrated music production company based in Glasgow which works predominantly with individuals who have special needs. In this case, the term *special needs* refers to individuals who have learning disabilities and/or physical impairments. The company aims:

- To provide access to creative music activities and professional training
- To facilitate integration between disadvantaged and non-disadvantaged individuals
- To challenge existing perceptions of disabilities
- To create employment opportunities.

SOP co-ordinates and delivers a range of musical activities including music education programmes, performance and recording-based activities, and music therapy interventions. Many of the SOP projects take the form of music workshops in which individuals with no previous experience of music-making are given the opportunity to explore their creativity through music. The music therapy work takes place in a number of different locations. One project, for example, involves a music therapist visiting a hospital regularly to work with children and adults, who are attending a day centre there, and who have a variety of severe learning disabilities and physical impairments. Other projects involve the therapist visiting schools and working with children who have autism. The music therapy work of SOP has been reported elsewhere by Dillon *et al.* (2000a,b).

In summary, the work of SOP falls under three broad headings: therapy, education and performance. These categories are not totally discrete and separate, however, but have some inter-related objectives and practices. The relationship between music education and music therapy has been discussed extensively in the literature (Ockelford, 2000). For example, a therapist with an interest in developing motor co-ordination may seek to develop musical skills such as playing a drum in time as a means to helping hand to eye co-ordination in participants (Young, 2000). However, the clinical nature of most music therapy emphasizes the developing musical and personal relationship between therapist and client (as exemplified by Magee in Chapter 11, this volume) and may not view development in specific musical skills as an objective (Bunt, 1994). Despite possible areas of overlap, music therapy should be viewed as a distinct and separate field of practice that requires a fully qualified clinician.

Interaction processes and skills development in music workshops

We begin by examining what we know about what occurs in the interactions between participants in SOP educational music workshops. The research reported here examined the observable changes in social and communicative skills which were the result of participation in these workshops, and suggests underlying processes that might account for these changes. The chapter then goes on to examine the reflections on participation in these and other SOP musical activities by some of the individuals involved. The two aspects of the research are linked by the theoretical approach we adopt which sees identities as being developed and changed in negotiation and collaboration with others. As a result of adopting this approach to identities, we look both at the social settings in which interactions occur and at the personal reflections of those involved in order to understand more fully the processes involved.

In a series of studies, MacDonald *et al.* (1999a) conducted an empirical examination of structured music workshops for individuals with learning difficulties run by SOP. The typical workshop programme is designed to develop the participants' rhythmic awareness by the use of both conventional and specialized percussion instruments. There may also be a focus on singing and keyboard skills, and there are opportunities for improvisation and exploration of musical instruments within the workshop format. In general, these workshops focus on developing the musical creativity of the participants.

In the MacDonald *et al.* (1999a) studies, one group ($n = 19$) participated in a typical 10-week music workshop programme, and were compared on a number of measures with one control group who took part in no activities for the same length of time ($n = 16$), and with a second control group who took part in cooking or art activities for 10 weeks ($n = 24$). The results indicated significant improvements in musical ability and self-perception of musical ability for participants in the workshop group in comparison with the other two groups. Perhaps this finding is not surprising given the nature of the different activities, but a significant improvement in more general communication skill measures was observed *only* in the music workshop group. None of the participants in either of the other groups made gains on any of the measures taken. A longitudinal investigation ($n = 12$, taken from the original group of 19) indicated that the gains made by the music workshop group remained 6 months after the intervention. The musical activities seemed to provide an environment that facilitated lasting developments for individuals with learning difficulties not only in their musical skills, but also in self-confidence (related to their musical ability) and in general communication skills.

The workshop programme in this particular study involved learning to play a Javanese Gamelan. Gamelan is a generic name for a set of percussion instruments consisting of tuned gongs, metallophones, cymbals and drums. These can be found throughout Malaysia and Indonesia and range in size from four to 40 instruments (Lindsay, 1989). An important feature of the Gamelan when working with a special needs population is the instruments' accessibility. Although mastery of the Gamelan requires dedication and perseverance to the same extent that mastery of any instrument does, complicated digital dexterity is not required to commence playing the instrument. Given these particular characteristics, the Gamelan caters for all levels of ability and is therefore an ideal instrument to use for music workshops. Its relative obscurity within Western cultures also makes it an ideal instrument for use with special needs populations as individuals can approach the Gamelan, as both listeners and performers, without any preconceived cultural stereotypes.

MacDonald and Miell (2000) suggest that it is the particular relationship between social and musical variables within the Gamelan workshops that help facilitate developments in communication. For example, the Gamelan workshop involved situations that required complex musical and social co-ordination. In order to play the Gamelan successfully in a group context, it is important to be able to follow changes in music that are signalled by the drummer. In Gamelan music, no conductor is present. Instead all communications are accomplished musically by one drum player leading and co-ordinating all the other musicians (Lindsay, 1989). Sustained effort is required by everyone to follow the variations in tempo that occur so that emphasis is placed on group-based communication. The musicians must also be able to integrate their own playing with the overall group in such a way that the individual elements come together to form a convincing whole. This process involves not only intense listening skills but also attending to subtle features of the interaction such as non-verbal communication.

Given that this research has provided evidence for the efficacy of the music intervention in terms of improved musical and communication skills, a key question for the next phase of the research emerged: what are the psychological mechanisms that underpin these developments? The relationship between the social and cognitive variables under study led to the development of a research project that focused on joint attention processes (O'Donnell *et al.*, 1999).

Joint attention

Joint attention is defined as a shared focus of attention on the same object by two individuals and is similar to the concept of 'shared social reality' (Rogoff, 1990). Both involve the need for a shared focus of activity or definition of the task and an agreed goal to work towards, and these are negotiated between partners or group members. As a theoretical construct, joint attention has been well explored in language development work (Hughes, 1998; Morales *et al.*, 1998; Sigman, 1998). For example, the children of mothers who spend a longer time in linguistically active joint attention are observed to have larger vocabularies and more developed syntactic structures (Tomasello and Todd, 1983; Tomasello, 1992, 1995).

In a development of the MacDonald *et al.* (1999a) studies reported above, a further study examined the interactions between individuals attending the music workshops to explore the possible relevance of joint attention processes in this setting. Independent raters watched short clips of participants in the experimental group and the control group communicating with another individual during the assessment sessions which took place before and after each workshop. They rated each participant on a number of aspects of communication, measuring the amount of joint attention present. The participants in the experimental group showed significant improvements over the 10-week workshop period in joint attention in comparison with the control group (O'Donnell *et al.*, 1999). This study provides evidence that the developments in communication skills which were observed as a result of participation in the music workshops can in fact be linked to developments in 'joint attention'.

Recent evidence suggests that joint attention is disrupted in children with atypical development (McCathren *et al.*, 1995; Harris *et al.*, 1996). For example, children with Down syndrome find situations of joint attention particularly difficult (Kasari *et al.*, 1995; Roth and Leslie, 1998). Such research suggests that individuals with special needs may have particular problems with joint attention. Given our evidence that participation in music workshops may be effective in developing joint attention skills, we suggest that working closely and co-ordinating with others on music activities, particularly playing the Gamelan, leads to these developments. For example, playing the Gamelan involves a combination of listening to instructions, paying attention to other people's performance and appropriately executing one's own performance in synchrony with others. It involves executing a planned sequence of actions in the context of a joint attention task (as indeed do many types of musical activity).

In summary, we have highlighted that structured music workshops can be effective in producing gains in musical ability, communication skills and joint attention, and we suggest that it is the particular relationship between musical, cognitive and social variables found in group music-making that promotes these gains. Thus, it appears that musical activities can be an intervention that meets both education and therapeutic objectives, and in this respect can be an excellent vehicle for producing developments in communication skills and musical ability.

Developing personal identities

This research has gone some way towards mapping the effects of participation in musical activities on various specific musical, social and communicative skills and uncovering a mechanism which might underlie these effects. This approach operates at a micro level, attempting to establish causal relationships between music interventions and certain specific musical and psychological variables, and we suggest that there will be important interactions between developments in these individual abilities and wider notions of personal and musical identity. Our research showed gains in key musical and psychological variables such as self-confidence and communication skills, and participation in music activities might also be expected to produce developments in more general beliefs, behaviours and feelings about the self and about musical abilities, i.e. about the participants' personal and musical identities. Experimental and observational research on the impact of participation in musical activities does not shed light upon these more general beliefs and identities of the people who participate in music activities, however, and so further research was required to focus more on this question.

In order to access individuals' own views of their identities, we carried out an exploratory study using in-depth interviews with a small sample of participants who had been involved with SOP between 1990 and 2000. Adopting this type of research method is appropriate, first since it is a useful way to access individuals' own personal accounts, from their own unique 'insider' perspective (MacDonald *et al.*, 1999b). The complex and sometimes contradictory nature of identities can be explored in detail through these extended accounts, and valuable information can be gained in the analysis of both the content of what is said, and the *ways* in which topics are talked about. Secondly, the method is compatible with the wider aims of SOP itself, which seeks to give a voice to all the individuals who work with the company, enabling them to take artistic control and help determine the way the company develops. Such an approach is perhaps demonstrated most graphically in one of their shows '*Irreparable Dolphins*', which focused on life histories and personal stories of individuals with special needs. These narratives formed the basis for a musical production that highlighted some of the realities of living with special needs for members of the company.

For the purposes of the research presented in this chapter, an experienced interviewer conducted interviews, which lasted between an hour and an hour and a half in the participants' own homes. The interviewer had been involved with some SOP performances and so was familiar to each of the individuals concerned. The interviews followed an informal structure covering the individual's early experiences of having a disability as a child and young person, including, where relevant, their experiences in schools and Adult Training Centres; their earliest involvement with music; how they became involved with SOP and their feelings about this involvement; and their sense of 'self' and how they felt this had changed if at all. Analysis of the interview material proceeded through a close listening to the data and inspection of transcripts. Repeated listenings led to the gradual emergence of identifiable themes in their talk about identity, which were then refined and checked back against the data from each interview using thematic analysis techniques (Denzin and Lincoln, 1998). The discussion below addresses three of these themes in more detail.

The view of identity adopted here is a social constructionist one, which has the following important implications for our conception of the nature of identity. The first is that identities are seen as being in a constant process of development, with individuals constructing and re-constructing identities which are provisional and subject to change, rather than fixed. A further implication is that identities are conceived of as relational, in that the process of development occurs through a process of negotiation and re-negotiation with individual others and with society at large. This relational nature of identities leads to the final important aspect of a social constructionist approach to identity, i.e. that plural or multiple identities are possible, with different relationships between the individual and other people enabling different identities to emerge and take priority at any one time for the person concerned. Both other individuals and society generally can be seen as at times trying to impose certain identities and positions on individuals that are in turn either accommodated to and developed, or resisted and challenged (Croghan and Miell, 1998, 1999).

We draw in the following discussion on the social model of disability, which asserts that in many respects the precise implications of being 'disabled' are tied more to individual perceptions of disability than to the physical features of the disability. In this sense, it can be argued that disabled identities are socially constructed, and not in fact dependent upon physiologically determined qualities. As Phoenix (2002) argues, this 'social model of disability' theorizes the everyday experiences associated with disability as not simply the result of biology. Instead, it demonstrates how an individual's physical condition interacts with the limitations imposed by other people in their expectations and reactions to the individual, and with the limitations imposed by the ways in which the environment is organized (such as only having access to a building by stairs) (Morris, 1993; Swain *et al.*, 1993; Begum, 1994; Murray *et al.*, 2001). The social model of disability emphasizes that very often it is the language we use to describe the lived experiences of individuals with disabilities that inhibits their opportunity for personal advancement rather than the physical features of the impairment itself. As a result, it is important to hear the voices of those with disabilities (Swain *et al.*, 1993; Keith, 1994), and the interviews reported below seek to do this, just as SOP continues to do in its work.

Theme 1: other people's expectations

According to the social model of disability, the degree to which any impairment impinges on everyday life depends more on the physical context and the views and reactions of others with whom the person is interacting than on the nature of the impairment itself. Each of the individuals interviewed here was aware of the impact of other people's expectations and prior assumptions about them, feeling that they were being judged on the basis of their appearance or assumed (lack of) competence rather than on their actual abilities. As is suggested by the social constructionist view, the views of others have important effects on the individual's sense of self. There is evidence in several of the extracts below of individuals struggling with the identities which others seek to impose on them and, in many places, of active resistance to these attempts to impose what are often seen as 'damaged' or 'spoiled' identities, defined by lack of ability more than anything else. This can take its toll on feelings of self-confidence, as Caroline expresses very directly in Extract 1 when discussing her worries and difficulties with finding accompanists (key to transcription conventions can be found in the Appendix at the end of this chapter (p. 178)):

Extract 1

C: I think, probably, (.) a lot of my lack of confidence does come from (.) my disability, you know (1) *wondering* whether people are (.) you know, making a judgement of you (.)

I: mm

C: you know, (.) *constantly* trying to (.) disprove it before they get a chance to (.) *make* up their mind, you know.

As she implies, she battles to get a chance to perform and be judged on her own merits before having other people's assumptions and expectations imposed on her. Music for Caroline is a powerful tool for helping to extend people's perceptions of who she is, playing a central role in her life as a means of establishing her multifaceted identity not only as a person with a particular impairment, but also as a musician amongst other things.

Theo describes the same relational difficulties with others who see him simply as 'disabled' rather than as a person with many different qualities and aspects of his identity. Until others heard him perform, they would avoid interacting directly with him but talk to whoever was with him (Extract 2), or talk about him as if he wasn't there (Extract 3):

Extract 2

T: (.) it makes it easier, sometimes, to talk to people, yeah (.) you know, having a, having a gift (.) because (.) at one time (.) people would come up and talk to my *Dad* instead of *me*, and (.) but now when they hear you singing [. . .] you know they'll come and talk to you. [. . .] It was great when SOP did the school tours, remember the *school* tours?

I: aye [interviewer was involved with this project]

T: it was *great* the kids never treated (.) the kids came up and asked for your autograph you know, just the same as an ordinary (.) an ordinary, just the same as they would (.) you know.

Extract 3

T: I remember I used to go up in the ambulance up to the hospital years ago (.) and there was this old woman she was always complaining about her illness (.) we used to call her 57 varieties! (both laugh) She used to always say about me, 'you know, he's in a wee world of his own there' (.) and you're sitting *listening*! (both laugh) and you're sitting listening 'oh aye, I'm in a wee world of my own here!' (laughs) (.) but there again, (.) that same old woman, I started a sing-song in the ambulance one time and she started to talk (.) she started to talk to me *normally*! (laughs) you know what I mean? (both laugh) so there you go [. . .] she forgot about the 'wee world of my own' when I started the sing-song! [. . .] The attitude changed.

In both Extracts 2 and 3, Theo points to an important change brought about by his music in the difficulties he experienced in interacting with others. When his identity as 'musician' became salient to them, rather than seeing him only as 'disabled', people began to relate to him directly rather than ignoring and by-passing him. In one case (Extract 2), this was in a professional context in which the audience asked him for autographs as they would of any performer, and although the other was not a professional context, music again served the purpose of facilitating interaction. Extract 3 highlights a very common and well-reported issue for individuals with disabilities; that they are often ignored in public situations.

The use of the terms 'ordinary' and 'normally' in Extracts 2 and 3 is telling, since they underline the point made by many disability researchers that to be seen and treated as 'ordinary' and 'normal' is so often in society to be seen as something different from having a disability. An important struggle for many people with impairments in dealing with people's expectations of them is to extend the use of the terms 'normal' and 'ordinary' beyond the able bodied community, which is so often what those terms imply.

For all participants, their perceptions of the shift in people's assumptions and expectations following a music performance was striking. Caroline saw this in very physical terms:

Extract 4

I: When you were thinking about doing music, were singing or whatever (.) what did it (.) give you? What did you get out of it?

C: I suppose there's always the (.) pure escapism of it (.) and there's that (.) um [...] I had this kind of (.) *strange* theory it's (.) the kind of theories you come up to cope with things yourself that don't always make sense to other people, but (.) it was this kind of idea that (.) although (.) I don't see myself as a (.) a very *elegant* person, or (.) you know (.) in (.) the conventional sense of the word, the way that I *move*, or the way that I *stand*, you know, just the way I see myself from a physical point of view anyway, I don't see myself that way as (.) um (.) but, (.) through (.) singing, you can create something that's (.) beautiful and elegant (.) despite what people were expecting, you know, (.) it doesn't fit with the image.

For Theo also, the key was the disjunction between what people might expect and what they actually heard at an SOP show:

Extract 5

I: D'you ever think about (.) what people are expecting to hear?

T: [...] maybe some would think (.) 'oh, these *disabled* folk what can they, you know, what can *they* do?' you know (laughs)

I: aye

T: but, I think (.) I think they get rather a (.) I think they get rather a shock when they (.) when they *hear* us!

What Theo and Caroline are emphasizing is the quality of what they can produce as musicians and how this has the power to confront the patronizingly low expectations held by others of their abilities. This links strongly with the second key theme to emerge in the interviews—the importance of the professional nature of SOP activities.

Theme 2: professionalism

A very important aspect of SOP work is the professionalism of the performances and the work needed to achieve this. The participants felt that the work they did with *SOP* was 'a complete professional job' (Extract 7) and that this became widely known, so that their audience came to expect a 'full professional sound' (from another part of the interview with Theo). In some ways, as Theo expresses in Extract 6, it was this professionalism that warranted the identities of both musician *and* person with a disability. The social constructionist view of identity as plural is one which in recent years has been drawn upon by disability researchers who argue that 'disabled' is not the only identity open to individuals with a disability, as is often assumed by many in society. As we can see here, other identities such as 'professional' and 'musician' are also made available, and are publicly recognized through participation in these activities (Morris, 1993; Swain *et al.*, 1993).

Extract 6

T: I feel, you know, it's uh (.) SOP did (.) certainly you know, (.) give me (.) the sort of uh, the thing I needed, as I said I'd given up (.), I'd given up trying to be a musician, I'd sort of (.) said, 'no, I'm not doing this any more, I'm not' (.) you know

I: Why'd you, why did you decide that?

T: I just (.) I (unclear) didn't know if I (.) I just used to do the odd spot in the likes of a local (.) local clubs and things (.) and I decided, I decided 'I wonder if they're really thinking 'he's a singer' or (.) it's just the old sympathy vote?' (.) I just stopped, I just stopped [...] then when things started to get a wee bit professional I thought 'this can't be bad!' (laughs) [Extract 6].

Central to his belief in himself as a musician is the sense that he is being evaluated critically as a musician by others, and not being given praise in a patronizing way, which he refers to more than once in the interview as 'the sympathy vote'. We can see in this statement the ethos of the company being adopted at an individual level by a musician involved in their activities. SOP takes an egalitarian approach to musical participation which begins from the assumption that everyone is musical, that everyone can access the basics of musical participation and as a result develop their confidence and ability and learn to communicate through music (MacDonald *et al.*, 1999a). As Extract 7 shows, Phil is ready to make critical appraisals of his own performance and demonstrates an awareness of the technical skills required to be an advanced player, using other advanced players against which to evaluate his own performance.

Extract 7

P: I've *done* difficult songs and all that, but, (.) I'm no (.) brilliant, I wouldn't turn and say, (.) I could do a song (.) unless I'd (.) played it a few times (unclear)

I: right

P: I'm no fast at getting round the fret board

I: uh huh

P: so (.) I couldn't (.) I mean I've seen some of the bass guitarists and there's some things I couldn't do (.) like, I can't *slap*, (.) I've *tried* slapping the bass but I can *not* do it (.)

I: aye

P: and I see other people doing it and, I'm like that, (.) I can *not* do that, I've tried it, but I can't do it.

The importance of the views of others is clear from what Phil says here and also from Theo's account in Extract 8 below. They both emphasize the extent to which they build on criticism offered by others or on their own comparison with the abilities of others in developing their emerging identities of musicians, and this is consistent with the social constructionist view of identities as relational. Importantly, for these views and comparisons to be taken seriously, they have to be seen as valid and not, in Theo's terms, purely 'the sympathy vote'.

Extract 8

T: like when folk came up and spoke to you, (.) they weren't giving you the *sympathy* vote any more, you know, you thought, (.) well (.) I must be, (.) I must be doing all right! You know! (laughs) (unclear) you didn't get all that pat on the head and that 'oh, that's very good son'

I: mm

T: I think sometimes if people thought you weren't very good (.) they would tell you, 'oh that was rotten!' or (.) I'd sometimes like to hear them *say* that! you know (laughs) (.) an honest, an honest *opinion*! you know (.)

I: yeah

T: Which, I (.) funnily enough (.) I never (.) I never (.) *got*, oh well you know apart from George (director) when things weren't going (unclear) (laughs) you know he (.) I mean George never tolerated it, he wanted a (.) he wanted a complete, which was right enough, he wanted a complete professional job!

I: yeah.

Theme 3: responsibility and empowerment

Linked in many ways to the issue of professionalism was the final theme of gaining empowerment and a sense of personal responsibility from performing with SOP. For the people interviewed, taking responsibility for the work involved in doing 'a professional job' was an important factor in feeling able to take on the identity of 'musician', or to broaden their access to different aspects of that identity. As Caroline explains in Extract 9, being given public credit for part writing a song that others critically acclaimed extended her range of musicianship to include that of song writing.

Extract 9

I: Did it [involvement with SOP] change your ideas about what (.) your (.) *potential* was as a musician or what (.) sort of things you (.) could do?

C: Yeah, absolutely, yeah, (.) I mean it made me (.) see that, (.) you know (.) I could sing this sort of music as well, you know (.) kind of, popular music as well, and that, um, (.) one of the songs as well in the show, (.) I kind of (.) helped George write the vocal melody for and I never really kind of (.) thought that I was doing anything at the time when we were just in, in the rehearsal space one (.) interval and we were just trying to write a tune and I never really (.) *thought* anything about it, and then I remember after the first night (laughs) meeting (unclear) all these press there giving it 'oh, wonderful' and this woman came up and she was like 'oh, that song, that was amazing' and I went 'yeah, it's a great song, it's beautiful' [...] and, I remember, (.) 10 minutes after I'd spoken to her, looking in a programme and I'd got *a credit* for part (.) writing the song and I didn't *know* that! (laughs) and I'd been (.) totally going 'oh it's a *lovely* song, it's *absolutely* amazing' (laughs) [...] but (.) I didn't really do anything, I just came up with a bit of the vocal (.) melody and I was like (.) 'so it's *that easy* at times (.) to do that' and ok it's (.) not always that easy, and George was doing, you know, did most of the work, (.) but (.) it was just the fact that (.) I (.) couldn't *believe* that my name was there, you know, that (.) you know, I'm not a composer, but, you know, why am I down as having helped compose this? I suppose I did, but it, it took a while to sink in and to realise that (.), you know, I'm, I'm never going to be a composer but, (.) you know, (.) I can (.) have some kind of, (.) you know, hand in that.

For Caroline, accessing a 'composer' identity further enhances the empowering effect that music has for her. It is something new for her and she is quite tentative in claiming this identity—emphasizing how she 'helped George' and explaining that he 'did most of the work' and that she 'didn't really do anything' and just 'had a hand in' the process. She is also at pains to point out her embarrassment when she thought she had been too boastful about 'her' song when talking to a woman after the show, and the numerous pauses and 'hedging about' in the extract above demonstrate that it is important to her to avoid further potential embarrassment. However, it is clear that this event was a very significant one for her, and that it was influential in enlarging and elaborating her identity as a musician. Again it is through the relationship with another that we can see new aspects of an identity emerging—through the close and supportive collaboration with George she now has at least some warranted access to the identity of songwriter and knows that she can 'come up with a vocal melody' again, having achieved it so successfully already.

Song writing or composing was a feature mentioned in all the interviews we conducted. The participants had all 'had a hand in' writing lyrics or music for at least one of the shows that SOP had performed, and this was an important feature of endorsing their identities as musicians. In shows such as '*Irreparable Dolphins*', entirely structured around personal narratives of disability, this had the effect not only of developing these skills to a professional level, but also of bringing to public attention views of disability from the perspective of those with disabilities, which was an important personal and political achievement for those who took part. As Theo expresses in Extract 10, having his voice heard and being taken seriously had been a long hard struggle against some of those in the training centres who thought they 'knew better'. He talks about how, although drama and music activities initially had been introduced into the Adult Training Centres by the councils, they were later withdrawn when staff felt they were no longer in control:

Extract 10

T: I think what upset them was, (.) I began to know a wee bit about things, maybe (.) maybe a wee bit more, you know, than (.) like (.) how you could get *paid*, you know [...] I think when we started getting a wee bit of professional work (.) we were getting the money, they were getting nothing, you know

I: aye

T: and because we knew, we began to *know* a wee bit more about things, we'd learnt a bit about things,

I: aye

T: they didn't sort of, sort of *like* it, you know!

I: aye, did

T: I mean they, they used to tell us at these centres, right, empower (.) 'you've got empowerment' they gave us this *empowerment*, right?

I: aye

T: But see as soon as you tried to make a *decision*? (.) Oh, you couldn't *do* that! (both laugh) you were an (.) you were an inferior (.) you know, you were a disabled person, they were the gaffers! (laughs) they knew what we wanted!

This experience is a common one and has been reported in other studies of the difficulties experienced by people with special needs in gaining a say in how their services are provided, and in achieving a real share in the responsibility of running their activities and day centres (Barnes, 1993). Other individuals interviewed here also talked about difficult times when individuals with disabilities were not given the power and opportunities to develop but instead had their actions defined by others. In Extract 11, Phil reflects on a 'performance' he saw in which this was strikingly shown:

Extract 11

P: I was sick the first time I went to (unclear) because I saw this (.) these two Down syndrome children

I: uh huh

P: on stage (.) and (.) they were up the front playing guitars(.) but they were *miming*, the boys at the back were playing (.) they weren't playing at all (.) in fact I don't even think they had *strings*

I: mm?

P: and then I thought that (.) I was really (.) I felt so *sad*.

Thus Phil demonstrates an awareness of some of the inherent problems and political issues in being involved in music from a special needs perspective and also demonstrates his own standards in terms of evaluating material produced by other people with special needs. It is clear that the developments in identity achieved through involvement with SOP music activities came about through a fundamentally different approach to that described in Extract 11. Everyone is encouraged to make and realistically evaluate their own contribution to the performance and to develop musically through their involvement. As a result, the range of identities open to individuals is extended, and becomes more complex. Central to this is the level of professionalism in all the activities, since this overcomes the perceived low expectations of others and gives a sense of empowerment.

Whilst these extracts have been drawn from a small-scale study of individuals' personal accounts of identity development following participation in music activities, they do identify some important and pervasive themes for understanding the powerful role which music can play in this process. The findings suggest that it would be useful to extend this study and explore the accounts offered by a wider range of individuals.

Conclusions

This chapter has discussed the social roots of personal identity; examining the detail of complex interactions between individuals involved in musical activities and the reflections on these interactions by some of the individuals involved, in particular the impact of such activities on their changing personal identities. We argue that musical activities can be particularly effective as catalysts for identity development because of the high degree of mutual engagement necessary between performers, and because of the impact of being involved in valued activities on their feelings of self-confidence and empowerment.

The results from the first studies reported here highlighted the impact that music interventions can have on discrete personal and social factors. The preliminary analysis of the interview material suggests that involvement in musical activities also has more general effects on the way in which people think about both themselves and their position within society. These two developments are related in that music can be thought of as not only facilitating specific changes in musical and psychological factors, but also as contributing to the identity projects in which the individuals are engaged. Whilst we have been focusing our debate upon the activities of one particular music company (SOP), this has been presented as an example of how any musical participation, suitably structured, can be an excellent vehicle for leading to musical and personal gains for participants. We do not believe that these effects will only be found with participants in SOP activities, but rather suggest that when music is employed for therapeutic/educational objectives in a structured and goal-directed way by individuals with musical expertise and training, then outcomes of the type reported here can be expected.

To sum up, as Theo explains in Extract 12 below, he has made profound and fundamental developments in personal identity through his involvement in SOP activities, and it has been important to explore the sites of such changes as well as individuals' reflections on these processes. For Theo and others, working with others in the professional theatre and music world was in some senses awe inspiring, and yet also made possible the identification of common efforts and ambitions amongst all in the show, transcending their other differences, and giving them a common identity as professional musicians and actors.

Extract 12

T: when I worked with (.) when I did that show with Wildcat [well known Scottish professional theatre company] you know, you really felt 'oh god, you're working with all these you know (.) (laughs) *people*' you know

I: uh huh

T: you know, it makes you feel (.) makes you feel (.) you must, you must have been, (.) you must have been *worth* something, you know (unclear) it's better not to get (.) you know too big headed about it, Gordon

I: aye

T: but you just feel, you feel different, you're working with *these people* you know—(laughs) you're probably *part* of these people (laughs) when you're in a show with them!, you know! But they're just the same, (.) they're no different from anybody, they're just the same as you and me.

Acknowledgements

We would like to thank Patrick O'Donnell and Graeme Wilson, Department of Psychology, University of Glasgow, for their help, comments and advice in completing this chapter. Tina Anderson and all the staff and musicians at Sounds of Progress made this research possible, and their ongoing support for our research activities is very much appreciated.

References

Barnes, C. (1993). *Disabling imagery and the Media*. Halifax: Ryburn Publishing.

Begum, N. (1994). Snow White. In L. Keith (ed.), *Musn't Grumble: Writing by Disabled Women*, pp. 25–39. London: Women's Press.

Bunt, L. (1994). *Music Therapy: An Art Beyond Words*. Routledge: London.

Croghan, R. and Miell, D. (1998). Strategies of resistance: 'bad' mothers dispute the evidence. *Feminism and Psychology*, **8**, 445–465.

Croghan, R. and Miell, D. (1999). Born to abuse? Negotiating identity within a discourse of impairment. *British Journal of Social Psychology*, **38**, 315–335.

Denzin, N.K. and Lincoln, Y.S. (ed.) (1998). *Collecting and Interpreting Qualitative Materials*. London, Sage.

Dillon, T., MacDonald, R.A.R. and Williams, K. (2000a). The effects of music therapy on social development and communication skills in two group's of moderate learning disabled children. Poster presented at *The 6th International Conference. Music Perception and Cognition*, Keele University, UK.

Dillon, T., MacDonald, R.A.R. and Williams, C. (2000b). Different drummers: evaluating music therapy sessions for children with learning difficulties. Presented at T*he Biannual Conference of the Society for Research in Psychology of Music and Music Education*, Leicester, UK.

Hargreaves, D.J. and North A.C. (ed.), (1997). *The Social Psychology of Music*. Oxford: Oxford University Press.

Harris, S., Kasari, C. and Sigmon, M.D. (1996). Joint attention and language gains in children with Down syndrome. *American Journal on Mental Retardation*, **100**, 608–619.

Hughes, C. (1998). Executive function in preschoolers: links with theory of mind and verbal ability. *British Journal of Developmental Psychology*, **16**, 233–253.

Kasari, C., Freeman, S., Mundy, P., and Sigman, M.D. (1995). Attention regulation by children with Down syndrome: coordinated joint attention and social referencing looks. *American Journal on Mental Retardation*, **100**, 128–136.

Keith, L. (ed.) (1994). *Musn't Grumble: Writing by Disabled Women*. London: Women's Press.

Lindsay, J. (1989). *Javanese Gamelan: Traditional Orchestra of Indonesia*. Oxford: Oxford University Press.

MacDonald, R.A.R. and Miell, D. (2000). Creativity and music education: the impact of social variables *International Journal of Music Education*, **36**, 58–68.

MacDonald, R.A.R., O'Donnell, P.J. and Davies, J.B. (1999a). Structured music workshops for individuals with learning difficulty: an empirical investigation. *Journal of Applied Research in Intellectual Disabilities*, **12**, 225–241.

MacDonald, R.A.R., Murray, J.L. and Levenson, V.L. (1999b). Staff attitudes towards individuals with intellectual disabilities and HIV/AIDS. *Journal of Applied Research in Intellectual Disabilities*, **12**, 348–358.

McCathren, R.B., Yoder, P.J. and Warren, S.F. (1995). The role of directives in early language intervention. *Journal of Early Intervention*, **19**, 91–101.

Miell, D. and MacDonald, R.A.R. (2000). Children's creative collaborations: the importance of friendship when working together on a musical composition. *Social Development*, **9**, 348–369.

Morales, M., Mundy, P. and Rojas, J. (1998). Following the direction of gaze and language development in 6-month-olds. *Infant Behavior and Development*, **21**, 373–377.

Morris, J. (1993). *Independent Lives: Community Care and Disabled People*. Basingstoke, UK: Macmillan.

Murray, J.L., MacDonald, R.A.R. and Levenson, V.L. (2001). Sexuality: policies, beliefs, and practice, *The Tizard Review*, **6**, 29–35.

Ockelford, A. (2000). Music in the education of children with severe or profound difficulties: issues in current UK provision, a new conceptual framework and proposals for research. *Psychology of Music*, **28**, 197–218.

O'Donnell, P.J., MacDonald, R.A.R. and Davies J.B. (1999). Video analysis of the effects of structured music workshops for individuals with leading difficulties. In D. Erdonmez and R.R. Pratt (ed.), *Music Therapy & Music Medicine: Expanding Horizons*, pp. 219–228. Saint Louis: MMB Music.

Phoenix, A. (2002). Identities and diversities. In Miell, D., Phoenix, A. and Thomas, T. (ed.), *Exploring Psychology*, pp. 43–95. Milton Keynes, UK: The Open University.

Rogoff, B. (1990). *Apprenticeship in Thinking: Cognitive Development in Social Context*. Oxford: Oxford University Press.

Roth, D. and Leslie, A.M. (1998). Solving belief problems: toward a task analysis. *Cognition*, **66**, 1–31.

Sigman, M. (1998). Change and continuity in the development of children with autism. *Journal of Child Psychology and Psychiatry and Allied Disciplines*, **9**, 817–827.

Swain, J., Finkelstein, V., French, S. and Oliver, M. (ed.) (1993). *Disabling Barriers—Enabling Environments*. London: Sage/Open University Press.

Tomasello, M. (1992). The social bases of language acquisition. *Social Development*, **1**, 67–87.

Tomasello, M. (1995). Joint attention as social cognition. In Moore, C., Dunham, P.J. *et al.* (ed.), *Joint Attention: Its Origins and Role in Development*, pp. 103–130. Hillsdale, NJ: Lawrence Erlbaum Associates, Inc.

Tomasello, M. and Todd, J. (1983). Joint attention and lexical acquisition style. *First-Language*, **4**, 197–211.

Young, H. (2000). Applications and reimbursement in RAS. Paper presented at *The Advances in Neurological Rehabilitation Conference*, Texas, USA.

Appendix: transcription key

(.) = pause
(1) = pause of one second or longer
emphasis in original speech is indicated by italics
where necessary, explanations of material are included within square brackets [ ]
material which could not be heard clearly or transcribed is written within parentheses ()
All names used are pseudonyms and use of the interview material in this way has been agreed with all participants.

CHAPTER 11

DISABILITY AND IDENTITY IN MUSIC THERAPY

WENDY L. MAGEE

Introduction

In the previous chapter, MacDonald and Miell presented data that revealed how acquiring musical skills within the shared experience of music workshops affects self-concepts and identity. This chapter will expand upon this with reference to music therapy. Drawing on the results of a research study (Magee, 1998), this chapter reveals the effects on personal identity when disability is acquired during adulthood, and examines the role of music in therapeutic interventions with individuals struggling with changes in their own identities. Particular emphasis is given to the therapeutic processes involved in music therapy, and to the potential for alliance between therapist and client in using music as an agent for change. The role of the music therapist in facilitating shifts in negative self-constructs will also be explored. The chapter will draw on the author's own research and many years of clinical experience with individuals who are living with complex neuro-disabilities which have been sustained through trauma or from chronic and progressive neurological illness. Similarly to the previous chapter, the data presented in this chapter draw from interview transcripts with a participant in a research study, revealing the participant's personal experience of therapy.

Background

Acquired neuro-disability stemming from trauma or illness results in potential changes on many levels in an individual's life. Most commonly, individuals who have sustained severe neurological damage through trauma or illness will become wheelchair dependent, reducing their independence. The ability to communicate verbally is also often affected by neuro-disability, either through the individual's inability to process or produce language with disorders stemming from brain damage (dysphasia) or through motor disorders which make speech laborious and difficult to understand (dysarthria). The latter may be overcome through technological devices, but these may not provide an immediate spontaneous means of communication for the individual.

Changes to physical and cognitive functioning alter how individuals perceive themselves, and how they are able to comprehend and interact with their environment, and others in it. As physical abilities change, levels of independence shift to greater dependence on others. This affects interpersonal relationships in terms of control, power and feelings of equality, in addition to dynamic emotional responses that may include feelings of anger or guilt (McKinlay and Watkiss, 1996). Most importantly, the individual may respond emotionally to all of these changes, experiencing a complex combination of loss, frustration, anger and bewilderment, which may in turn lead to fundamental changes in 'self' and 'identity'.

Many intimate, social and even family relationships do not survive such dramatic changes (Brooks, 1984; Tyerman, 1996). Individuals who have sustained such disabilities may have very complex medical and care needs which cannot be met within the home environment, necessitating frequent hospitalization or residential care. This can result in difficulties with access to the external world and little potential for developing new relationships. Even if physical disabilities do not prevent access to the external world, personality and cognitive changes experienced as a result of acquired brain injury can affect the quality of relationships with significant others (Oddy, 1984).

These changes may take place gradually, as in the case of progressive chronic illness, or quite suddenly, as a result of a traumatic incident, stroke or other neurological illnesses with sudden onset, such as meningitis. After severe brain damage from any of these events, the individual is often faced with varying degrees of physical and psychosocial disabilities which are likely to be chronic in nature (McKinlay and Watkiss, 1996).

In an earlier chapter of this book, different identities were seen to emerge through relationships which individuals either accommodate or resist (see MacDonald and Miell, Chapter 10). However, changes caused by chronic disability result in what has been termed a 'spoiled identity' (Charmaz, 1991). An individual who is isolated from the external world due to hospitalization may not be able to challenge such self-constructs, nor readily to claim alternative identities. In fact, individuals living with chronic illness and disability have been found gradually to scale down their self-expectations, resulting in the identity of a 'salvaged self' (Charmaz, 1987).

Individuals who are able to transcend the body, and come to terms with their losses, are more likely to develop new self-concepts. This process has been called the 'reconstitution of self', which aims to address the 'damaged' identity resulting from acquired illness (Conrad, 1987; Corbin and Strauss, 1987). Control is one key concept in this process; control over one's changing body and changing abilities, control over one's life when the future is unknown, and control in defining images of 'self'. In her long-term study of individuals living with chronic illness, Charmaz (1991) suggests that control is central to the maintenance of self-esteem. After the loss of self and feelings of wholeness which chronic disability may cause, new self-concepts can only be reconstructed with the discovery of new actions, thereby transcending the changes which have taken place in the body.

Individuals living with chronic disability or illness may experience loss of control over their present and future, which may raise questions about whether they will live, or whether indeed they want to. The individual is at risk of becoming increasingly isolated. Prolonged immersion in illness takes its toll upon social relationships and self, translating directly into emotional isolation and loneliness. People can become isolated in this way, after living with degenerative illness and complex disability over many years. Furthermore, having acquired complex disabilities from illness or trauma, they may experience continual change due to the degenerative nature of their illness.

Music therapy and disability

Music therapy is a clinical intervention which can be defined as the planned and intentional use of music to meet an individual's social, psychological, physical and spiritual needs within an evolving therapeutic relationship (Magee and Davidson, 2000). In the therapy session, the therapist and client explore the client's world together, basing all interaction on the client's own musical utterances or musical preferences. Clinical improvisation is a widely used technique in music therapy, in which the therapist and client spontaneously generate musical dialogues and forms in mutual partnership. Music's ability to transcend the barriers of spoken language mean that it can be used with individuals who are not able to communicate verbally for reasons of ability or culture.

The role of musical culture in personal identity, discussed elsewhere in this book, is an important consideration for the music therapist. When verbal communication with clients is impossible, music is often able to provide a common language by which the therapist may relate to the client. Understanding the semantics of an individual's musical culture and the meaning of music in that culture have been found to be essential for the therapist to establish rapport with the client (Maratos, 1997; Pavlicevic, 1997).

Published clinical case studies of music therapy in neuro-disability refer to the power of music to address issues pertaining to identity and self-constructs as a response to music (Aldridge *et al.*, 1990) and within the therapeutic process (McMaster, 1991; Purdie and Baldwin, 1994; Magee, 1999a). In a group study of music therapy with patients with multiple sclerosis, the themes which emerged during verbal discussions after free clinical improvisations were disability, uncertainty, anxiety, depression and loss of self-esteem (Lengdobler and Kiessling, 1989). Using music therapy to form a new aesthetic identity which transcends the physical has also been discussed with respect to chronic illness and the dying (Aldridge, 1995, 1996). Recent music therapy research has applied qualitative paradigms to examine both the therapeutic process taking place in the music and changes in self-constructs (Smeijsters and Van Den Berk, 1995; Magee, 1999b; Magee and Davidson, 1999).

Music in the hospital setting

During an 11-year period of clinical work with individuals who have acquired neuro-disabilities, the author has worked alongside individuals who have been coping with enormous and irreversible changes in their lives. In a large residential and rehabilitation setting, music is offered in differing formats. Music that is played on a ward radio or in a shared bedroom environment risks being invasive as it is likely to be someone else's choice, with little individual control over the style of music or volume. Weekly concerts which take place centrally can provide a change from the ward environment, and an event to share with visiting friends or family. Music played in weekly religious services of differing faiths offers a refuge for contemplation on a spiritual and private level. Recreational music-making run on a drop-in basis offers a chance for fun, informal interaction and distraction from the hard work of a rehabilitation programme. This range of informal opportunities to enjoy music reflects how many of us access and use music in the external world, i.e. shared within social or recreational environments, for private contemplation or as respite in the privacy in our own homes.

Music therapists normally will not be involved in such recreational activities, as this potentially could offer conflicting messages to a client. Recreational activities using music are opportunities for distraction with an emphasis on pleasure and enjoyment. This contrasts with music therapy sessions, in which music is central, and in which clients are encouraged and supported in expressing less superficial and more difficult emotional responses. By offering consistent messages to clients, and not becoming associated with the two different music settings, the therapist establishes boundaries. These are essential in order for clients not to feel under pressure to 'perform' in music therapy sessions, nor to reveal only 'positive' emotional responses. It is essential for clients to understand that the therapist is able to tolerate even the most difficult emotional expressions.

The music therapy treatment process

Within nearly all health care settings in the UK, the music therapy treatment process involves referral, assessment, intervention based on client-focused aims, evaluation of the client's progress related to aims, and discharge. Referral to music therapy occurs in response to active health needs following specified referral criteria. Referral criteria vary according to the needs of the client group with whom the therapist is working. Broadly speaking, the need for music as a therapeutic intervention in most clinical or educational settings is indicated by communication disorders, active mental health needs including problems with emotional self-expression, challenging behaviour or difficulties with social skills and relationship development.

Referral is made most often by a member of the multidisciplinary team. Following referral, the therapist carries out an assessment with the individual which determines the individual's priority needs, identifies how music therapy might address these and sets goals in line with those of the multidisciplinary team. Depending on the individual's needs, assessment and treatment sessions may include active participation in exploration of instruments, joint clinical improvisation, and singing improvised and pre-composed songs.

The 'therapeutic process' is the process of change and development which takes place during the period of therapy, in which client and therapist work together towards meeting the specified goals. This also encourages the client to take some responsibility for change, and to understand that the therapy setting is different from a purely recreational experience. Change is monitored and recorded through clinical documentation of sessions. Treatment goals and aims are revised accordingly and, where possible, with the client him/herself. Development and review of the therapy process usually is monitored through clinical supervision. Treatment may be in individual sessions, or in group sessions, dependent on the client's need.

Reports on individual developments are made to the multidisciplinary team or to relevant external bodies (such as funding authorities), whilst maintaining the client's right to confidentiality. State-registered music therapists are bound to this by a professional code of ethics, and by legislation for the protection of data. Discharge from therapy may take place for any one of a number of reasons, which include the client's needs changing to indicate that therapy is no longer needed. This process normally evolves slowly over a period of time, indicated by a positive growth in the client which is usually expressed in an outward wish to try new experiences. The therapist and client work together towards an ending. Endings in therapy are always prepared for, unless ending is due to the client's unexpected death. This does happen, and needs to be supported within the supervisory relationship.

In the author's experience of meeting and working with individuals who have experienced many changes, certain patterns emerge in individuals' responses. Observations made by myself and by music therapy colleagues reveal that after changes in physical functioning, individuals often may be focused solely on being able to use their hands again, or to walk again. These abilities appear integral to feelings of independence. For clients with limited or no means of verbal communication, interactions which depend on either speech or language comprehension result in feelings of frustration, distress and lowered motivation. Feelings of dependency increase when the individual needs to rely on others to initiate communicative exchanges.

Clients often have unknown cognitive abilities, particularly when they have no consistent means of communicating 'yes' or 'no', which is the first step in cognitive assessment. Clinicians may not know the degree of the clients' awareness of their environment, their level of comprehension, nor the degree of insight they have into their changed circumstances. A particular pattern which emerges is one in which mood problems develop as clients become more aware of what has happened to them, or that they can no longer return home. This commonly presents as reduced responses within therapy sessions, or as withdrawing from others' attempts to interact. Hence, motivation is the key to continuing treatment successfully.

The nature of multidisciplinary assessment, involving goal-oriented tests and assessments, often presents the individual with abilities they can no longer demonstrate. The use of music as a treatment medium may provide a more exploratory environment which focuses on what the individual *is* able to achieve. This can be particularly useful for joint multidisciplinary sessions which allow other team members to observe the individual 'achieving' rather than 'failing'. Active participation in the music therapy session provides opportunities for a different experience of 'self', in which the individual may experience feelings of success, developing skill and increased independence, i.e. feelings of ability rather than disability.

Music therapy research

Historically, music therapy in Britain has been used with clinical populations who were non-verbal, such as children and adults with moderate to profound learning difficulties and communication disorders (Nordoff and Robbins, 1971; Alvin, 1978). This is one factor which influenced early research projects in Britain, in both the data recorded and the methods used for analysis, which tended to be quantitative in nature. Hence, until recently, much of the empirical research in music therapy has presented outcomes of behavioural responses to music therapy intervention or has compared treatment effects (Bunt, 1985; Oldfield, 1986; Odell, 1987).

However, the adopted quantitative designs did not foster investigation of the effects of music therapy intervention on variables such as emotional states and self-constructs. Increasingly, an awareness has grown that the inter- and intrapersonal developments and processes which take place in music therapy have not been examined or measured empirically. At the completion of a quantitative study comparing the effects of music therapy intervention with an alternative intervention, Odell (1995) recommended single case design studies looking at smaller numbers of research subjects. She succinctly summarizes the conflicts for music therapists embarking on quantitative research by discussing the dilemma of how, as researcher, she looks at '...observable phenomena in the research...' whereas the focus of her clinical work tends to be on the '...much more intangible process of developing relationships and internal processes within client/ patient groups' (Odell, 1995, p. 110). It is this dilemma which has deterred many music therapists from attempting the challenge of research.

Within psychotherapeutic treatments, personal growth and emotional change are the primary principles of intervention. It has therefore been difficult to develop quantitative behavioural studies which investigate and reveal information about the essence of the events taking place in music therapy. It is these underlying processes for which clinicians are hungry, to help inform clinical work. As the clinical populations with whom music therapists work have broadened in recent years to include individuals who are able to articulate their personal experiences, there is a trend towards researching the effects of music therapy with participants who are able to verbalize the effects (Smeijsters and Van Den Berk, 1995; Lee, 1996; Magee, 1998). As a result, there is a growing body of research revealing how music therapy affects inter- and intrapersonal phenomena, such as relationship development, constructs of identity and emotional states.

There is a substantial body of empirical research with neuro-disabled populations demonstrating significant positive effects of a technique known as 'rhythmic auditory stimulation' (RAS), which involves practising the motor activities affected by pathology to metronomic pulse sequences embedded into rhythmically accentuated music. The results of a series of studies have shown significant improvements in gait parameters using RAS with normals (Thaut et al., 1992), with patients undergoing rehabilitation after stroke (Thaut et al., 1993), with Parkinson's disease (Thaut et al., 1996) and with traumatic brain injury (Hurt et al., 1998). However, a similar study with Huntington's disease patients found that although gait velocity was modulated during self-paced and external metronome cueing, significant improvements in gait did not occur during external musical cueing (Thaut et al., 1999).

Findings such as these offer important evidence of music's effectiveness as a treatment medium in physical rehabilitation programmes. This is essential in the current climate of a health care system seeking interventions which have been shown to be effective in both treatment effects and costs. However, for many music therapists working within psychotherapeutic treatment models, using music in this way would not be considered to address the client's holistic needs, optimizing the full potential of music as an emotionally expressive and interactive medium. This debate of 'outcome versus process' is a significant one within the international music therapy community, with different needs emerging for practitioners, managers and researchers. With the existing research in mind, the inadequate empirical investigation of implicit processes stimulated the research presented here. The case study in this chapter is taken from a study which aimed to reveal the changes in identity during music therapy clinical intervention for individuals living with chronic degenerative illness (Magee, 1998).

A research study investigating the role of music therapy in chronic neurological illness

The aim of this research (Magee, 1998) was to explore as closely as possible individuals' experiences in music therapy and gain insight into what music therapy really offers those living with chronic and progressive neurological illness. Although the existing empirical investigations provide evidence that music is effective as a treatment medium through quantitative designs, these studies have reduced the role of the therapist in this process to little more than an external metronome (Thaut *et al.*, 1993, 1996; Hurt *et al.*, 1998). As discussed above, the reductionist approach of measuring behavioural parameters has failed to depict the gestalt effect of music therapy as a treatment medium including emotional as well as interpersonal factors. The current research study therefore set out to identify the role of the therapist in facilitating change and to examine broader effects on identity. Because these were recognized as being implicit processes rather than explicit observable behaviours, a qualitative methodology was adopted.

Data were collected from six individuals who participated in individual music therapy for a period of 6 months. A combination of data sources included observational data, such as the musical, verbal and behavioural responses within sessions, in addition to primary data collected in focused interviews with the participants. The interviews gathered information, in the participants' own words, about what had happened during the session. As with the data collected in the study described by MacDonald and Miell in Chapter 10, the overall emphasis in this study was on the participants' own experiences, rather than on the therapist offering an interpretation of events. In order to do this, data were analysed using open and axial coding modified from grounded theory (Strauss and Corbin, 1990). This ensured that analyses and further interpretations were firstly grounded in the participants' perspective, gained from the process of open coding. Trustworthiness and triangulation were ensured through means which reflected typical clinical intervention, such as taking clinical material to supervision, checking with the multidisciplinary team, and prolonged involvement and persistent observation during a 6-month period of therapy. These processes have been described in detail elsewhere (Magee and Davidson, 1999, 2000).

The phenomena which emerged from open coding analysis of the six participants' data related directly to self-constructs, supporting the notion that changes in self-concepts take place in music therapy. These concepts tended to be bipolar in nature, possessing either a positive or a negative weighting. For example, emergent concepts such as disability, dependence, loss of skills, failure and a general sense of loss were negatively weighted, whereas positively weighted self-concepts encompassed ability, independence, developing skill, achievement and success, ownership and creativity. All of these concepts were temporal in nature, i.e. individuals compared what they were able to do since acquiring disability with what they were able to achieve before.

Concepts relating to identity were related directly to the musical experience, i.e. individuals often presented at the start of sessions with lowered mood and arousal states, poor motivation and low responsiveness. Often individuals would make openly negative statements, such as 'I'm not too good today', or 'I can't do much today'. The act of joint music-making visibly changed mood states, which were evident through greater spontaneity of motor or verbal responses, changes in vocal tone colour, higher levels of motivation to respond or increased stamina to continue.

Extracts from axial coding analysis of a single case study will illustrate how self-constructs pertaining to identity changed through involvement in clinical improvisation within the therapy setting. This case study was selected as it was one of the clearest in revealing how the music therapy process shifted feelings of identity in a positive way for the individual involved.

Case study: 'Jessie'

The research participant, who we shall call 'Jessie', was a woman of minority ethnic origin who was in her 50s at the time of this study. She had started showing symptoms of Multiple Sclerosis, a chronic progressive neurological illness, 13 years prior to this study and lived with a chronic progressive form of the illness. She often referred to her past career as a professional in the health service with a great sense of pride about how she had helped others, particularly those who were vulnerable. She had minimal contact with her family, who lived in another part of Britain.

At the time of this study, she was wheelchair dependent. Although she had functional use of her hands and arms, she was fully dependent on others for all activities of daily living and general mobility because of profound visual impairment. Her independence was, therefore, severely limited. She also experienced delusional beliefs which were attributed to organic brain damage from her disease. The isolation caused by being disabled and blind was exacerbated by her mental health problems, as she refused all offers of therapeutic group activities and even recreational events in which she could have participated. She spent most of her day sitting in her wheelchair by her bedside, not moving physically outside the limits of her wheelchair, listening to the radio. Neuropsychological tests revealed difficulties with conceptual thinking and with memory. She was also assessed to have a 'mild' level of anxiety and to be within a 'moderate' range of depression.

As a result of her complex neuro-disabilities, Jessie was extremely isolated and severely restricted in her independence by visual impairment. Because she was mentally alert, she had insight into her situation, which resulted in periods of low mood, combined with fatigue and pain. Despite her long residence in Britain, she still referred to her country of birth as 'home', and often expressed a wish to return there and experience the familiar aspects of the culture in which she had grown up. An extract of Jessie's interview data illustrates the experience of the spoiled identity which has already been mentioned. Alongside Jessie's text are the conceptual categories which emerged through open coding.

Extract 1

Well, I **wish I could write my own letters, I've got**	DISABILITY AND DEPENDENCE
lots of letters to write. I miss contact with	ISOLATION
all my friends. I don't know where they are	LOSS
since I came here. I **didn't write to**	RELATIONSHIP OVER TIME
them **because when I was blind in the**	CHANGING ABILITIES
right eye I thought the left eye would	
come better and I'd see better to write.	
But **it got worse, and I can't see at all to**	DISABILITY INCREASED OVER TIME
read or write. And **I lost contact with a lot**	
of friends . . . which is a shame really, because	LOSS
I don't know where they are, and they	ISOLATION
don't know where I am. . . . I lost touch with all of	LOSS AND ISOLATION
them. With every one. And **that upsets me**	RELATES NON-COPING TO SELF
sometimes. Sometimes at night **the tears comes down,**	
and I thought, **why is this happening to**	SEEKS SENSE FRAMEWORK
me, what have I done?	(COPING)

This extract reveals, as a consequence of chronic illness and severe disability, that Jessie experienced changes to her identity involving feelings of loss of ability, increasing dependence and isolation. She experienced changes over time in all of these feelings. Jessie rarely experienced the positive aspects of the concept of 'ability', except for when she talked about her professional past, particularly in her ability to help and care for others, giving her a sense of achievement. This contrasted starkly with the isolation of her current experience and the role reversal as she found herself dependent on others. Her reaction to this loss was to withdraw herself further from any opportunities to challenge the experience, and she did this by actively refusing participation in any event. This reduced the opportunities for novel experiences which might have challenged her ongoing sense of disability, loss and dependence, and offered her a chance to experience feelings of challenge or success in an activity. She therefore increased her control through active refusal, but in doing so increased her isolation and reinforced her disabled identity overall. Jessie had a severely damaged sense of identity due to the devastating effects of her illness. Her loss was experienced on many different levels: emotionally, interpersonally, and within her self-concepts.

The musical material used in Jessie's sessions involved both pre-composed familiar music of personal meaning to her, and spontaneously co-improvised music. Personal meaning attributed to pre-composed music was established in verbal discussion with Jessie both at the outset of therapy and within sessions as therapy progressed and as she referred to songs. Both types of music were included, as the aim of this study was to make an exploratory comparison between the two. It was within the clinical improvisations, however, that Jessie engaged more readily and actively, and became more animated. Clinical improvisations always began with an exploration of the range of instruments available from which she would choose. Jessie's musical utterances in her exploration of instruments were typically highly rhythmic, with syncopated variations of an energetically driving nature, which were both matched and developed in musical fragments by the therapist, i.e. contrasting syncopations interspersed with longer chord values were offered to hold her driving fragments. The main aim was to capture and match the energy behind her playing, particularly in terms of the emotional intensity of her music.

Usually she chose small hand-held percussion instruments, such as African shakers, in the early parts of sessions. Jessie held a cultural identification with these instruments, which brought her much pleasure. Within the main improvisation activities, she usually chose a combination of pitched percussion instruments, such as bass xylophone, alto metallophone, cymbal, drum or windchimes with hard felt beaters. These instruments would be placed around her, usually angled on boom stands so that they were within immediate reach. Time was spent orientating her to their location at the start as she could not locate them independently due to her visual loss. Although she would begin improvisations predominantly on one instrument, she typically became increasingly confident in reaching out to other instruments as the improvisation continued. As she became more aroused and involved, she tended to alternate between instruments more rapidly. Improvisations would end in varied ways. Sometimes she would announce that she needed to stop, as she was tired. On occasions when the therapist pulled back from matching her driving music and attempted to 'hold' her musically by offering sustained chords, she became anxious, thinking that the music had stopped and she had missed the cue. It was essential for the therapist to remain sensitive to all the nuances of the musical and communicative interaction taking place.

Improvisations were not analysed verbally with her at the end of the session. Any attempt at verbal analysis often caused her to withdraw, as she was less articulate and confident in her verbal material than in her musical self. It was acknowledged that the primary experience for her was purely in the music and the intersubjective experience which it involved. At the end of sessions, however, as part of the primary data collection, Jessie was led into a gentle discussion about her experience of the music in which the therapist/researcher used prompts to gain insights in Jessie's own words. This was more successful on some occasions than others, and the therapist needed to remain sensitive to Jessie's primary emotional needs and state on any one day and allow that to lead the interview.

In Jessie's experience of clinical improvisation, aspects of her self-concepts were challenged directly and repeatedly. In discussing her experience of improvisation in music therapy, positive self-constructs emerged which were directly related to her experience of the music.

Extract 2

. . . but this is quite different,

this is a different type of music. Cause it's

something which **I can play**, to   ABILITY

make sound, ... and **we**	OWNERSHIP
try to correspond together	HIGH INTERACTION
with it and **get the rhythm right,** and	CHALLENGE
the sound, **just to see if we can do something**	HIGH INTERACTION
about it, you know **make sounds seem nice**	CHALLENGE
or better.	

In Extract 2, she hints at the role of the therapist. Jessie frequently used the term 'correspond' to mean 'coming together' in the music. In Extract 3, she describes the shift in mood and arousal which she experienced during the act of joint music-making:

Extract 3

I just seem to play, play,	
play, and um, **playing something,**	ACHIEVEMENT
it feels *professional*, as if it's something	INCREASED SKILL
you're really doing that you learnt to do,	INCREASED SKILL
you know. . . . I think **improvising takes more**	INCREASED MOOD/AROUSAL
energy. I think **improvising I get**	
more and more interesting, and get more	INCREASED MOOD/AROUSAL
energy, more and more. Sort of, you know.	
It feels as if you're doing something really	INCREASED SKILL
professional.	

Extract 4

. . . because it's like it's	
something you're achieving . . . **on your**	ACHIEVEMENT
own over time . . . you know, **you're achieving**	INCREASED INDEPENDENCE OVER TIME
something of your own . . . you're improvising	OWNERSHIP
all the time, going on and on and on, really	
enjoy what you're doing, you know,	POSITIVE EMOTION
making your own song, or your words,	OWNERSHIP
and you're carrying on . . . quite nice	
cause **you can continue as much as**	CONTROL

you like . . . you **feel like you're**

doing something. You know   ACHIEVEMENT

. . . **achieving something.**   ACHIEVEMENT

The concepts emerging from her data in these descriptions of clinical improvisation include feelings of ownership, ability, achievement, independence, success and increased feelings of skill. The emotional experience also emerged as feelings of motivation and an increased sense of arousal.

Extract 5

MT: *I wonder whether you're able to describe to me in your own words how it feels improvising together?*

It feels lovely. It feels rhythmy. We're   EMOTION

playing rhythm together all the time.   HIGH INTERACTION

We correspond together quite well.   HIGH INTERACTION

MT: *What's that experience like for you?*

It's a lovely experience Wendy. A   HIGH EMOTION

beautiful experience. Cheers me up   MOOD CHANGE

anyway. **Feels better afterwards.**   TEMPORAL COMPARISON

All of these emerging concepts were important, as they contrasted dramatically with the lack of opportunities in her life to experience feelings of skill:

Extract 6

But also improvising . . . suppose you playing

something, you **sort of learning as you**   DEVELOPING SKILL

go along. It feels as if you're singing a

song, and you're **carrying on and on and**   INCREASED MOTIVATION

on with it, and you're singing more and   INCREASED MOTIVATION

more as you go along, and you're learning   DEVELOPING SKILL

what you are singing, or what you are playing.

It's like a song itself, like you're

singing something and you know, although

you're not using any words, but carrying on and

it's all there.

Improvising was perceived as a skill which developed over time, heightening feelings of motivation. Feelings of success resulted from the experience of independence and ownership. Her sense of isolation was reduced through the shared interactive experience.

Extract 7

MT: *What about the music between us?*

I think **we are corresponding well. Corresponding**	HIGH INTERACTION
well ... ... That's why it was **coming so**	SUCCESS
good, because **we weren't saying anything,**	HIGH INTERACTION
just playing and listening to each other, and	HIGH INTERACTION
follow one another and playing what you	HIGH INTERACTION

were playing. Makes it nice.

In Extract 7, Jessie refers to the non-verbal interactive experience of improvisation. This starts to highlight the therapist's role as a validator of Jessie's non-verbal emotional experience. Jessie's description also develops an understanding of how the therapeutic interaction differs from the experience of playing on one's own, or playing along to someone else's music. The outcome of her experience of clinical improvisation was a positive sense of self, which differed so markedly from her usual experience.

Her over-riding therapeutic experience within music therapy was the heightened sense of able identity, achieved through clinical improvisation. Given the material in Jessie's interview data, the most influential factor in her experience of music therapy was the disabled view she held of herself at the outset of the sessions. The experience of improvisation facilitated a great change in how she perceived herself, as it presented a challenge to her disabled identity. Jessie gained a different experience of her abilities within improvisation. She felt increased ability through the creative process and, through being challenged in this way, felt 'skilled'. Furthermore, independence and ownership within the improvisation increased her feelings of success. Most importantly, through the interactive experience of clinical improvisation, she felt validated in her emotional experience.

Discussion

In Chapter 2, Colwyn Trevarthen hypothesized that music

... has the capacity to give emotional companionship, and to heal, because it supports intrinsic, neurobiologically founded needs for qualities of human communication that are organized with musicality...

For the individual isolated through disability or hospitalization, music is a medium which can be shared and worked with in a mutual way, unlike other media. Adopting the client's musical utterances stimulates the emotional memory of care as an infant, and offers a means for enabling the individual's damaged identity to emerge and regenerate. Through interacting 'with the expression of motive forces in other human beings' in clinical improvisation, the client has subconscious memories of interacting non-verbally as an infant. As Trevarthen states, '... affective understanding with others is the development of a secure recognized and valued identity being somebody placed in the world with others ... "making sense" of oneself'.

For Jessie, this experience of a heightened sense of self occurred through her inter-relating in clinical improvisation. Jessie's primary therapeutic need was for meaningful interaction on an emotional level, in which her emotional responses to the many losses she had experienced as a consequence of chronic illness were heard and accepted. This was her core experience in the clinical improvisations. The role of the therapist within the improvisation was to validate both Jessie's emotional experience and, through the non-verbal musical interaction, her experience of a different self, centred around positive constructs.

Relating the findings of this case study to the broader study (Magee, 1998), the data collected from a group of six individuals included many references to interactional qualities in the music, for example 'sharing', 'corresponding', 'interaction'. Clinical improvisation provided a vehicle by which the solo physical experience developed, through the therapeutic process, into an emotional/musical duet, reflecting many aspects of identity reconstitution as described by Corbin and Strauss (1987):

Through continued self and other validation of each successful performance—however altered, changed, or flawed the performances may be—the ill person begins once more to achieve a sense of identity integration, a feeling of wholeness about identity. Receiving performance validation from others is essential' (Corbin and Strauss, 1987, p. 275).

For the therapist working with individuals with chronic illness, it is essential to understand that all tasks are measured as performance. Indeed, music therapy was another forum in which to monitor illness by noting tiny changes in physical, vocal or cognitive performance. However, the act of clinical improvisation was experienced as increasingly interactive over time, as individuals sought and gained feedback for their 'performance' through the therapist's music. This feedback did not exist only in terms of musical performance and its components, such as volume and rhythm, but also in the emotional intensity of the musical sounds. In this way, the act of clinical improvisation served to offer the experience of emotional validation as well.

The results of this study with a group of individuals living with chronic neurological illness suggest that, through the act of improvising, individuals changed their self-perceptions (Magee, 1998). This process was a positive one, despite it being an acknowledgement of the loss of and change in abilities due to the impact of illness. Through the expressive medium of music, the emotional responses to these changes (such as, for example, frustration, loss or anger) could be expressed in ways which words did not allow. The co-improvised music, with its expressive power, validated the individual's emotional experience. However, this did not occur for all individuals nor in all instances. When this process failed to take place, analysis revealed that the experience of improvisation was registered as a purely physical experience in which individuals measured their physical performance.

The manner in which Jessie played out control in her life is also a significant feature of this case study. Jessie gained control over her loss and dependence by actively refusing novel activities which may have allowed her opportunities to develop new skills. This increased her control in one sense, but also served to reinforce her isolation and disabled identity. Clinical improvisation within a therapeutic relationship provided her with opportunities to experience control and discovery of new skills through the interactive elements of spontaneous, non-verbal music-making. Although her sense of identity was severely damaged, the seeds of the process described as 'identity reconstitution' (Corbin and Strauss, 1987) were evident in Jessie's heightened emotional responses within improvisation, as she moved towards a greater sense of wholeness.

The similarities in the interview data produced in the earlier chapter by MacDonald and Miell (Chapter 10) and the data given here are extraordinary, and warrant closer comparison. We must ask in what respects the two musical activities (Gamelan workshop and clinical improvisation in music therapy) differ, and whether the underlying processes of shifting identities are similar in any way. There are certainly similarities between Jessie, and the participant quoted in Extract 3 of Chapter 10, in each person's experience of shifting identities from 'disabled person' to include that of 'musician'.

There are also qualitative differences between these two different musical interactions and the processes taking place which are important to highlight. The Gamelan workshops were led and co-ordinated by one drum player signalling changes. In both Gamelan workshops and music therapy interactions, there is a complex co-ordination between musical and social interactions which requires listening skills and non-verbal communication. However, whereas the music played in the Gamelan workshop is goal-driven to play as an ensemble member, in music therapy, the music played is based on the individual's personal expression and emotional needs, with an emphasis on the interpersonal exchange. Furthermore, the music within therapeutic interventions is analysed in consideration of the overall interpersonal aspects. This is a fundamental difference between playing in group music workshops and clinical improvisation in music therapy.

The theme of 'feeling professional' is present in both sets of data. The participant in MacDonald and Miell's interviews who developed his sense as a professional musician did so because he knew that he was being evaluated critically as a musician, rather than being given the 'sympathy vote' (Extract 7). Indeed, critical evaluation from the audience and director underpinned the shift to feeling professional by invalidating the limited view of them held by others (particularly professionals), and the limitations imposed by environments.

This is crucially different from the music therapy session, in which a client's initial fear of being critically evaluated often inhibits participation early on in therapy. It is essential for an understanding to be reached that the music is not an 'object' or an outcome to be achieved, but rather a shared language for expression. The primary emphasis is on the process of interpersonal relating rather than the outcome. Clients may experience the outcome of an improvisation as a denial of their disabilities. However, the therapist must follow clients and support them, rather than placing expectations upon them, or evaluating their performances on criteria of musical ability. The therapy session must remain a space for clients to experience their optimum abilities, but also to express their emotional response to their loss. Critical evaluation, in which the therapist takes on a 'teacher/director' role, potentially could damage self-development rather than promoting it.

Jessie reflects the picture of chronically ill individuals who are 'so immersed in illness that they cannot readily claim other identities in the external world' or 'move on' from their preoccupation with loss (Charmaz, 1987). The external world did not exist for Jessie, through either visual images, physical presence or access. Opportunities to claim a more able identity were therefore very limited, and immensely difficult for her. Trevarthen states that

The foundations of all psychological co-operation or intersubjectivity are to be found in a sense of movement and in detection of the generation of qualities of movement in other bodies. It is in "future sense", the anticipatory, generative mental image of a movement and of its likely sensory consequences that the parameters of intersubjective communication are defined.

In the case study presented here, we can only speculate as to how the intersubjective experience of clinically improvising with another may have been one of the few times in which Jessie gained a psychological sense of another. Through interactive music-making which was responsive to all of her musical utterances, Jessie was able to anticipate another's actions and be a mutual part of them. In doing so, she experienced a stronger, more confident and vital sense of self.

The process of isolation for chronically ill individuals stems from shifts in self-perception, strained social relationships and changed relationships with intimates caused by the increasing dependence on others. Individuals living with neurological illness may have lost the ability to communicate fluently and spontaneously through words, may have lost many supportive and intimate connections in their lives, or may be living with physical and emotional pain which finds little relief or respite. The interpersonal connections which can take place within improvisation provide support through a musical relationship which is essentially non-verbal. This can provide reassurance through the reflection and development of musical ideas, and may by-pass the need for language altogether. The individual in the case study reported here was unable to gain reassurance in this way in her verbal interactions. As an emotional medium, music can express, convey, hold and support in ways which words cannot.

Jessie had little opportunity for change, development or progress in her life. Within sessions, she frequently expressed the wish to die, and yet the extracts given from her data in this chapter indicate that her experience of improvisation gave her hope, and a sense of development. Feelings of motivation for chronically ill individuals result from developing personal identities which encompasses future selves, reflecting their hopes and aspirations. Through improvisation, Jessie gained motivation and increased levels of arousal stemming from a changed sense of self. This was observable in her behaviour during and immediately after sessions, which contrasted greatly with the depressed affective state and reduced energy levels which she displayed before them. There was no evidence or investigation, however, of whether these heightened mood states generalized to general living situations or were sustained over time. That was outside the remit of this particular research project, and in itself is a much broader issue.

The results of this study show that through active music therapy, isolation is reduced, thereby enabling individuals to challenge their concepts of self. Clinical improvisation centres around the interactive relationship on an equal basis through the physical act of playing, and this involves dependency. Dependency is critical in forming concepts of self and identity, as individuals with chronic illness express a greater fear of dependence, debility and abandonment than of death itself (Charmaz, 1991). The experience of clinical improvisation stimulates shifts in identity, and can therefore be an effective means of addressing the 'spoiled identity'. The case study reported in this chapter illustrates that the interactive nature of clinical improvisation with individuals with chronic disability and illness may provide validation of positive feelings of self-esteem and identity. Feelings of identity can be changed through an intervention which by-passes language, stems from and feeds into the emotional self, and addresses the need for intimacy with others. Clinical improvisation is able to facilitate the emergence of new and undiscovered skills, and to develop a wholeness of self, thereby shifting identity to reach a preferred sense of self.

Acknowledgements

The work research is part of doctoral research undertaken whilst registered at the Department of Music, University of Sheffield. In particular, the author would like to thank the research participants who took part in this study and also acknowledge the contribution made by Dr Jane W. Davidson, University of Sheffield, who supervised this research. The Royal Hospital for Neuro-disability received a proportion of its funding to support this paper from the NHS Executive. The views expressed in this publication are those of the author and not necessarily those of the NHS Executive.

References

Aldridge, D. (1995). Spirituality, hope and music therapy in palliative care. *The Arts in Psychotherapy*, 22, 103–109.

Aldridge, D. (1996). *Music Therapy Research and Practice in Medicine*. London: Jessica Kingsley Publishers.

Aldridge, D., Gustorff, D. and Hannich, H.-J. (1990). Where am I? Music therapy applied to coma patients. *Journal of the Royal Society of Medicine*, 83, 345–346.

Alvin, J. (1978). *Music Therapy for the Autistic Child*. Oxford: Oxford University Press,.

Brooks, N. (1984). Head injury and the family. In N. Brooks (ed.), *Closed Head Injury: Psychological, Social and Family Consequences*, pp. 123–147. Oxford: Oxford University Press.

Bunt, L. (1985). Music therapy and the child with a handicap: evaluation of the effects of intervention. PhD thesis, London: Department of Music, City University.

Charmaz, K. (1987). Struggling for a self: identity levels of the chronically ill. In J. Roth and P. Conrad (ed.), *Research In the Sociology of Health Care: A Research Annual. The Experience and Management of Chronic Illness*, Vol. 6, pp. 283–321. London: JAI Press Inc.

Charmaz, K. (1991). *Good Days, Bad Days. The Self in Chronic Illness and Time*. New Brunswick: Rutgers University Press.

Conrad, P. (1987). The experience of illness: recent and new directions. In J. Roth and P. Conrad (ed.), *Research In the Sociology of Health Care: A Research Annual. The Experience and Management of Chronic Illness*, Vol. 6, pp. 1–31. London: JAI Press Inc.

Corbin, J. and Strauss, A. (1987). Accompaniments of chronic illness: changes in body, self, biography, and biographical time. In J. Roth and P. Conrad (ed.), *Research In the Sociology of Health Care: A Research Annual. The Experience and Management of Chronic Illness*, Vol. 6, pp. 249–281. London: JAI Press Inc.

Hurt, C.P., Rice, R.R., McIntosh, G.C. and Thaut, M.H. (1998). Rhythmic auditory stimulation in gait training for patients with traumatic brain injury. *Journal of Music Therapy*, 35, 228–241.

Lee, C. (1996). *Music At The Edge: The Music Therapy Experiences of a Musician Living With AIDS*. London: Routledge.

Lengdobler, H. and Kiessling, W.R. (1989). Gruppenmusiktherapie bei multipler Sklerose: Ein erster Erfahrungsbericht. *Psychotherapie, Psychosomatik, Medizin und Psychologie*, 39, 369–373.

Magee, W. (1998). 'Singing my life, playing my self'. Investigating the use of familiar pre-composed music and unfamiliar improvised music in clinical music therapy with individuals with chronic neurological illness. Unpublished doctoral dissertation, University of Sheffield, UK, #9898.

Magee, W. (1999a). Music therapy in chronic degenerative illness: reflecting the dynamic sense of self. In D. Aldridge (ed.), *Music Therapy in Palliative Care*, pp. 82–94. London: Jessica Kingsley Publishers.

Magee, W. (1999b). 'Singing my life, playing my self': song based and improvisatory methods of music therapy with individuals with neurological impairments. In T. Wigram and J. De Backer (ed.), *Clinical Applications of Music Therapy in Developmental Disability, Paediatrics and Neurology*, pp. 201–223. London: Jessica Kingsley Publishers.

Magee, W.L. and Davidson, J.W. (1999). Changing self-concepts through music therapy: a study of music therapy in chronic neurological illness using modified grounded theory. Poster presented at *The 9th World Congress of Music Therapy*, Washington DC.

Magee, W.L. and Davidson, J.W. (2000). Identity in chronic neurological disability: finding an able 'self' in music therapy. In C. Woods, G.B. Luck, R. Brochard, S.A. O'Neill and J.A. Sloboda (ed.), *Proceedings of the 6th International Conference on Music Perception and Cognition*. Keele, Staffordshire, UK. Department of Psychology. CD-ROM.

Maratos, A. (1997). Musical polyglossia: one step further towards a client-based approach. *British Journal of Music Therapy*, 11, 24–25.

McKinlay, W.W. and Watkiss, A.J. (1996). Long-term management. In F.D. Rose and D.A. Johnson (ed.), *Brain Injury and After: Towards Improved Outcome*, pp. 119–142. Chichester, UK: Wiley & Sons.

McMaster, N. (1991). Reclaiming a positive identity: music therapy in the aftermath of a stroke. In K.E. Bruscia (ed.), *Case Studies in Music Therapy*, pp. 547–560. Philadelphia: Barcelona Publishers.

Nordoff, P. and Robbins, C. (1971). *Therapy in Music for Handicapped Children*. London: Gallancz.

Oddy, M. (1984). Head injury and social adjustment. In N. Brooks (ed.), *Closed Head Injury: Psychological, Social and Family Consequences*, pp. 108–122. Oxford: Oxford University Press.

Odell, H. (1987). Music therapy and the elderly mentally ill. Unpublished M.Phil. thesis. London: City University.

Odell, H. (1995). Approaches to music therapy in psychiatry with specific emphasis upon a research project with the elderly mentally ill. In T. Wigram, B. Saperston and R. West (ed.), *The Art and Science of Music Therapy: A Handbook*, pp. 83–111. The Netherlands: Harwood Academic Publishers.

Oldfield, A. (1986). The effects of music therapy on a group of profoundly mentally handicapped adults. M. Phil, London: City University.

Pavlicevic, M. (1997). Culture, cross-culture and multi-culture. *British Journal of Music Therapy*, 11, 56.

Purdie, H. and Baldwin, S. (1994). Music therapy: challenging low self-esteem in people with a stroke. *British Journal of Music Therapy*, 8, 19–24.

Smeijsters, H., and Van Den Berk, P. (1995). Music therapy with a client suffering from musico-genic epilepsy: a naturalistic qualitative single-case research. *The Arts in Psychotherapy*, **22**, 249–263.

Strauss, A. and Corbin, J. (1990). *Basics of Qualitative Research. Grounded Theory Procedures and Techniques*. Newbury Park, CA: Sage Publications, Inc.

Thaut, M.H., McIntosh, G.C., Prassas, S.G. and Rice, R.R. (1992). Effect of rhythmic auditory cuing on temporal stride parameters and EMG patterns in normal gait. *Journal of Neurological Rehabilitation*, **6**, 185–190.

Thaut, M.H., McIntosh, G.C., Prassas, S.G. and Rice, R.R. (1993). Effect of rhythmic cuing on temporal stride parameters and EMG patterns in hemiparetic gait of stroke patients. *Journal of Neurological Rehabilitation*, **7**, 9–16.

Thaut, M.H., McIntosh, G.C., Rice, R.R., Miller R.A., Rathburn, J. and Brault, J.M. (1996). Rhythmic auditory stimulation in gait training for Parkinson's disease patients. *Movement Disorders*, **11**, 193–200.

Thaut, M.H., McIntosh, G.C., Miltner, R., Lange, H.W., Hurt, C.P. and Hoemberg, V. (1999). Velocity modulation and rhythmic synchronization of gait training in Huntington's disease. *Movement Disorders*, **14**, 808–819.

Tyerman, A. (1996). The social context. In F.D. Rose and D.A. Johnson (ed.), *Brain Injury and After: Towards Improved Outcome*, pp. 97–118. Chichester, UK: Wiley & Sons.

NAME INDEX

SUBJECT INDEX